Garfield
chews the fat

BY JIM DAVIS

Ballantine Books • **New York**

2008 Ballantine Books Trade Paperback Edition

Published in the United States by Ballantine Books, an imprint of The Random House Publishing Group, a division of Random House, Inc., New York.

BALLANTINE and colophon are registered trademarks of Random House, Inc.

Originally published in slightly different form in the United States by Ballantine Books, an imprint of The Random House Publishing Group, a division of Random House, Inc., in 1989.

ISBN 978-0-345-49170-1

Printed in China

www.ballantinebooks.com

9 8 7 6 5 4 3

Garfield impressions

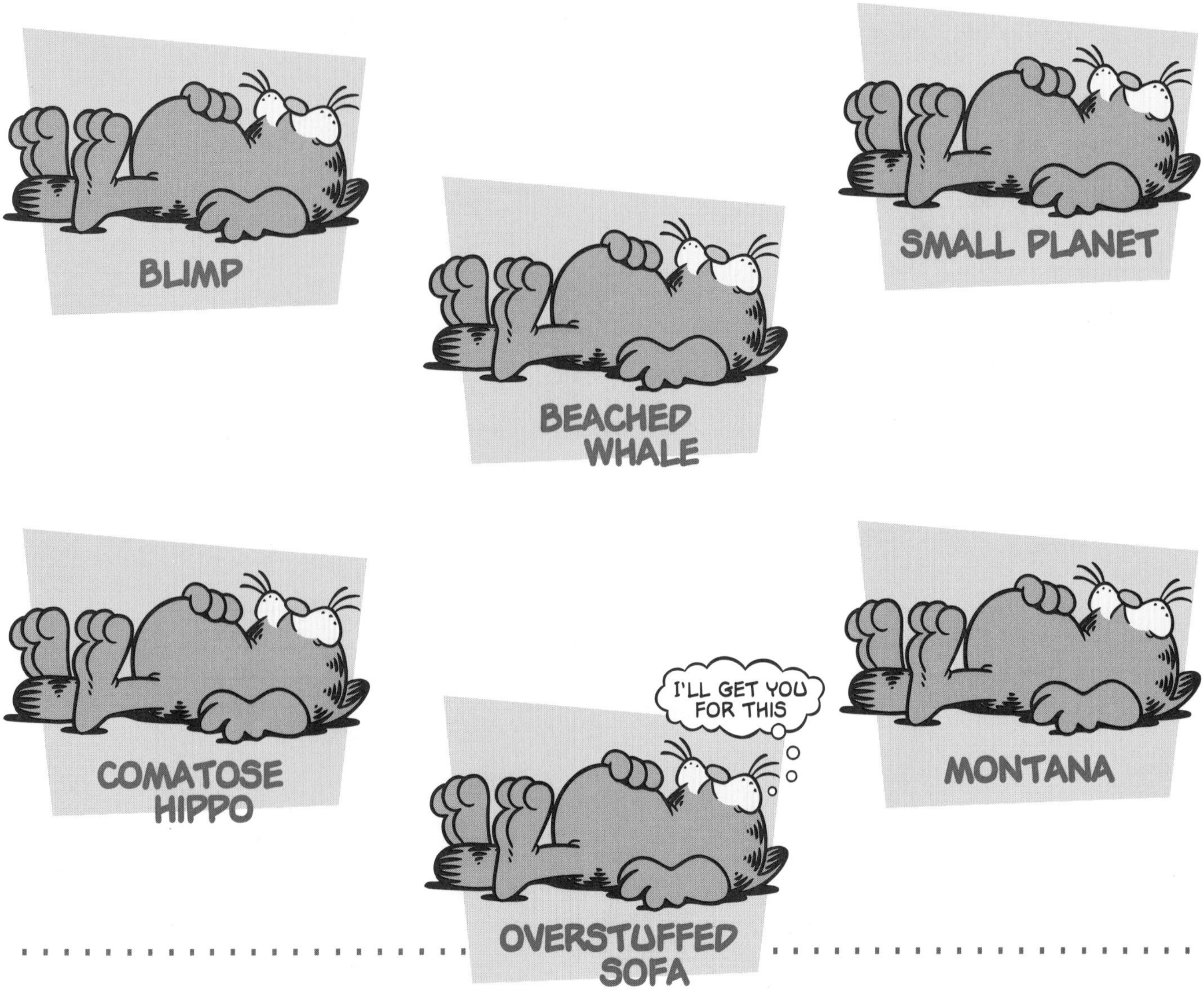
BLIMP
BEACHED WHALE
SMALL PLANET
COMATOSE HIPPO
I'LL GET YOU FOR THIS
OVERSTUFFED SOFA
MONTANA

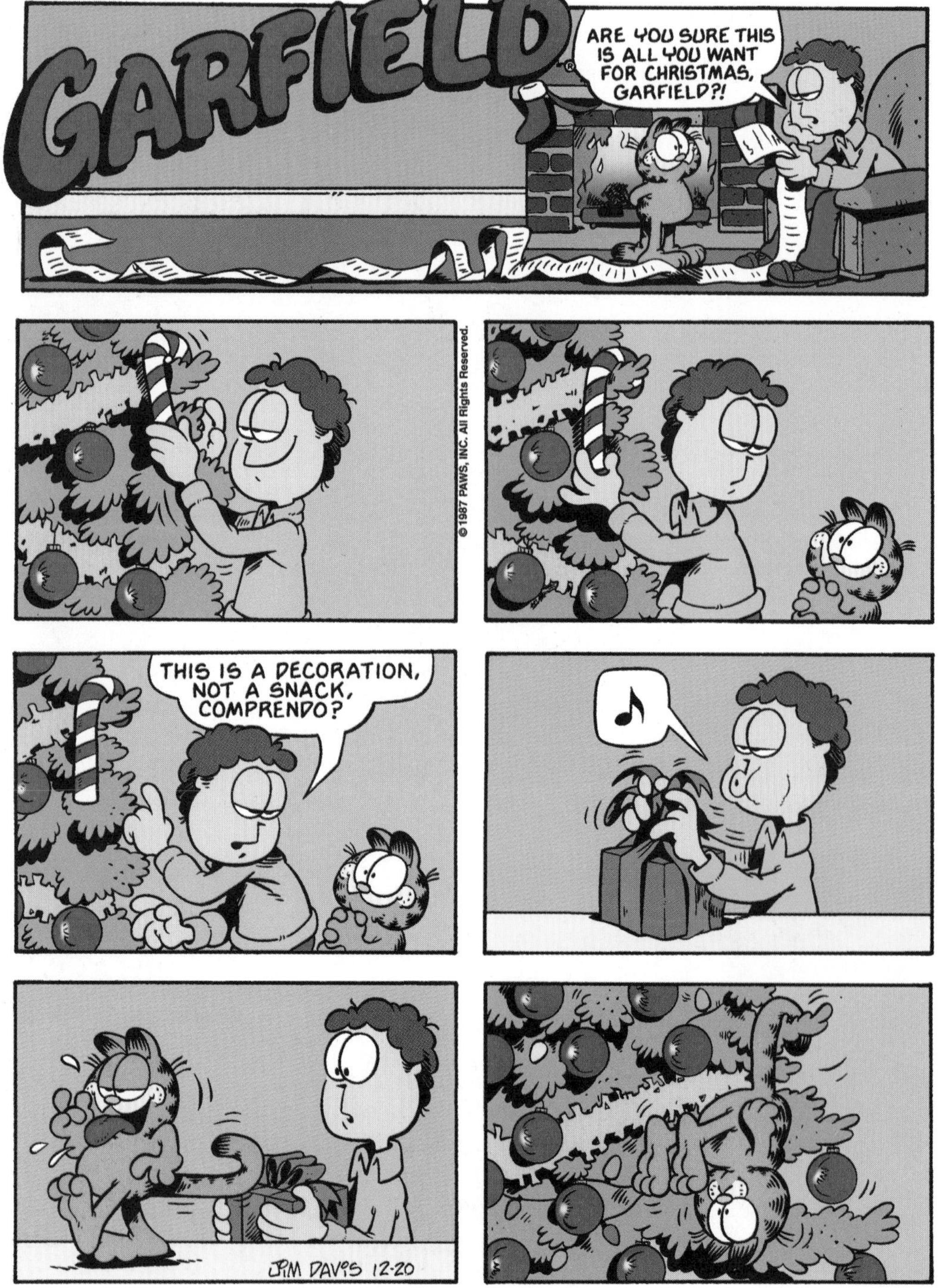
GARFIELD
ARE YOU SURE THIS IS ALL YOU WANT FOR CHRISTMAS, GARFIELD?!
© 1987 PAWS, INC. All Rights Reserved.
THIS IS A DECORATION, NOT A SNACK, COMPRENDO?
♪
JIM DAVIS 12-20

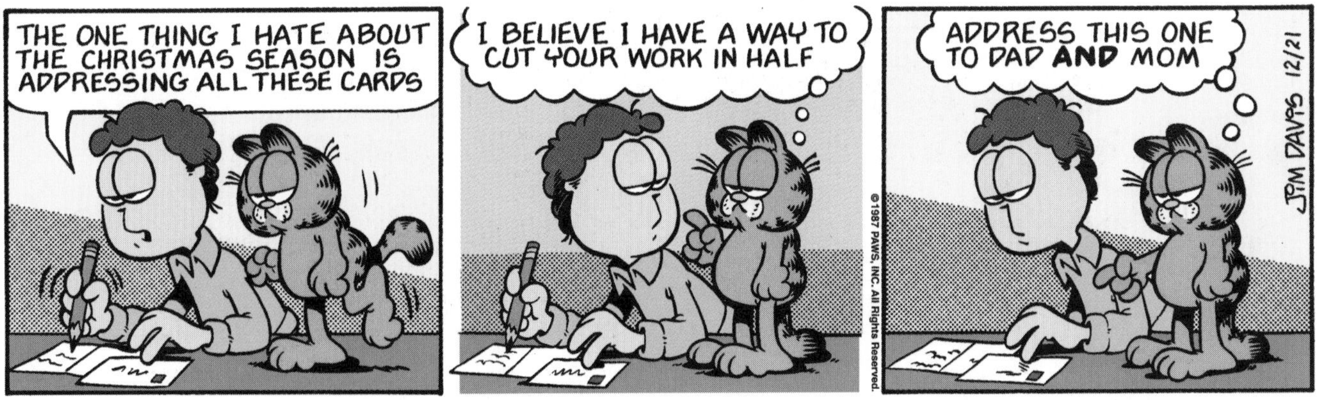
THE ONE THING I HATE ABOUT THE CHRISTMAS SEASON IS ADDRESSING ALL THESE CARDS
I BELIEVE I HAVE A WAY TO CUT YOUR WORK IN HALF
©1987 PAWS, INC. All Rights Reserved.
ADDRESS THIS ONE TO DAD **AND** MOM
JIM DAVIS 12/21

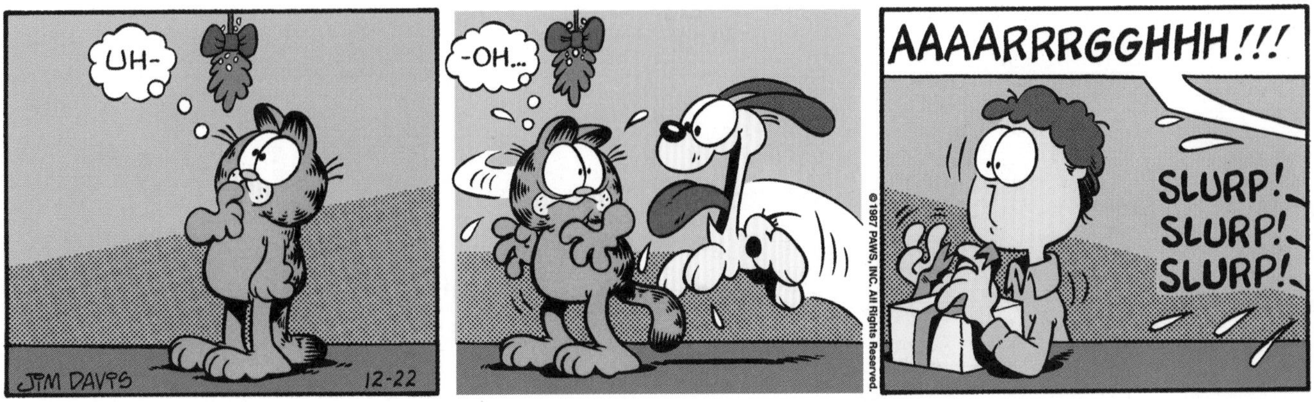
UH-
JIM DAVIS
12-22
-OH...
©1987 PAWS, INC. All Rights Reserved.
AAAARRRGGHHH!!!
SLURP!
SLURP!
SLURP!

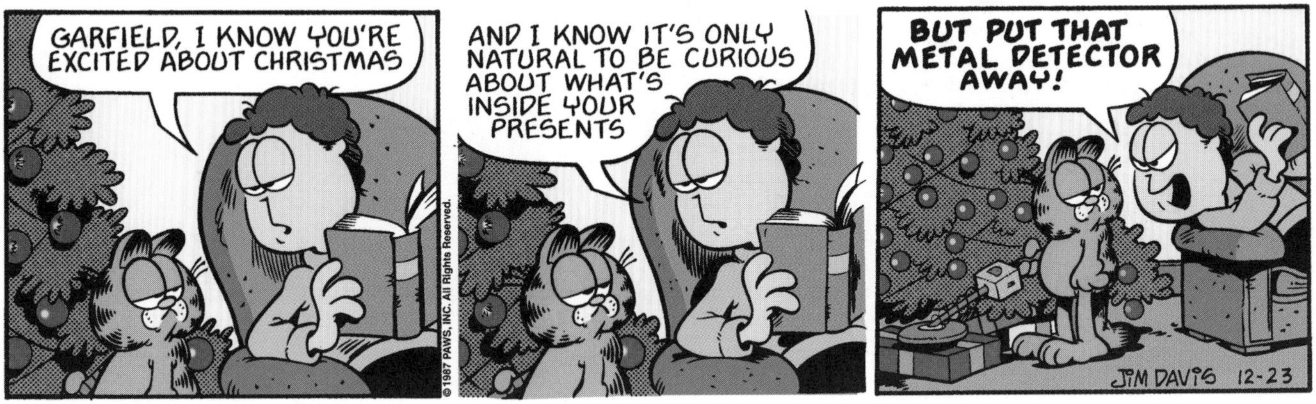
GARFIELD, I KNOW YOU'RE EXCITED ABOUT CHRISTMAS
©1987 PAWS, INC. All Rights Reserved.
AND I KNOW IT'S ONLY NATURAL TO BE CURIOUS ABOUT WHAT'S INSIDE YOUR PRESENTS
BUT PUT THAT METAL DETECTOR AWAY!
JIM DAVIS 12-23

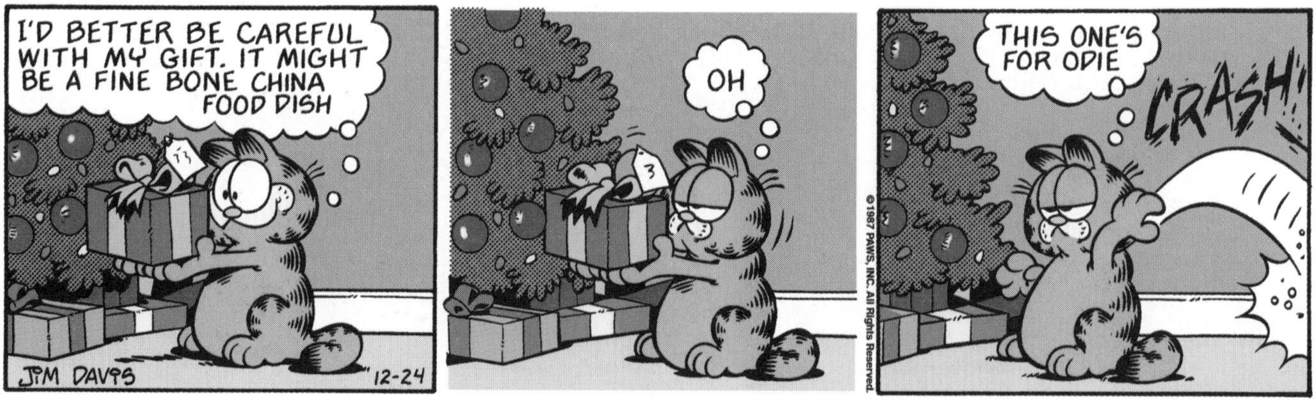
I'D BETTER BE CAREFUL WITH MY GIFT. IT MIGHT BE A FINE BONE CHINA FOOD DISH
JIM DAVIS
12-24
OH
© 1987 PAWS, INC. All Rights Reserved.
THIS ONE'S FOR ODIE
CRASH!!

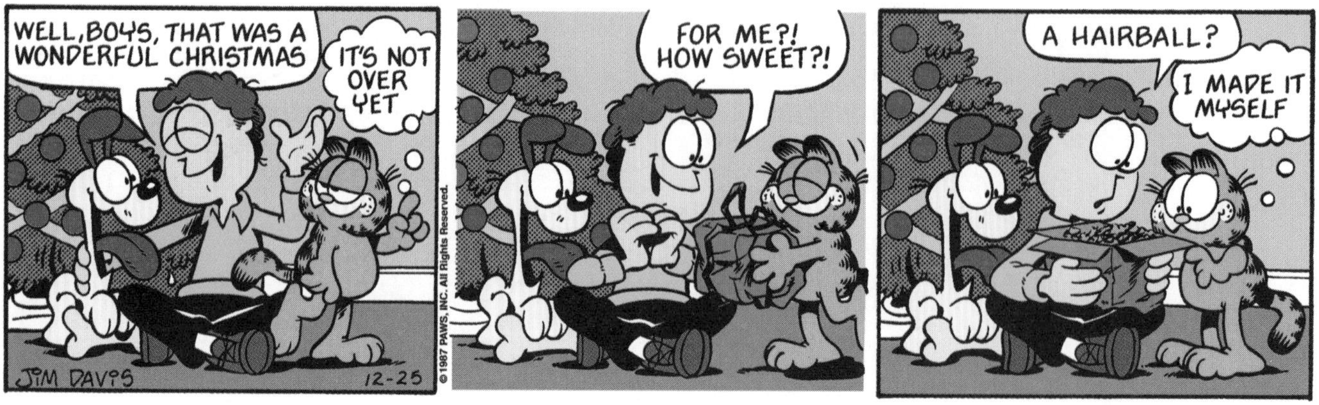
WELL, BOYS, THAT WAS A WONDERFUL CHRISTMAS
IT'S NOT OVER YET
JIM DAVIS
12-25
© 1987 PAWS, INC. All Rights Reserved.
FOR ME?! HOW SWEET?!
A HAIRBALL?
I MADE IT MYSELF

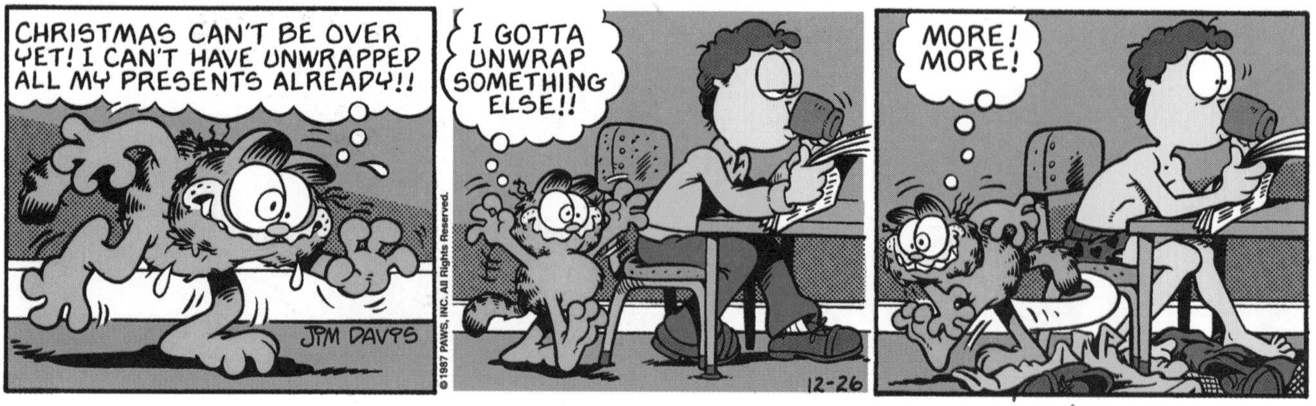
CHRISTMAS CAN'T BE OVER YET! I CAN'T HAVE UNWRAPPED ALL MY PRESENTS ALREADY!!
JIM DAVIS
© 1987 PAWS, INC. All Rights Reserved.
I GOTTA UNWRAP SOMETHING ELSE!!
12-26
MORE! MORE!

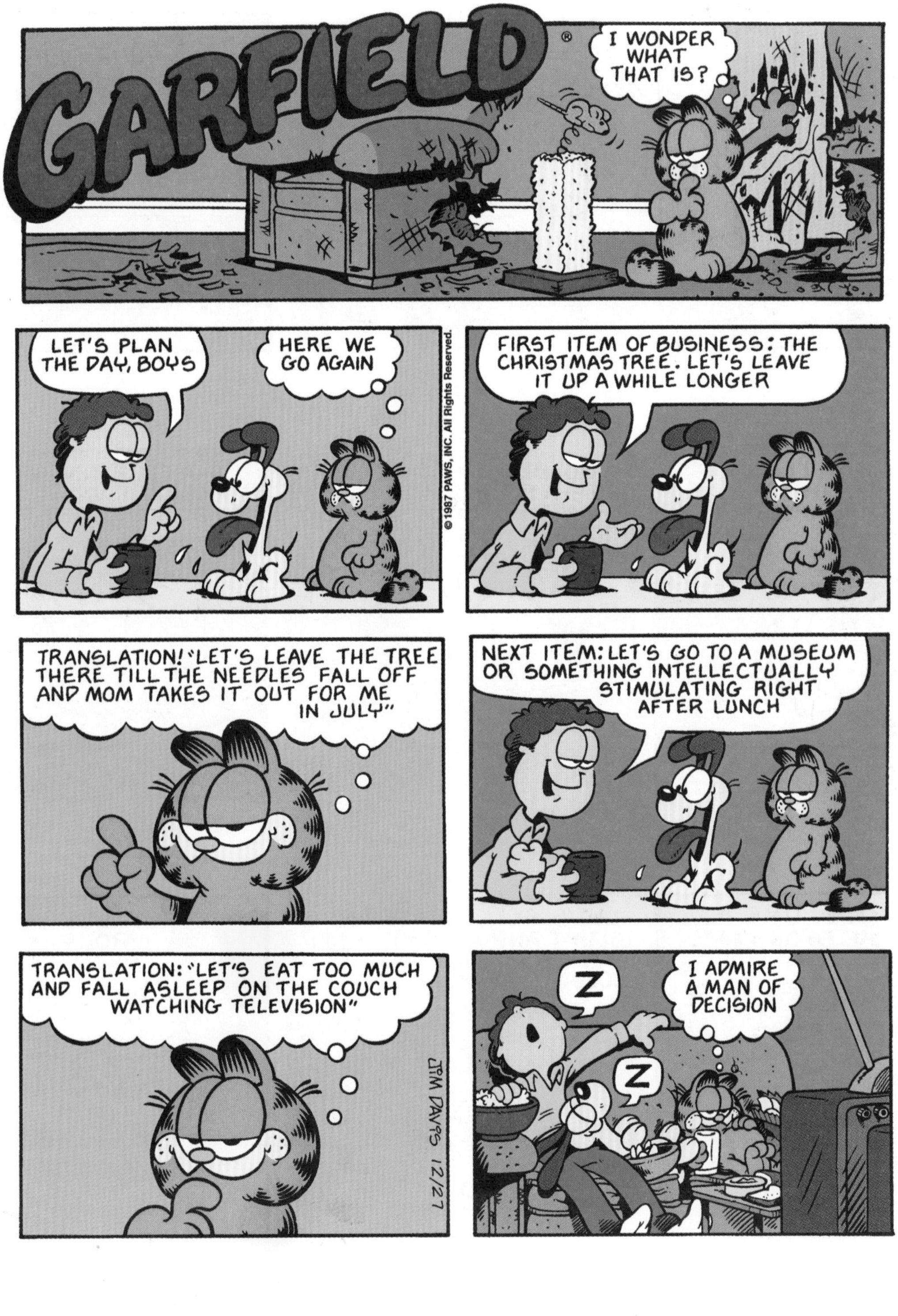

GARFIELD®
I WONDER WHAT THAT IS?
LET'S PLAN THE DAY, BOYS
HERE WE GO AGAIN
©1987 PAWS, INC. All Rights Reserved.
FIRST ITEM OF BUSINESS: THE CHRISTMAS TREE. LET'S LEAVE IT UP A WHILE LONGER
TRANSLATION! "LET'S LEAVE THE TREE THERE TILL THE NEEDLES FALL OFF AND MOM TAKES IT OUT FOR ME IN JULY"
NEXT ITEM: LET'S GO TO A MUSEUM OR SOMETHING INTELLECTUALLY STIMULATING RIGHT AFTER LUNCH
TRANSLATION: "LET'S EAT TOO MUCH AND FALL ASLEEP ON THE COUCH WATCHING TELEVISION"
JIM DAVIS 12/27
Z
Z
I ADMIRE A MAN OF DECISION

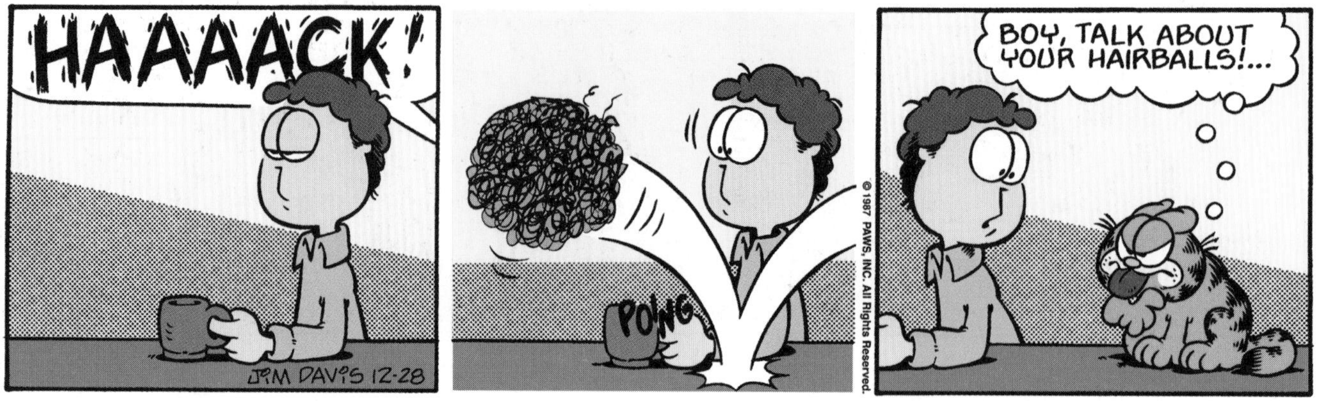
HAAAACK!
JIM DAVIS 12-28
POING
© 1987 PAWS, INC. All Rights Reserved.
BOY, TALK ABOUT YOUR HAIRBALLS!...

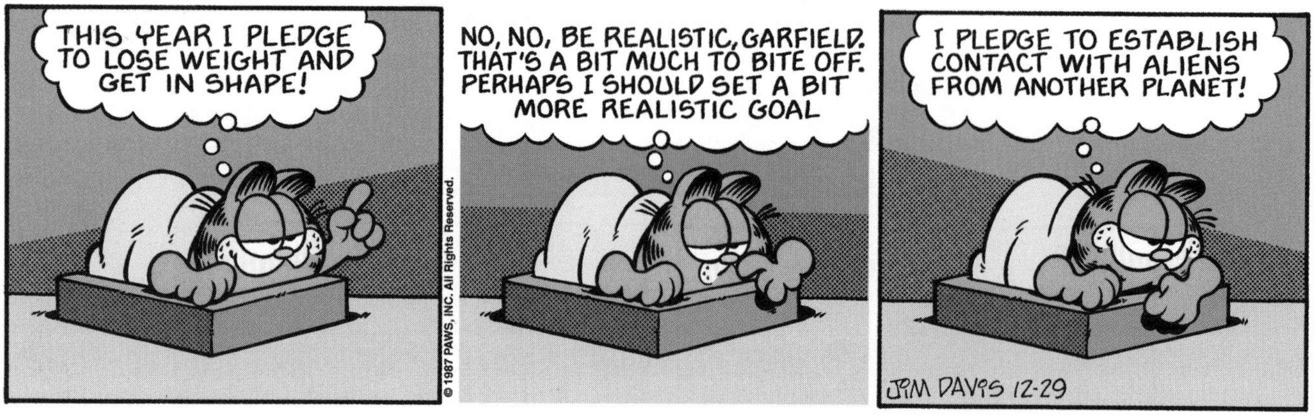
THIS YEAR I PLEDGE TO LOSE WEIGHT AND GET IN SHAPE!
© 1987 PAWS, INC. All Rights Reserved.
NO, NO, BE REALISTIC, GARFIELD. THAT'S A BIT MUCH TO BITE OFF. PERHAPS I SHOULD SET A BIT MORE REALISTIC GOAL
I PLEDGE TO ESTABLISH CONTACT WITH ALIENS FROM ANOTHER PLANET!
JIM DAVIS 12-29

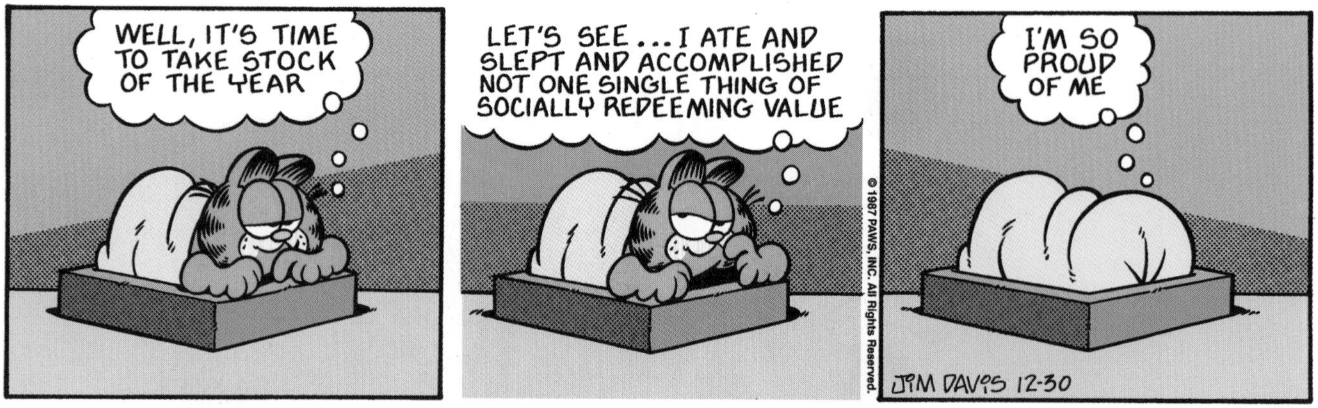
WELL, IT'S TIME TO TAKE STOCK OF THE YEAR
LET'S SEE ... I ATE AND SLEPT AND ACCOMPLISHED NOT ONE SINGLE THING OF SOCIALLY REDEEMING VALUE
© 1987 PAWS, INC. All Rights Reserved.
I'M SO PROUD OF ME
JIM DAVIS 12-30

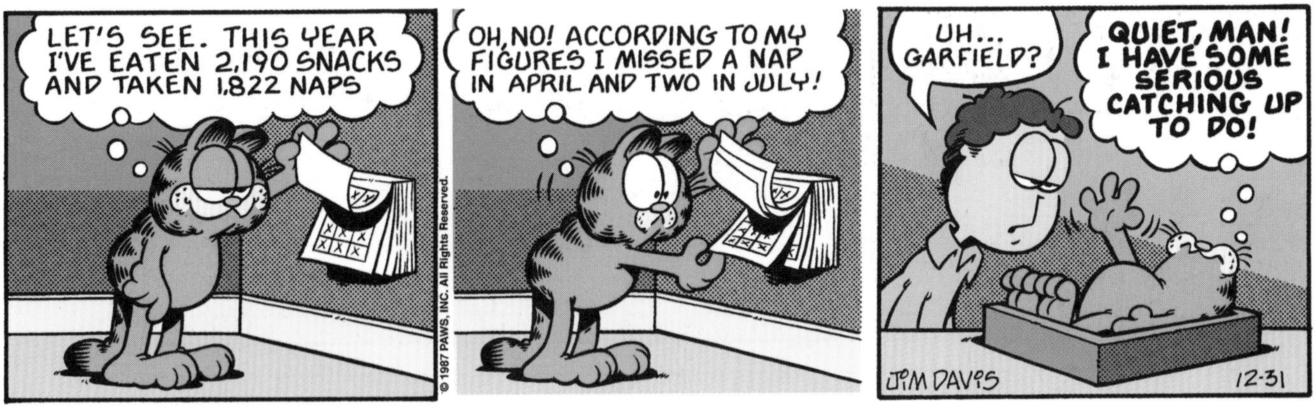
LET'S SEE. THIS YEAR I'VE EATEN 2,190 SNACKS AND TAKEN 1,822 NAPS
OH, NO! ACCORDING TO MY FIGURES I MISSED A NAP IN APRIL AND TWO IN JULY!
UH... GARFIELD?
QUIET, MAN! I HAVE SOME SERIOUS CATCHING UP TO DO!
JIM DAVIS
12-31

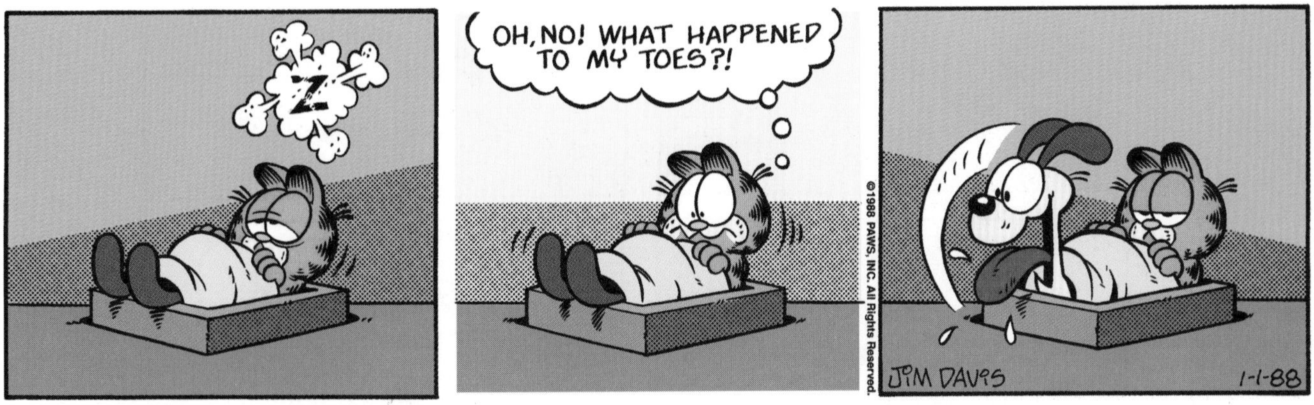
Z
OH, NO! WHAT HAPPENED TO MY TOES?!
JIM DAVIS
1-1-88

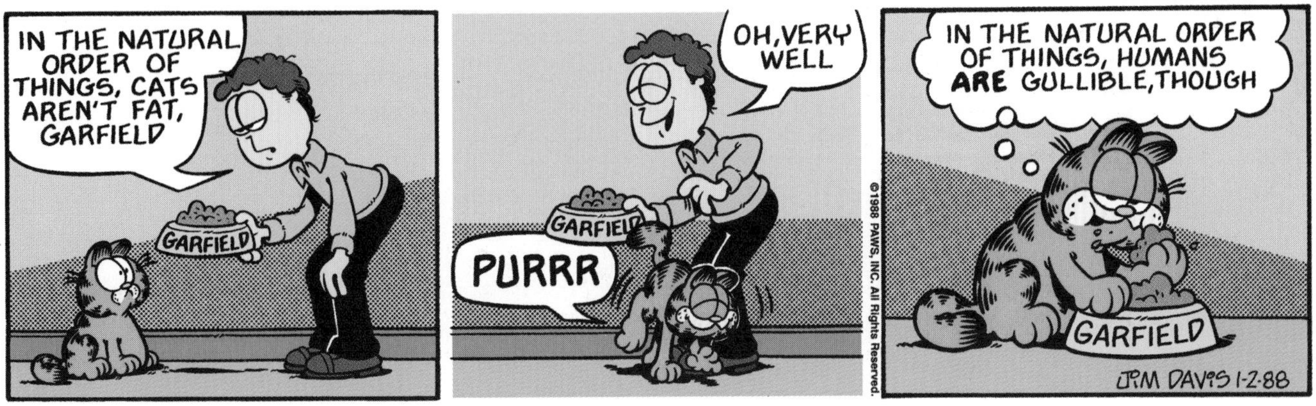
IN THE NATURAL ORDER OF THINGS, CATS AREN'T FAT, GARFIELD
GARFIELD
OH, VERY WELL
GARFIELD
PURRR
IN THE NATURAL ORDER OF THINGS, HUMANS **ARE** GULLIBLE, THOUGH
GARFIELD
JIM DAVIS 1-2-88

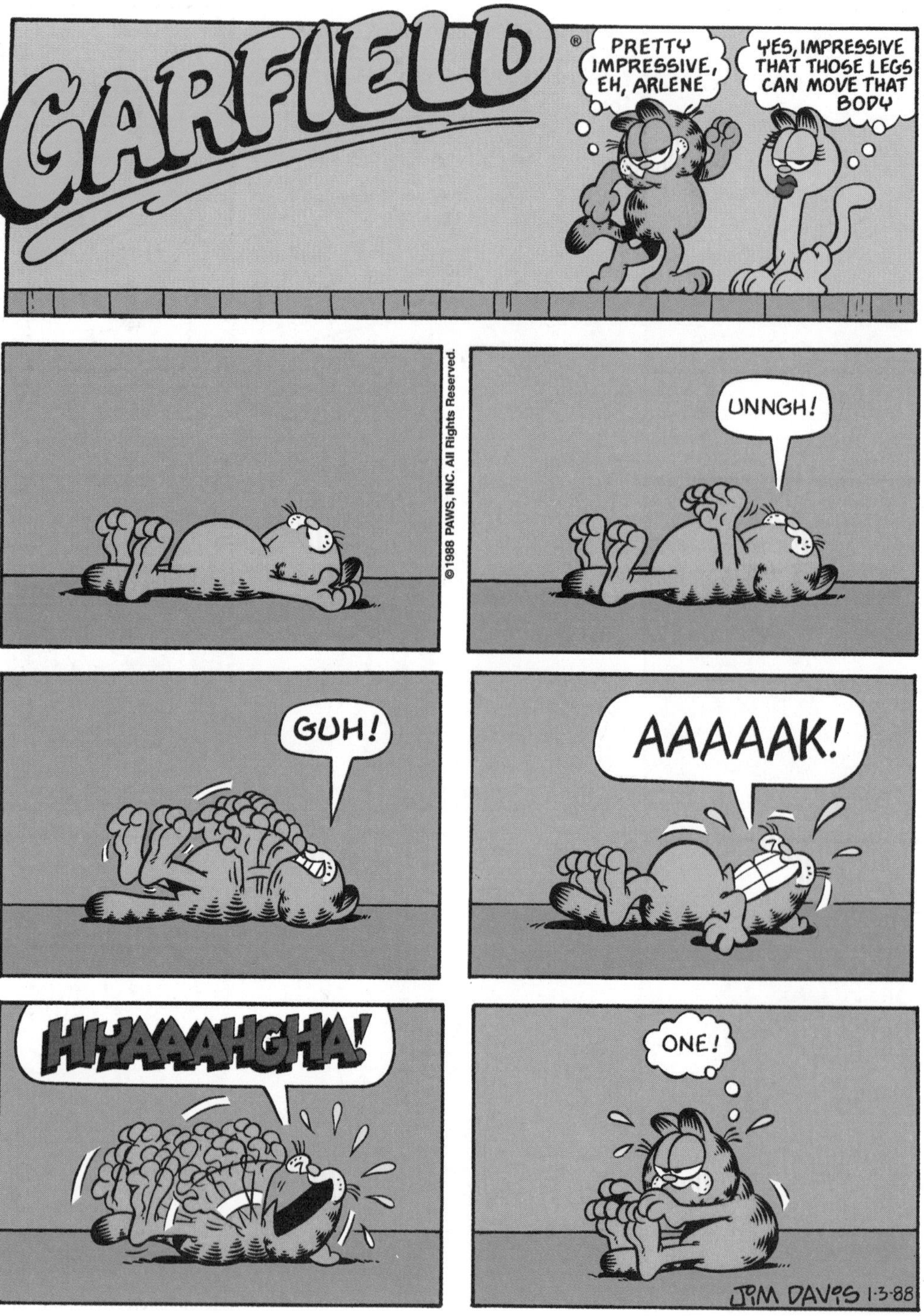
GARFIELD®
PRETTY IMPRESSIVE, EH, ARLENE
YES, IMPRESSIVE THAT THOSE LEGS CAN MOVE THAT BODY
©1988 PAWS, INC. All Rights Reserved.
UNNGH!
GUH!
AAAAAK!
HIYAAAHGHA!
ONE!
JIM DAVIS 1-3-88

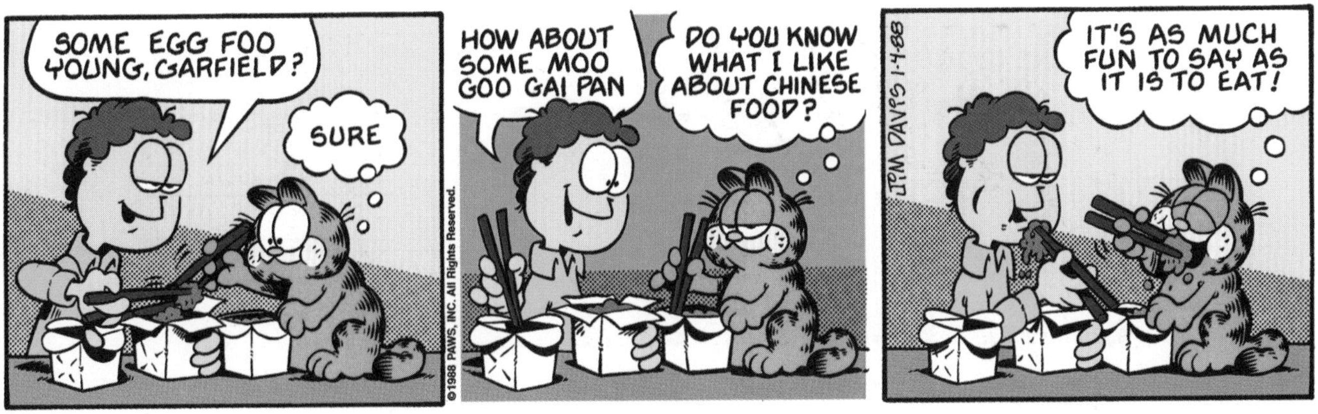
SOME EGG FOO YOUNG, GARFIELD?
SURE
©1988 PAWS, INC. All Rights Reserved.
HOW ABOUT SOME MOO GOO GAI PAN
DO YOU KNOW WHAT I LIKE ABOUT CHINESE FOOD?
JIM DAVIS 1-4-88
IT'S AS MUCH FUN TO SAY AS IT IS TO EAT!

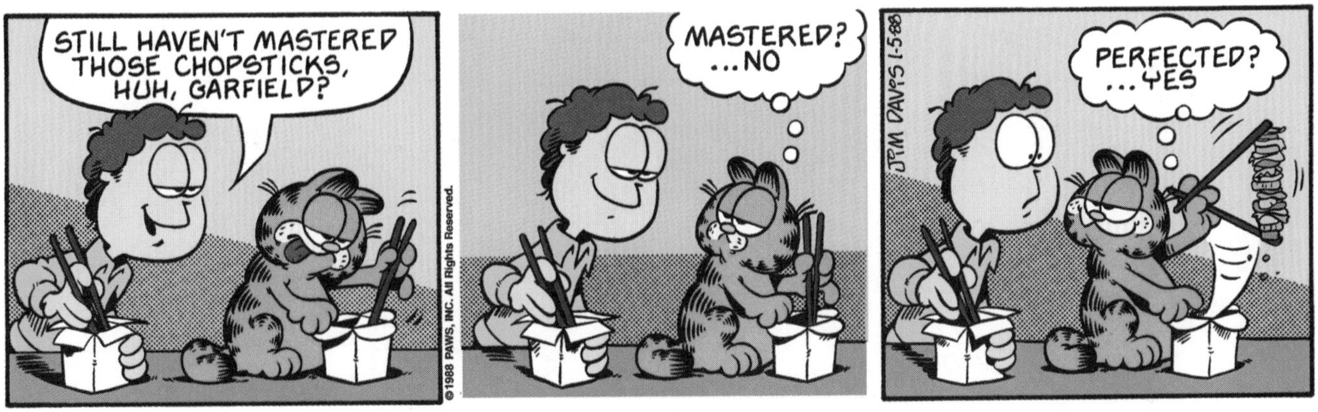
STILL HAVEN'T MASTERED THOSE CHOPSTICKS, HUH, GARFIELD?
©1988 PAWS, INC. All Rights Reserved.
MASTERED? ...NO
JIM DAVIS 1-5-88
PERFECTED? ...YES

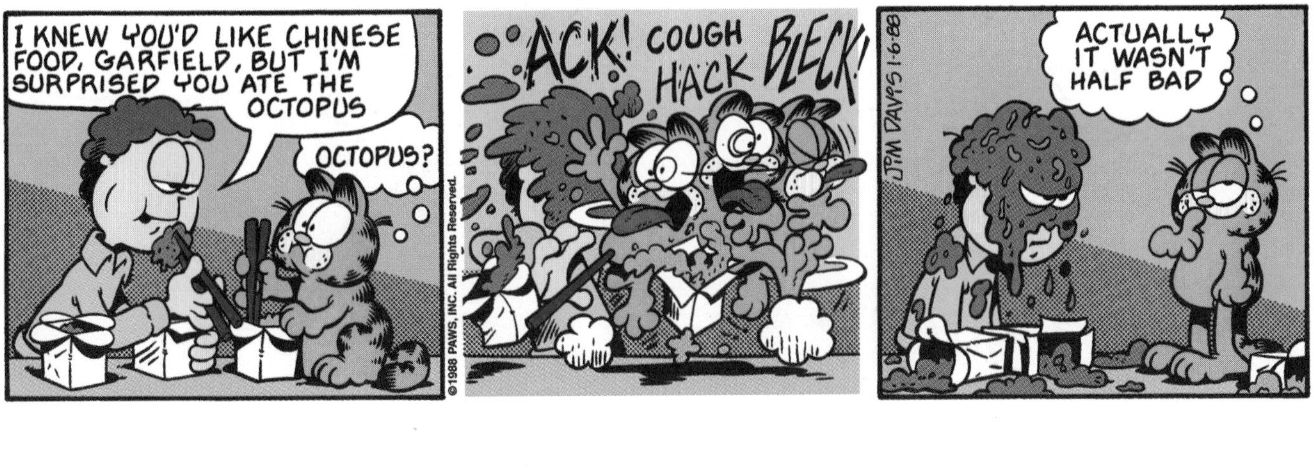
I KNEW YOU'D LIKE CHINESE FOOD, GARFIELD, BUT I'M SURPRISED YOU ATE THE OCTOPUS
OCTOPUS?
©1988 PAWS, INC. All Rights Reserved.
ACK! COUGH HACK BLECK!
JIM DAVIS 1-6-88
ACTUALLY IT WASN'T HALF BAD

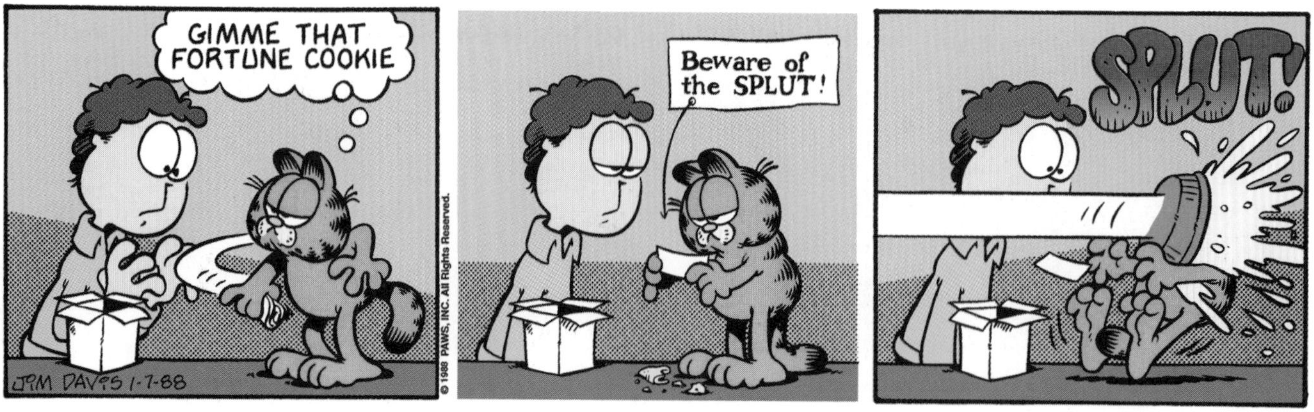
GIMME THAT FORTUNE COOKIE
JIM DAVIS 1-7-88
© 1988 PAWS, INC. All Rights Reserved.
Beware of the SPLUT!
SPLUT!

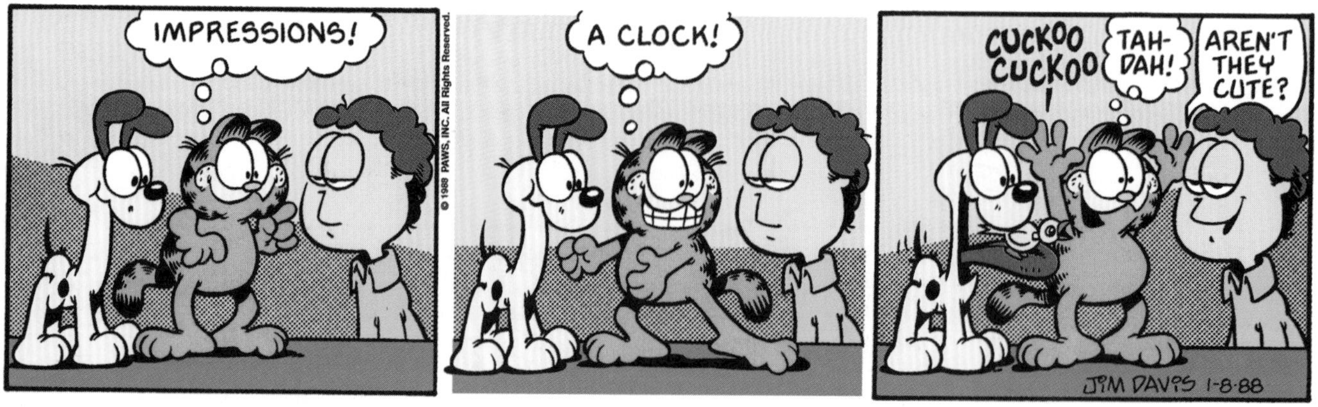
IMPRESSIONS!
© 1988 PAWS, INC. All Rights Reserved.
A CLOCK!
CUCKOO CUCKOO
TAH-DAH!
AREN'T THEY CUTE?
JIM DAVIS 1-8-88

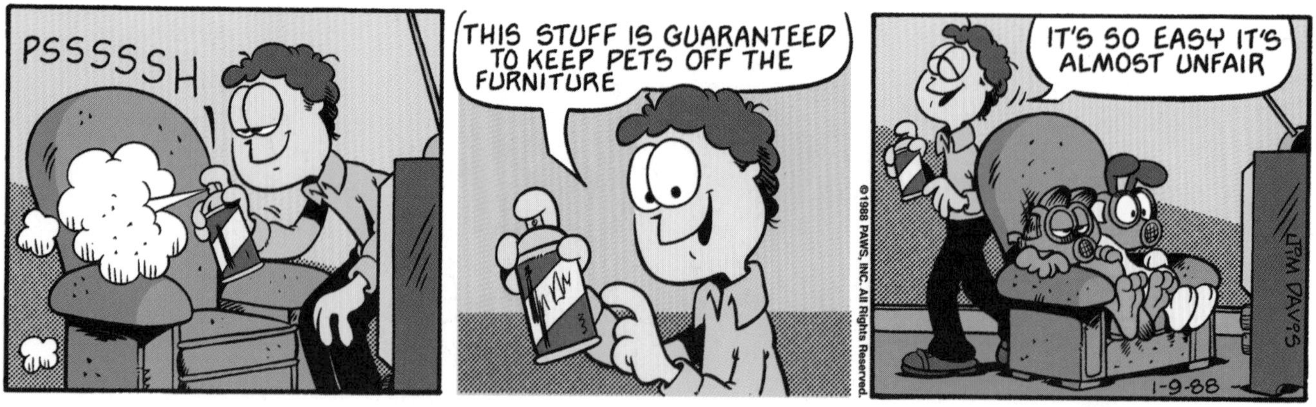
PSSSSSH
THIS STUFF IS GUARANTEED TO KEEP PETS OFF THE FURNITURE
©1988 PAWS, INC. All Rights Reserved.
IT'S SO EASY IT'S ALMOST UNFAIR
JIM DAVIS
1-9-88

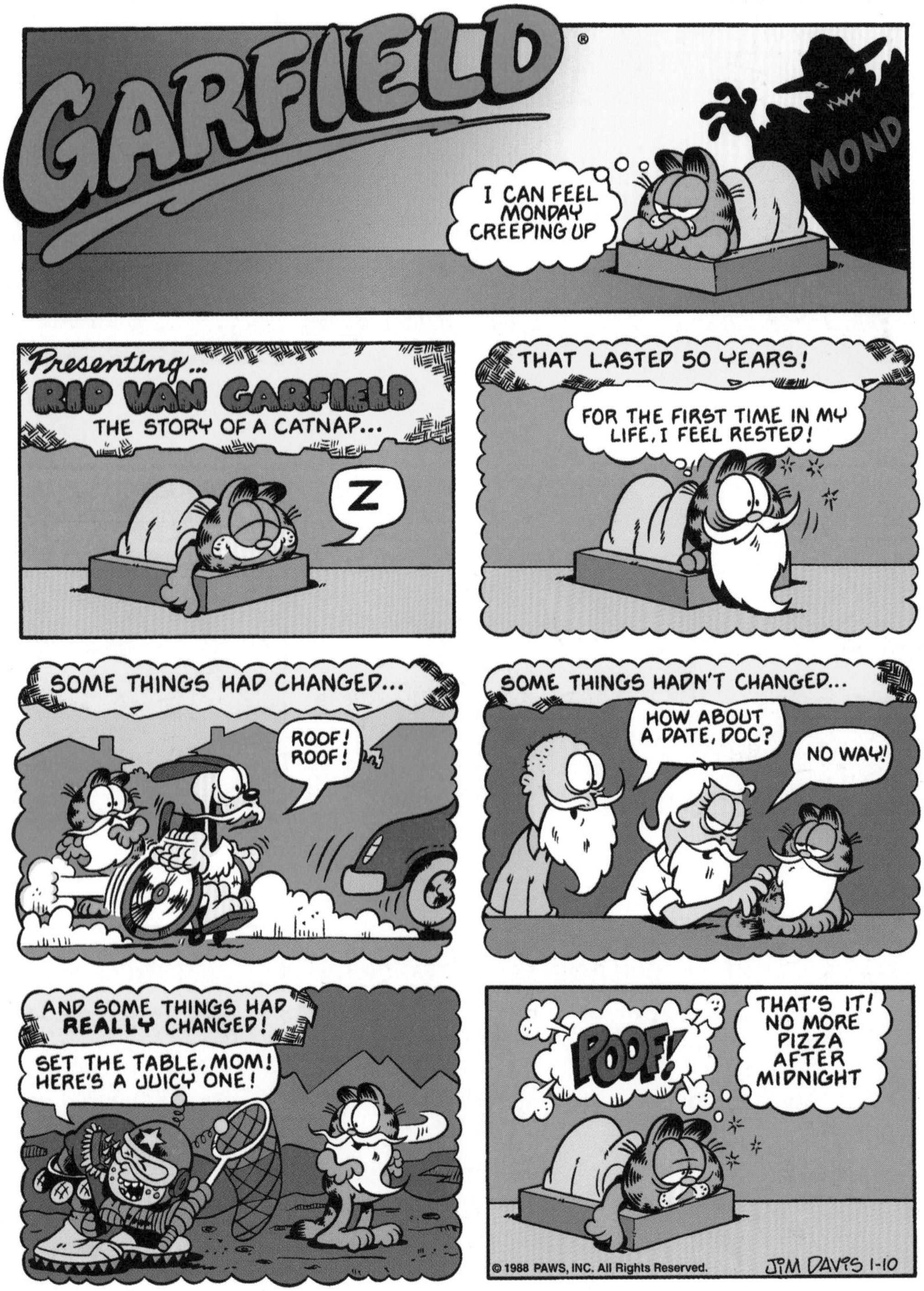
GARFIELD®
MOND
I CAN FEEL MONDAY CREEPING UP
Presenting... RIP VAN GARFIELD
THE STORY OF A CATNAP...
Z
THAT LASTED 50 YEARS!
FOR THE FIRST TIME IN MY LIFE, I FEEL RESTED!
SOME THINGS HAD CHANGED...
ROOF! ROOF!
SOME THINGS HADN'T CHANGED...
HOW ABOUT A DATE, DOC?
NO WAY!
AND SOME THINGS HAD REALLY CHANGED!
SET THE TABLE, MOM! HERE'S A JUICY ONE!
POOF!
THAT'S IT! NO MORE PIZZA AFTER MIDNIGHT
© 1988 PAWS, INC. All Rights Reserved.
JIM DAVIS 1-10

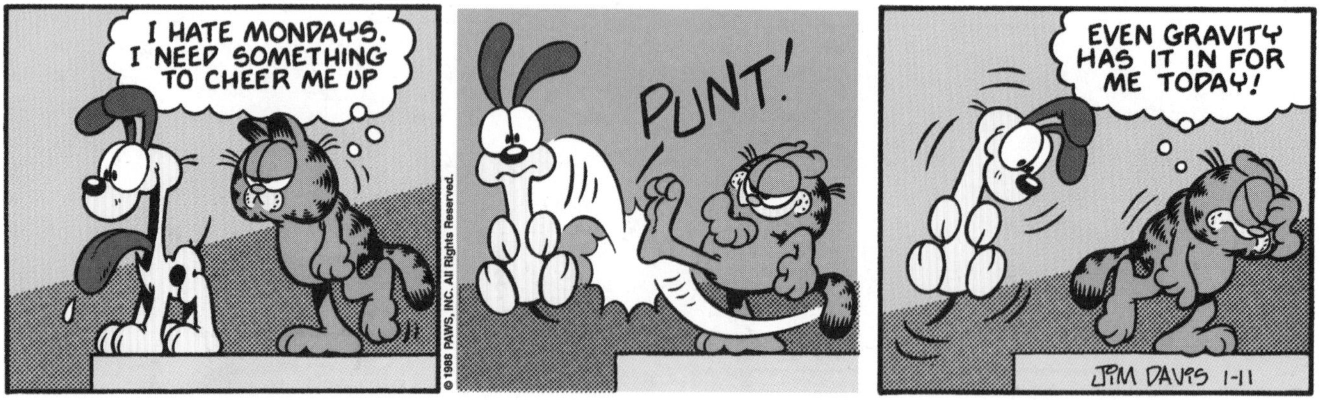
I HATE MONDAYS. I NEED SOMETHING TO CHEER ME UP
PUNT!
© 1988 PAWS, INC. All Rights Reserved.
EVEN GRAVITY HAS IT IN FOR ME TODAY!
JIM DAVIS 1-11

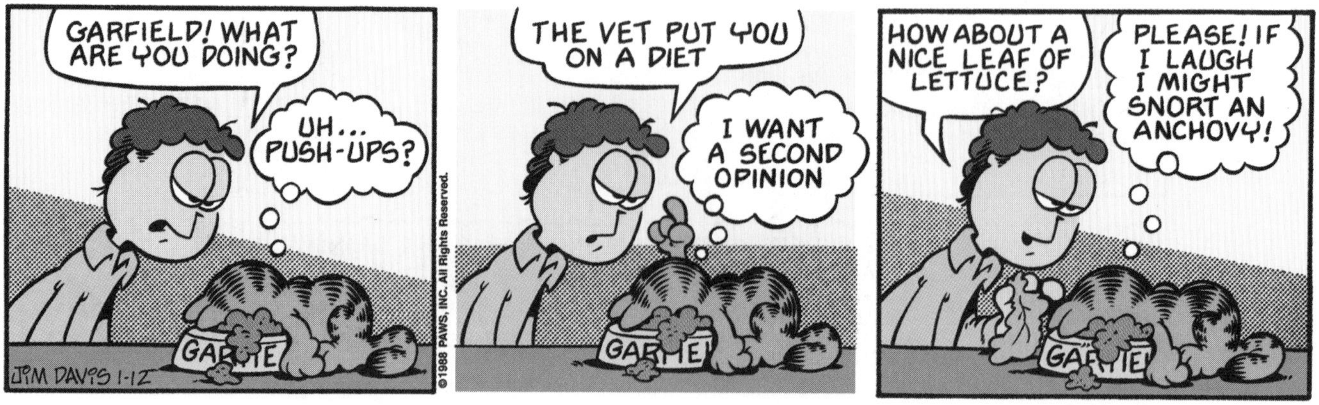
GARFIELD! WHAT ARE YOU DOING?
UH... PUSH-UPS?
JIM DAVIS 1-12
© 1988 PAWS, INC. All Rights Reserved.
THE VET PUT YOU ON A DIET
I WANT A SECOND OPINION
HOW ABOUT A NICE LEAF OF LETTUCE?
PLEASE! IF I LAUGH I MIGHT SNORT AN ANCHOVY!

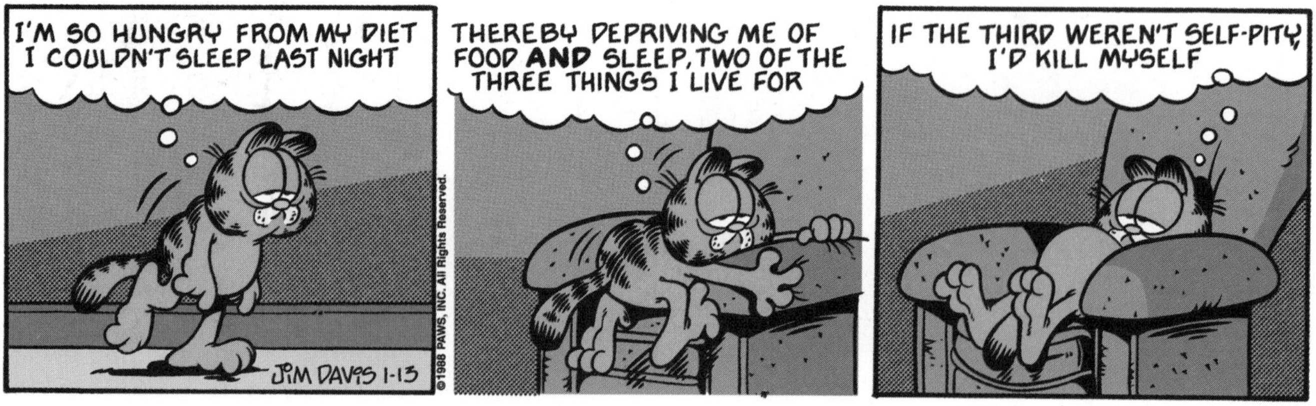
I'M SO HUNGRY FROM MY DIET I COULDN'T SLEEP LAST NIGHT
JIM DAVIS 1-13
© 1988 PAWS, INC. All Rights Reserved.
THEREBY DEPRIVING ME OF FOOD **AND** SLEEP, TWO OF THE THREE THINGS I LIVE FOR
IF THE THIRD WEREN'T SELF-PITY, I'D KILL MYSELF

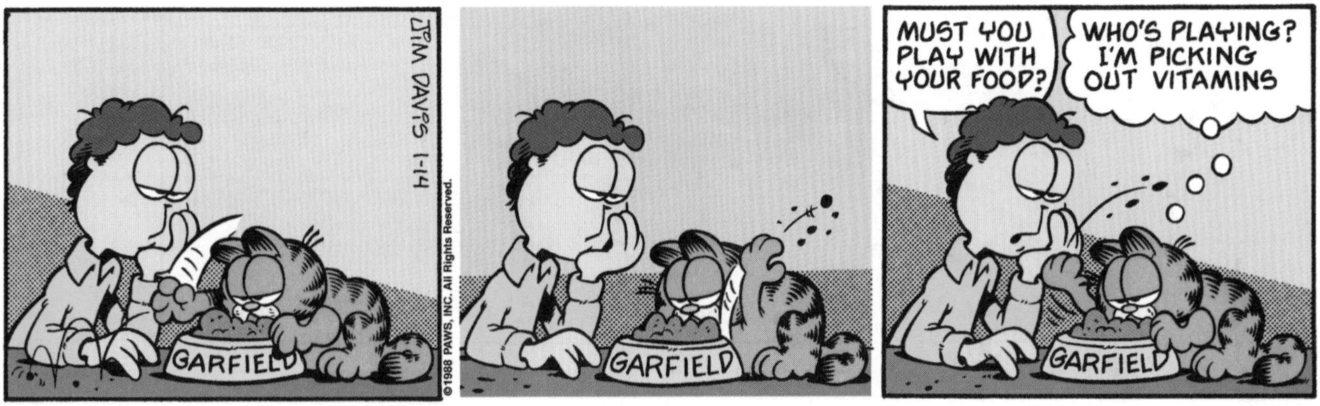
JIM DAVIS 1-14
©1988 PAWS, INC. All Rights Reserved.
MUST YOU PLAY WITH YOUR FOOD?
WHO'S PLAYING? I'M PICKING OUT VITAMINS
GARFIELD

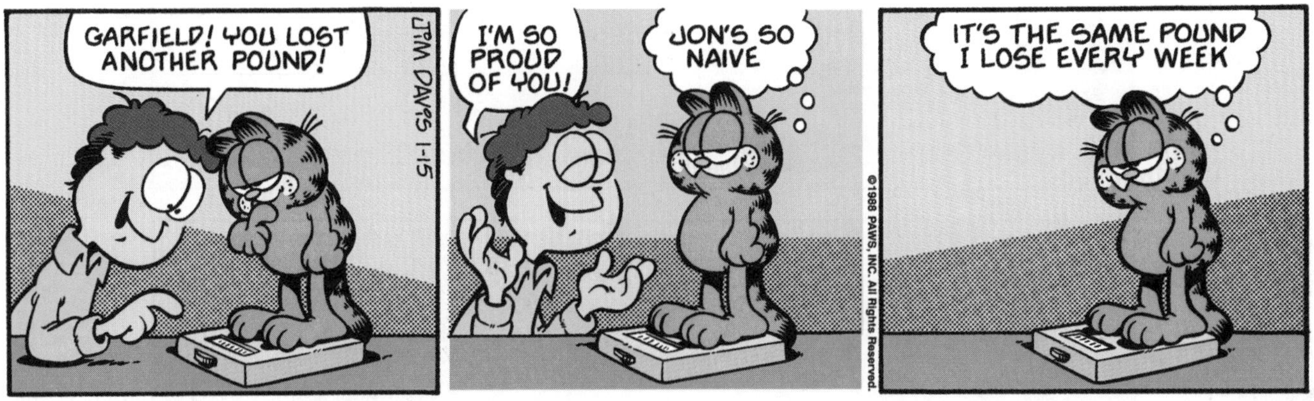
GARFIELD! YOU LOST ANOTHER POUND!
JIM DAVIS 1-15
I'M SO PROUD OF YOU!
JON'S SO NAIVE
©1988 PAWS, INC. All Rights Reserved.
IT'S THE SAME POUND I LOSE EVERY WEEK

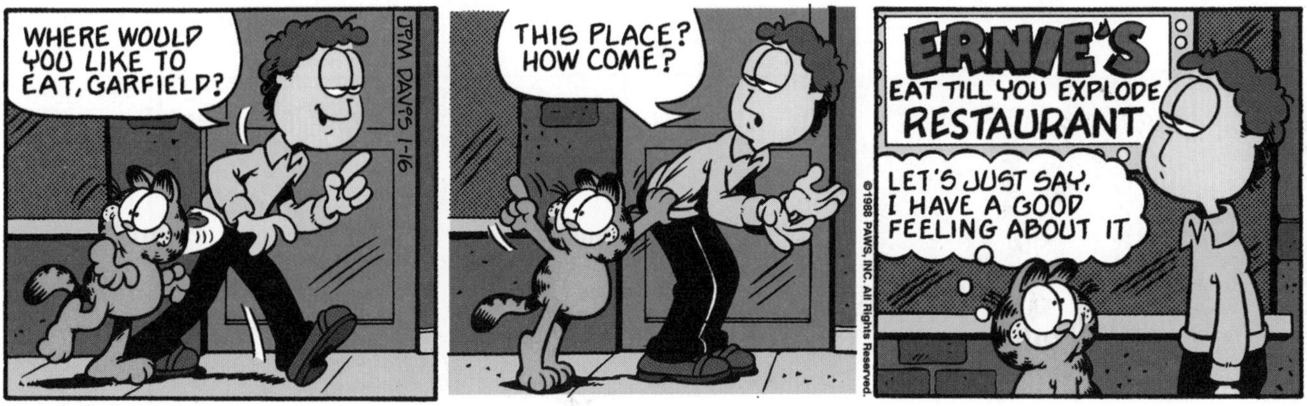
WHERE WOULD YOU LIKE TO EAT, GARFIELD?
JIM DAVIS 1-16
THIS PLACE? HOW COME?
©1988 PAWS, INC. All Rights Reserved.
ERNIE'S
EAT TILL YOU EXPLODE
RESTAURANT
LET'S JUST SAY, I HAVE A GOOD FEELING ABOUT IT

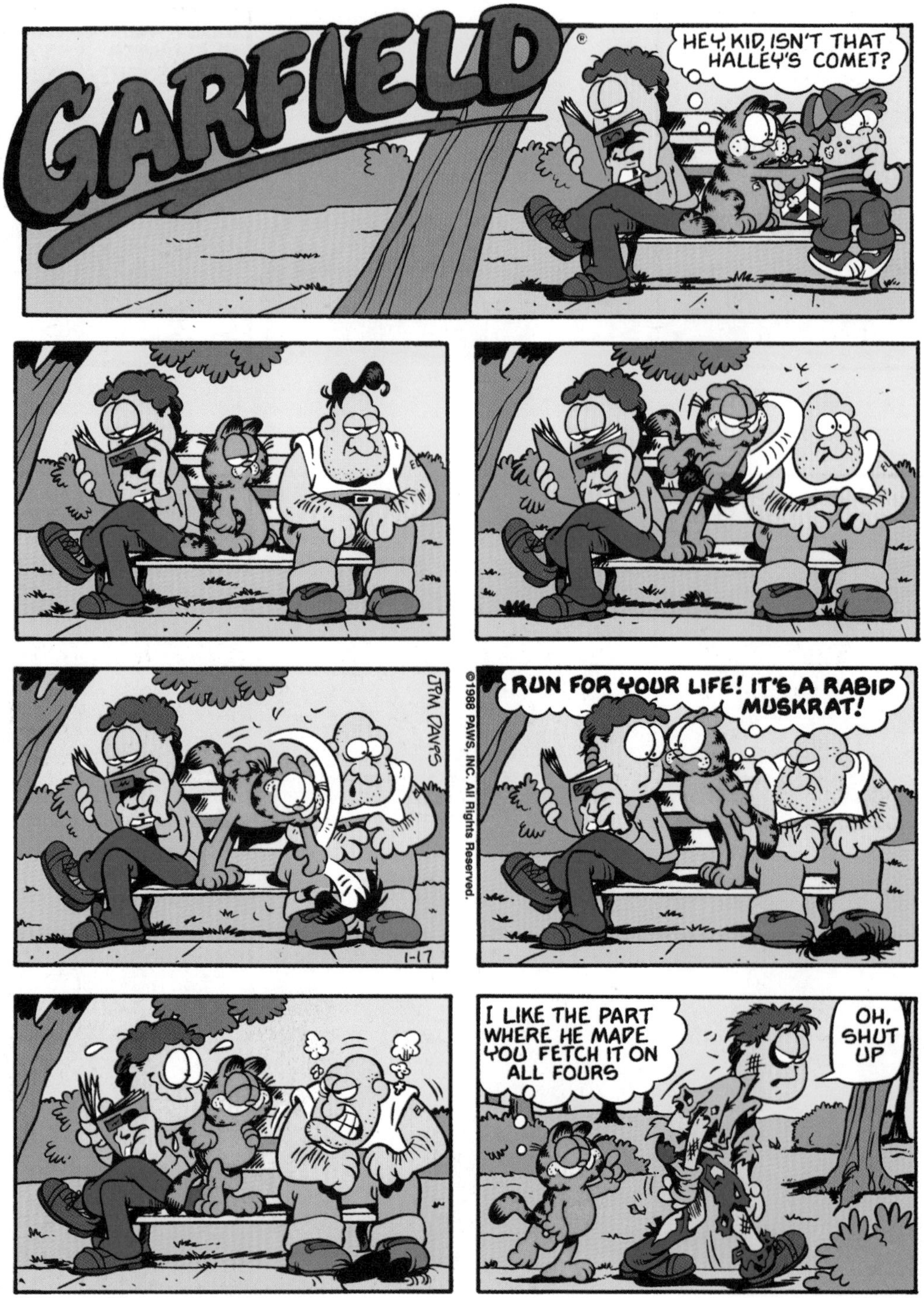
GARFIELD
HEY, KID, ISN'T THAT HALLEY'S COMET?
JIM DAVIS
©1988 PAWS, INC. All Rights Reserved.
1-17
RUN FOR YOUR LIFE! IT'S A RABID MUSKRAT!
I LIKE THE PART WHERE HE MADE YOU FETCH IT ON ALL FOURS
OH, SHUT UP

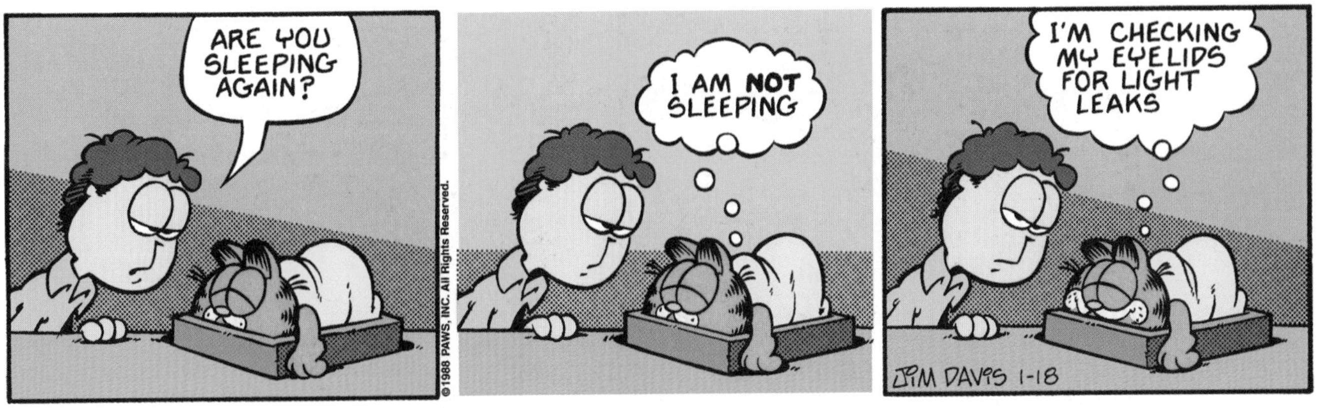
ARE YOU SLEEPING AGAIN?
© 1988 PAWS, INC. All Rights Reserved.
I AM **NOT** SLEEPING
I'M CHECKING MY EYELIDS FOR LIGHT LEAKS
JIM DAVIS 1-18

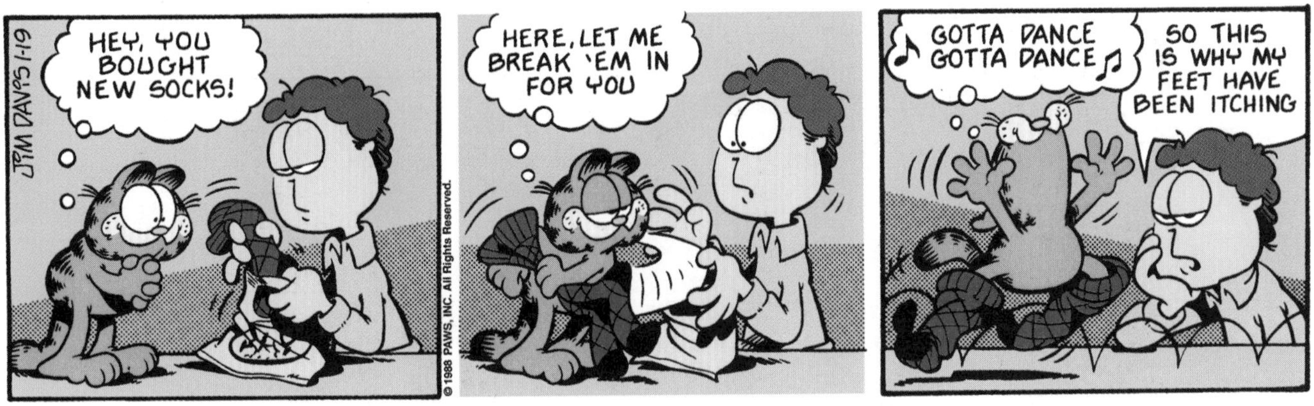
JIM DAVIS 1-19
HEY, YOU BOUGHT NEW SOCKS!
© 1988 PAWS, INC. All Rights Reserved.
HERE, LET ME BREAK 'EM IN FOR YOU
GOTTA DANCE GOTTA DANCE
SO THIS IS WHY MY FEET HAVE BEEN ITCHING

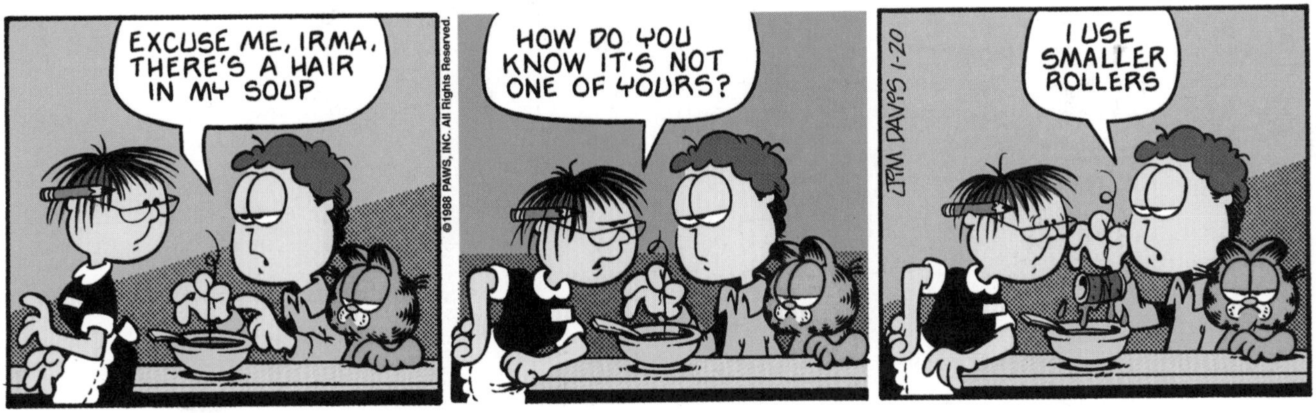
EXCUSE ME, IRMA, THERE'S A HAIR IN MY SOUP
© 1988 PAWS, INC. All Rights Reserved.
HOW DO YOU KNOW IT'S NOT ONE OF YOURS?
JIM DAVIS 1-20
I USE SMALLER ROLLERS

HEY, LOOK, GARFIELD. ODIE'S STANDING ON HIS HEAD!
SO?
JIM DAVIS 1-21
ISN'T THAT AMAZING?!
NOT REALLY
© 1988 PAWS, INC. All Rights Reserved.
HOW DOES HE DO THAT?
I GLUED HIS HEAD TO THE TABLE

THEY SAY CATS CAN SEE IN THE DARK
JIM DAVIS
1-22
© 1988 PAWS, INC. All Rights Reserved.
HEY! IT'S TRUE! I **CAN** SEE!
CLICK
I SEE A WHOLE LOT OF DARK

I SHALL NOW DERIVE GREAT PLEASURE FROM KICKING ODIE OFF THIS TABLE
CRASH!
© 1988 PAWS, INC. All Rights Reserved.
THAT WAS DARNED INCONSIDERATE!
JIM DAVIS 1-23

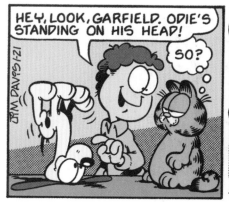

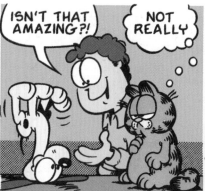

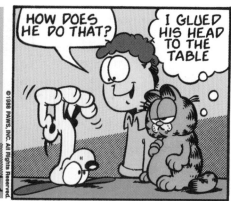

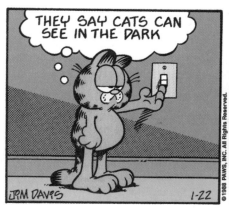

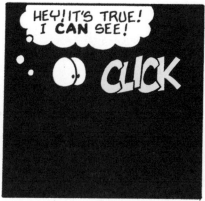

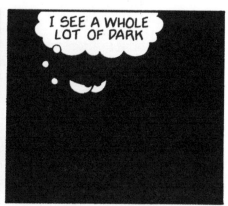

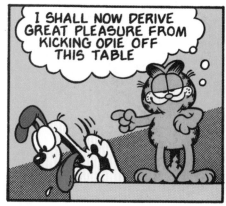

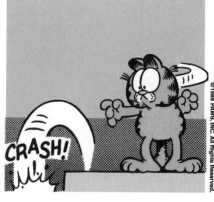

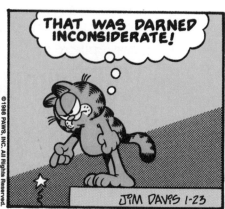

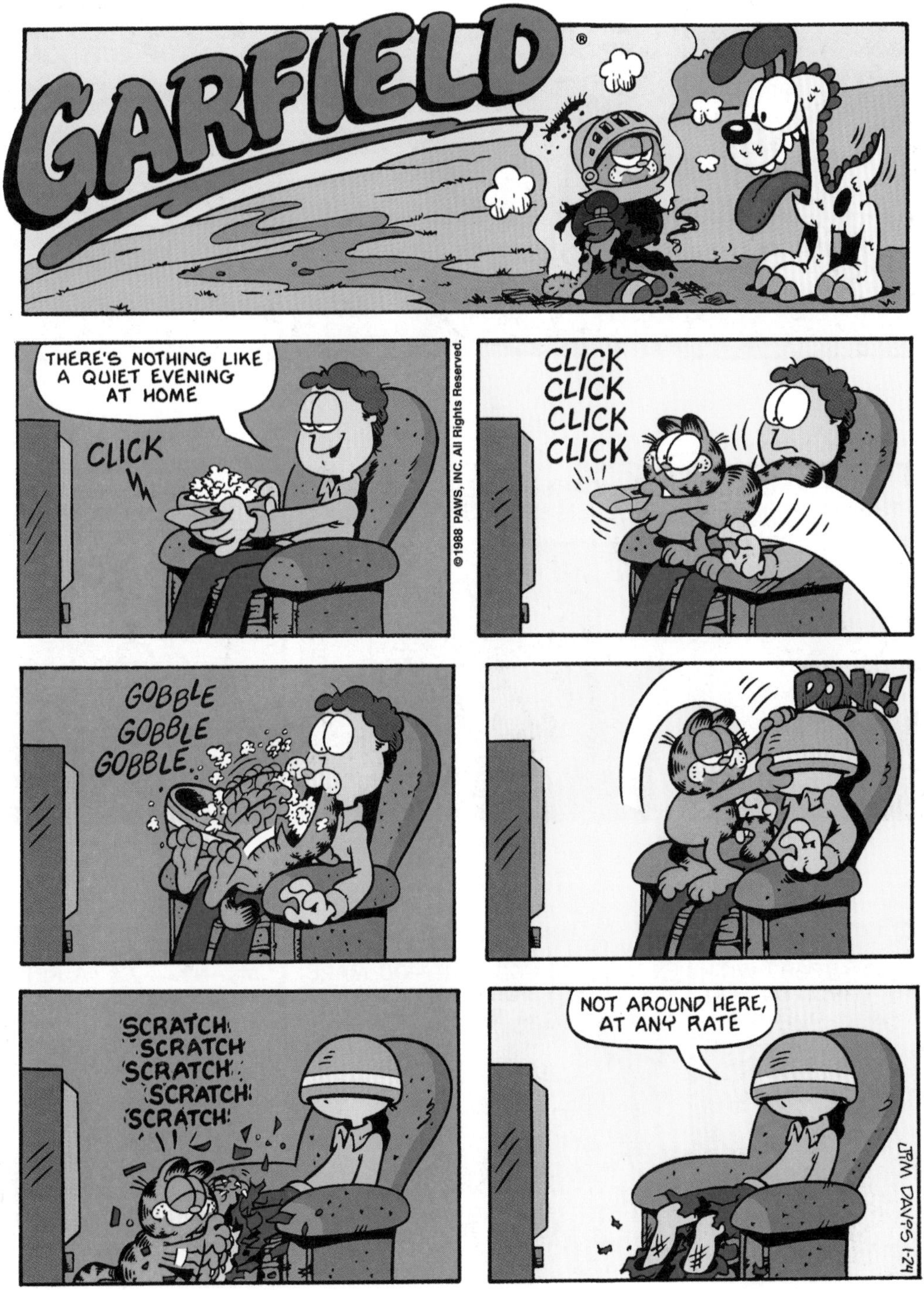
GARFIELD®
THERE'S NOTHING LIKE A QUIET EVENING AT HOME
CLICK
©1988 PAWS, INC. All Rights Reserved.
CLICK CLICK CLICK CLICK
GOBBLE GOBBLE GOBBLE...
DONK!
SCRATCH SCRATCH SCRATCH SCRATCH SCRATCH
NOT AROUND HERE, AT ANY RATE
JIM DAVIS 1-24

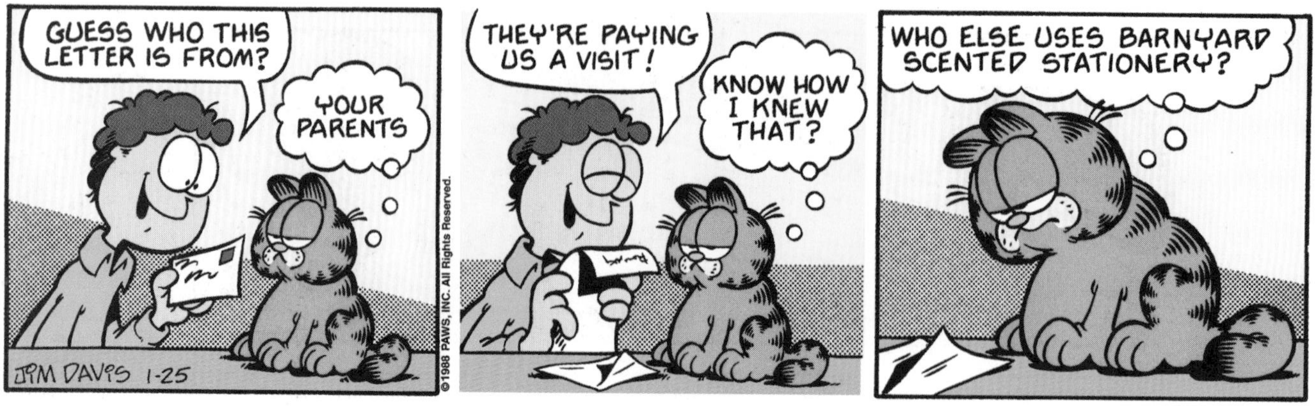
GUESS WHO THIS LETTER IS FROM?
YOUR PARENTS
JIM DAVIS 1-25
©1988 PAWS, INC. All Rights Reserved.
THEY'RE PAYING US A VISIT!
KNOW HOW I KNEW THAT?
WHO ELSE USES BARNYARD SCENTED STATIONERY?

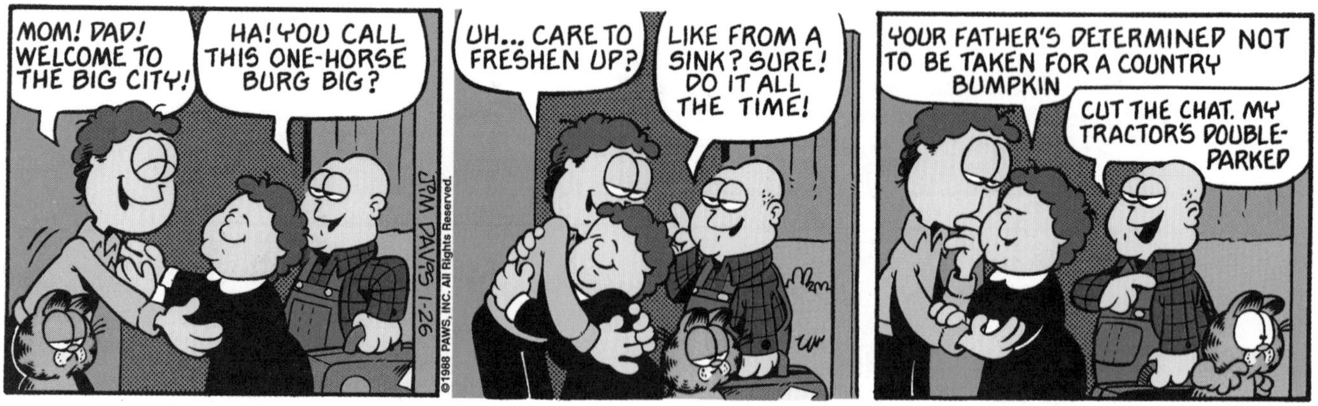
MOM! DAD! WELCOME TO THE BIG CITY!
HA! YOU CALL THIS ONE-HORSE BURG BIG?
JIM DAVIS 1-26
©1988 PAWS, INC. All Rights Reserved.
UH... CARE TO FRESHEN UP?
LIKE FROM A SINK? SURE! DO IT ALL THE TIME!
YOUR FATHER'S DETERMINED NOT TO BE TAKEN FOR A COUNTRY BUMPKIN
CUT THE CHAT. MY TRACTOR'S DOUBLE-PARKED

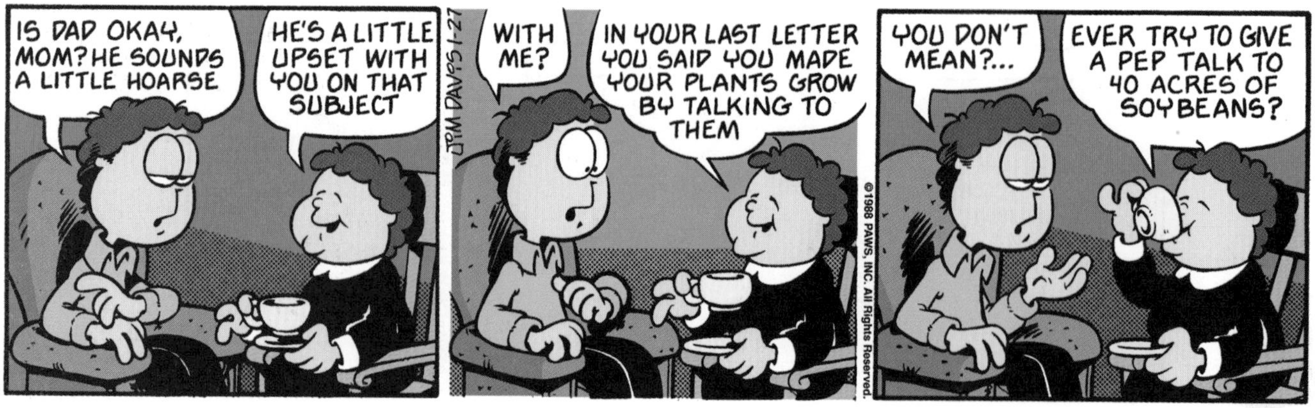
IS DAD OKAY, MOM? HE SOUNDS A LITTLE HOARSE
HE'S A LITTLE UPSET WITH YOU ON THAT SUBJECT
JIM DAVIS 1-27
WITH ME?
IN YOUR LAST LETTER YOU SAID YOU MADE YOUR PLANTS GROW BY TALKING TO THEM
©1988 PAWS, INC. All Rights Reserved.
YOU DON'T MEAN?...
EVER TRY TO GIVE A PEP TALK TO 40 ACRES OF SOYBEANS?

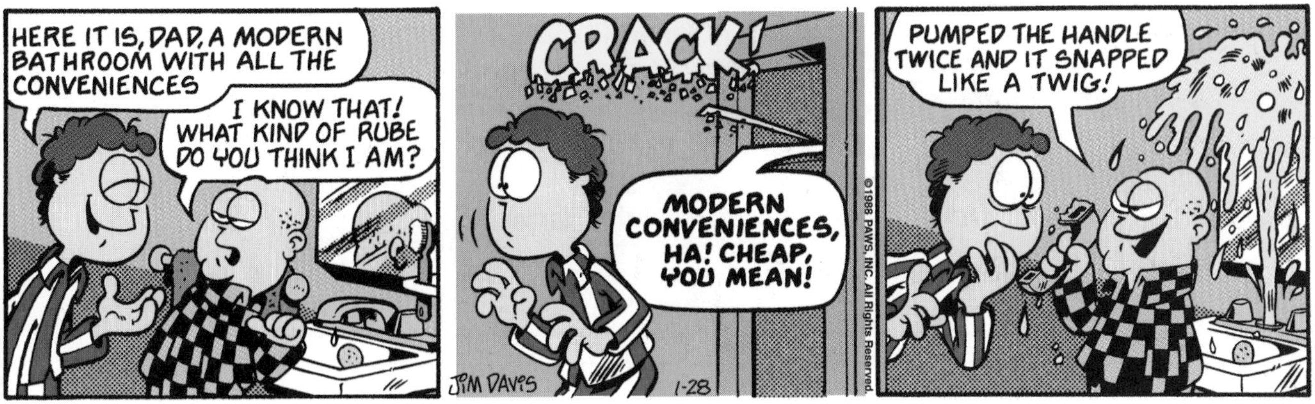
HERE IT IS, DAD, A MODERN BATHROOM WITH ALL THE CONVENIENCES
I KNOW THAT! WHAT KIND OF RUBE DO YOU THINK I AM?
CRACK!
MODERN CONVENIENCES, HA! CHEAP, YOU MEAN!
JIM DAVIS 1-28
©1988 PAWS, INC. All Rights Reserved.
PUMPED THE HANDLE TWICE AND IT SNAPPED LIKE A TWIG!

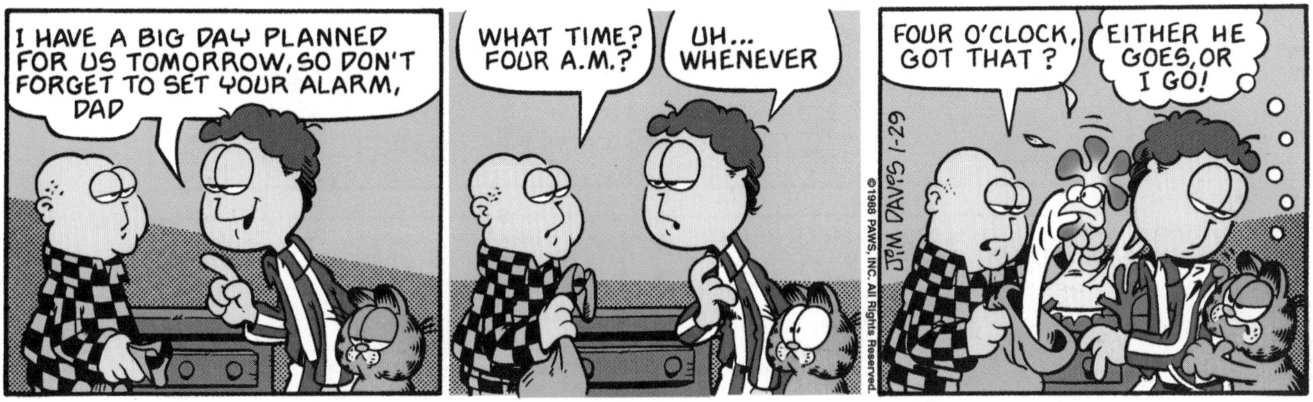
I HAVE A BIG DAY PLANNED FOR US TOMORROW, SO DON'T FORGET TO SET YOUR ALARM, DAD
WHAT TIME? FOUR A.M.?
UH... WHENEVER
©1988 PAWS, INC. All Rights Reserved.
JIM DAVIS 1-29
FOUR O'CLOCK, GOT THAT?
EITHER HE GOES, OR I GO!

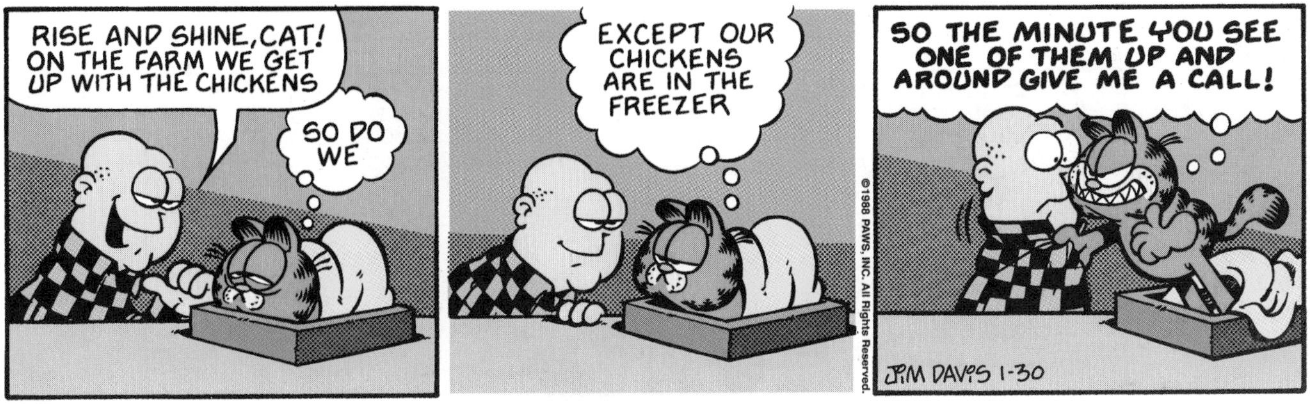
RISE AND SHINE, CAT! ON THE FARM WE GET UP WITH THE CHICKENS
SO DO WE
EXCEPT OUR CHICKENS ARE IN THE FREEZER
©1988 PAWS, INC. All Rights Reserved.
SO THE MINUTE YOU SEE ONE OF THEM UP AND AROUND GIVE ME A CALL!
JIM DAVIS 1-30

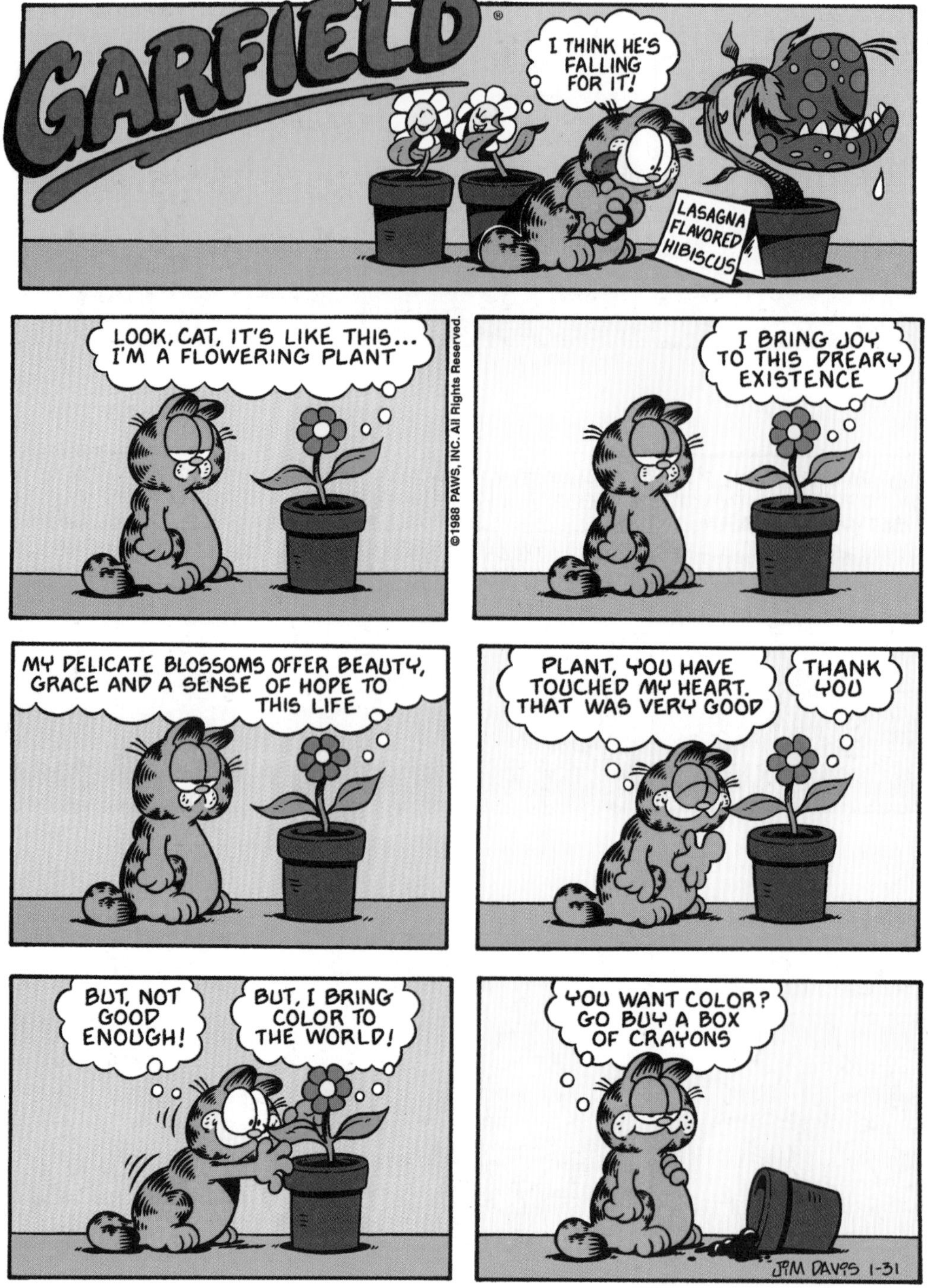
GARFIELD
I THINK HE'S FALLING FOR IT!
LASAGNA FLAVORED HIBISCUS
LOOK, CAT, IT'S LIKE THIS... I'M A FLOWERING PLANT
I BRING JOY TO THIS DREARY EXISTENCE
MY DELICATE BLOSSOMS OFFER BEAUTY, GRACE AND A SENSE OF HOPE TO THIS LIFE
PLANT, YOU HAVE TOUCHED MY HEART. THAT WAS VERY GOOD
THANK YOU
BUT, I BRING COLOR TO THE WORLD!
BUT, NOT GOOD ENOUGH!
YOU WANT COLOR? GO BUY A BOX OF CRAYONS
JIM DAVIS 1-31

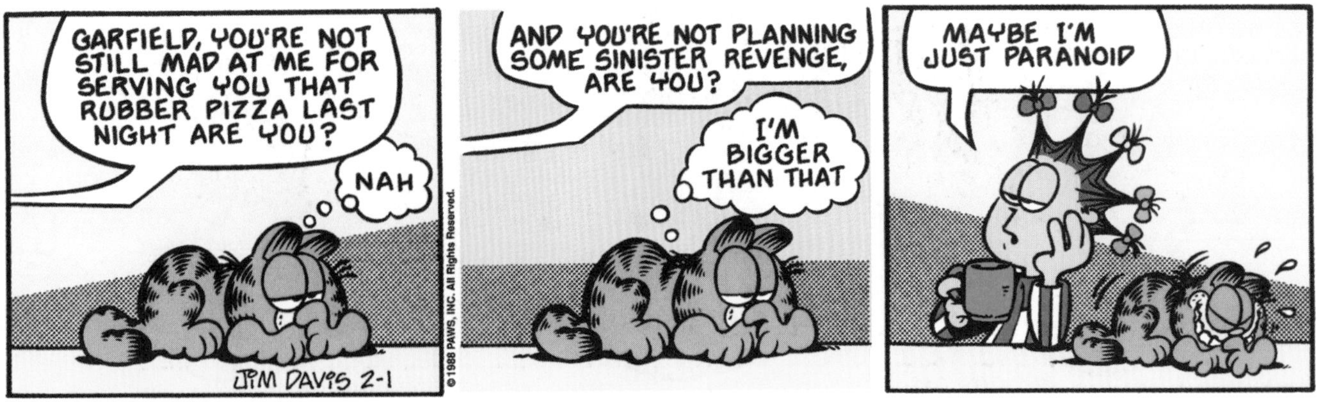
GARFIELD, YOU'RE NOT STILL MAD AT ME FOR SERVING YOU THAT RUBBER PIZZA LAST NIGHT ARE YOU?
NAH
JIM DAVIS 2-1
©1988 PAWS, INC. All Rights Reserved.
AND YOU'RE NOT PLANNING SOME SINISTER REVENGE, ARE YOU?
I'M BIGGER THAN THAT
MAYBE I'M JUST PARANOID

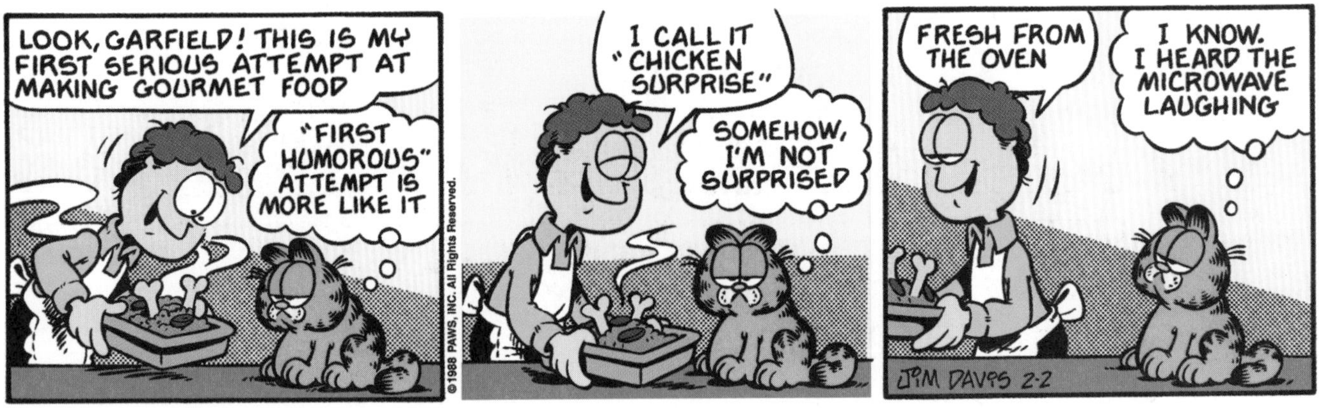
LOOK, GARFIELD! THIS IS MY FIRST SERIOUS ATTEMPT AT MAKING GOURMET FOOD
"FIRST HUMOROUS" ATTEMPT IS MORE LIKE IT
©1988 PAWS, INC. All Rights Reserved.
I CALL IT "CHICKEN SURPRISE"
SOMEHOW, I'M NOT SURPRISED
FRESH FROM THE OVEN
I KNOW. I HEARD THE MICROWAVE LAUGHING
JIM DAVIS 2-2

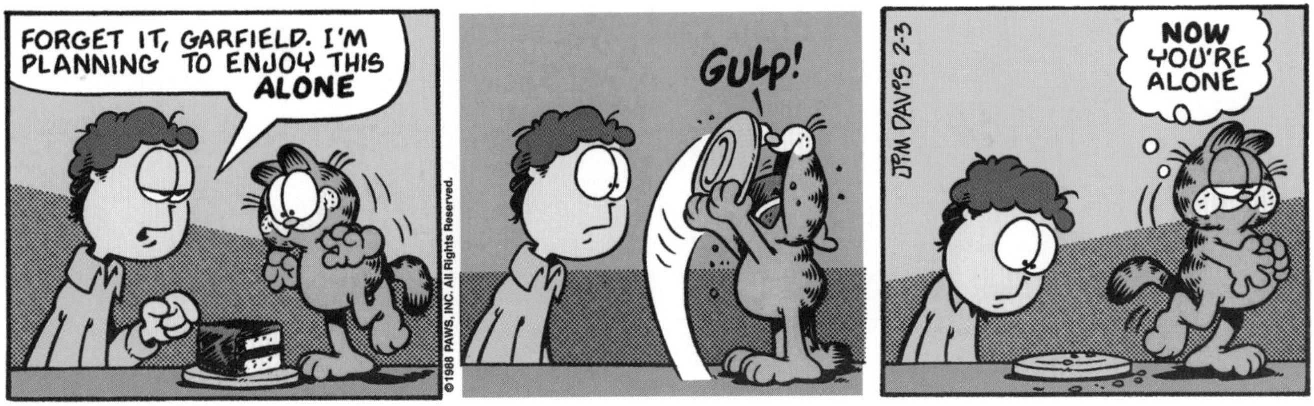
FORGET IT, GARFIELD. I'M PLANNING TO ENJOY THIS **ALONE**
©1988 PAWS, INC. All Rights Reserved.
GULP!
JIM DAVIS 2-3
NOW YOU'RE ALONE

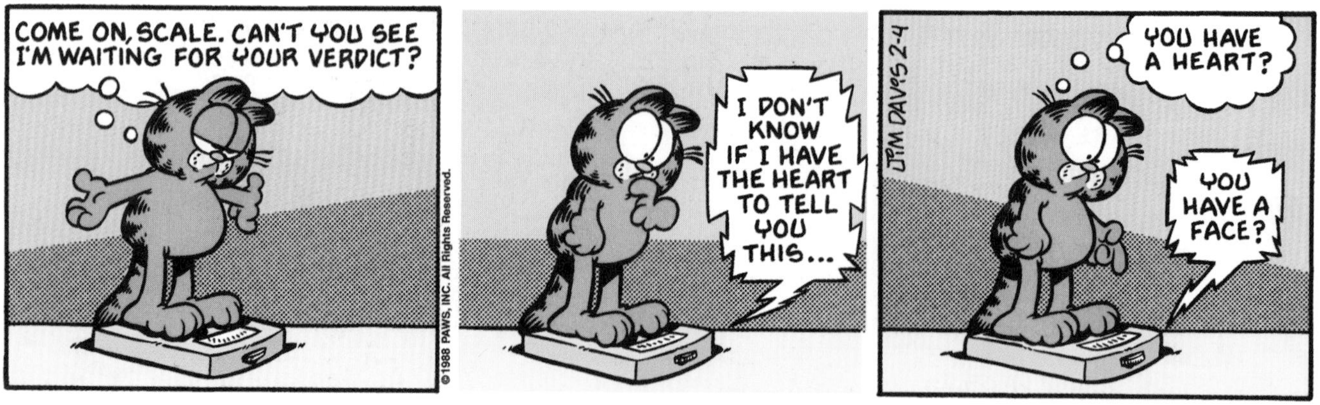
COME ON, SCALE. CAN'T YOU SEE I'M WAITING FOR YOUR VERDICT?
©1988 PAWS, INC. All Rights Reserved.
I DON'T KNOW IF I HAVE THE HEART TO TELL YOU THIS...
JIM DAVIS 2-4
YOU HAVE A HEART?
YOU HAVE A FACE?

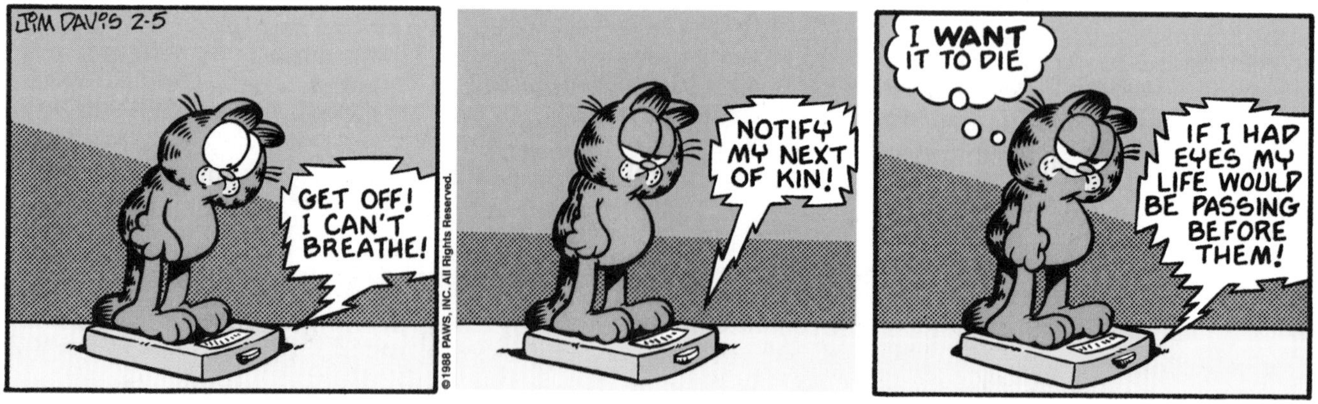
JIM DAVIS 2-5
GET OFF! I CAN'T BREATHE!
©1988 PAWS, INC. All Rights Reserved.
NOTIFY MY NEXT OF KIN!
I WANT IT TO DIE
IF I HAD EYES MY LIFE WOULD BE PASSING BEFORE THEM!

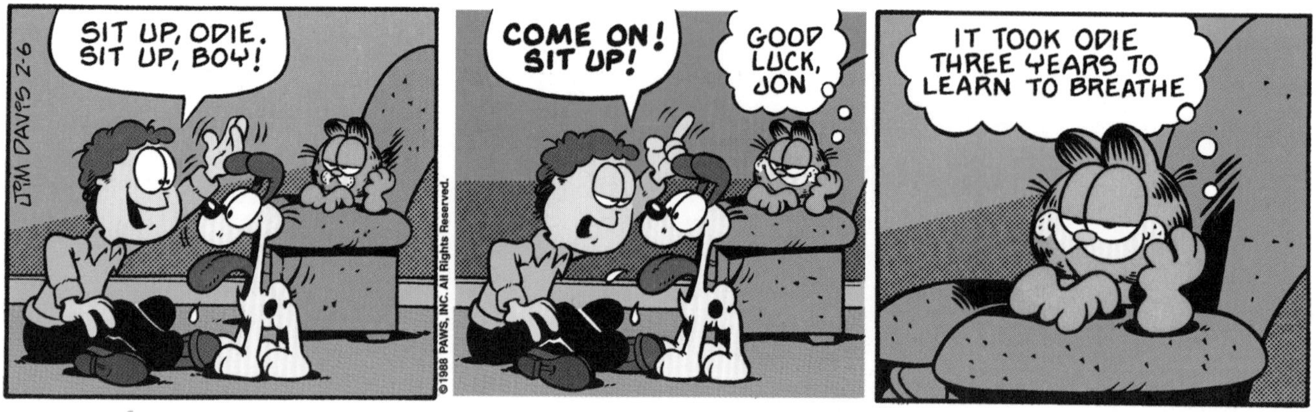
JIM DAVIS 2-6
SIT UP, ODIE. SIT UP, BOY!
©1988 PAWS, INC. All Rights Reserved.
COME ON! SIT UP!
GOOD LUCK, JON
IT TOOK ODIE THREE YEARS TO LEARN TO BREATHE

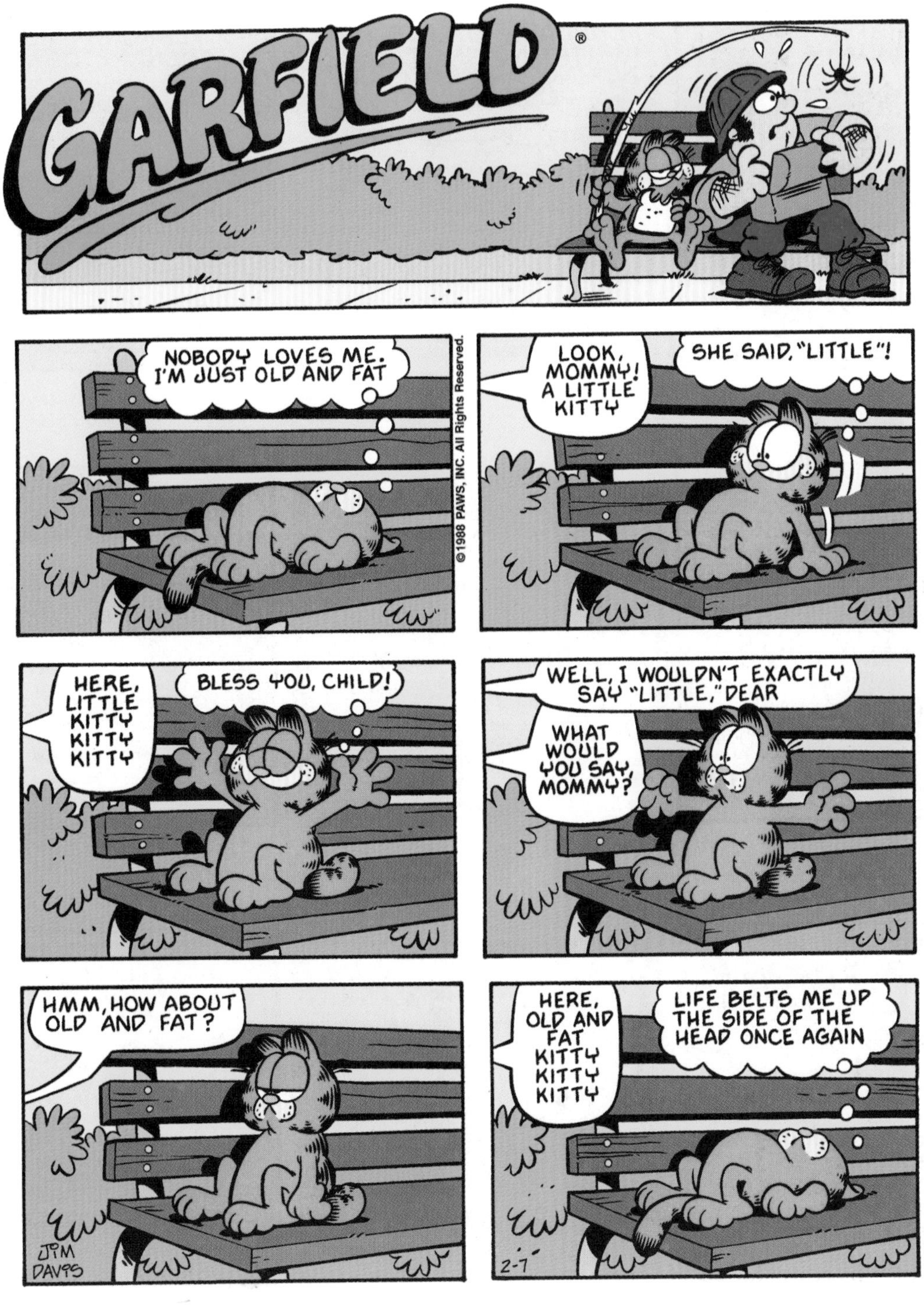
GARFIELD®
NOBODY LOVES ME. I'M JUST OLD AND FAT
©1988 PAWS, INC. All Rights Reserved.
LOOK, MOMMY! A LITTLE KITTY
SHE SAID, "LITTLE"!
HERE, LITTLE KITTY KITTY KITTY
BLESS YOU, CHILD!
WELL, I WOULDN'T EXACTLY SAY "LITTLE," DEAR
WHAT WOULD YOU SAY, MOMMY?
HMM, HOW ABOUT OLD AND FAT?
JIM DAVIS
HERE, OLD AND FAT KITTY KITTY KITTY
LIFE BELTS ME UP THE SIDE OF THE HEAD ONCE AGAIN
2-7

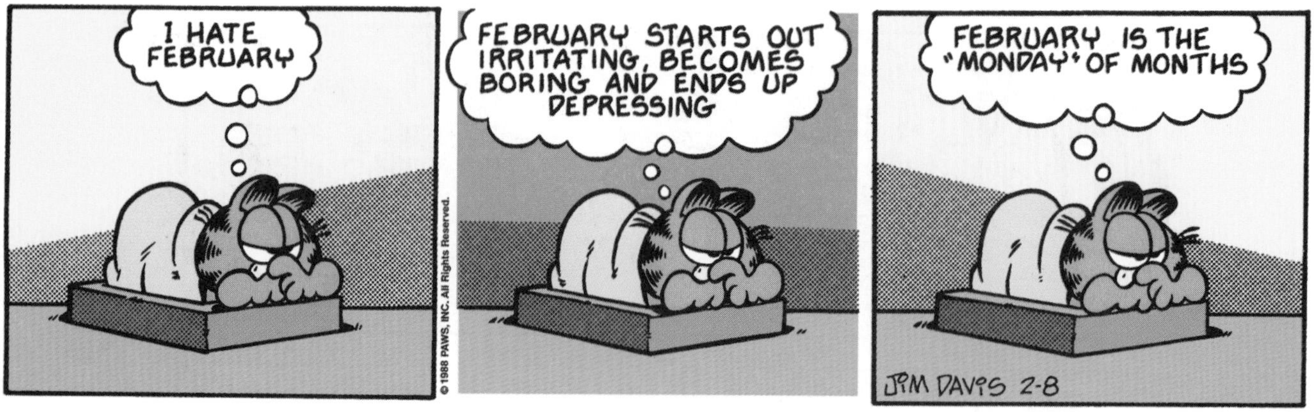
I HATE FEBRUARY
FEBRUARY STARTS OUT IRRITATING, BECOMES BORING AND ENDS UP DEPRESSING
FEBRUARY IS THE "MONDAY" OF MONTHS
JIM DAVIS 2-8
© 1988 PAWS, INC. All Rights Reserved.

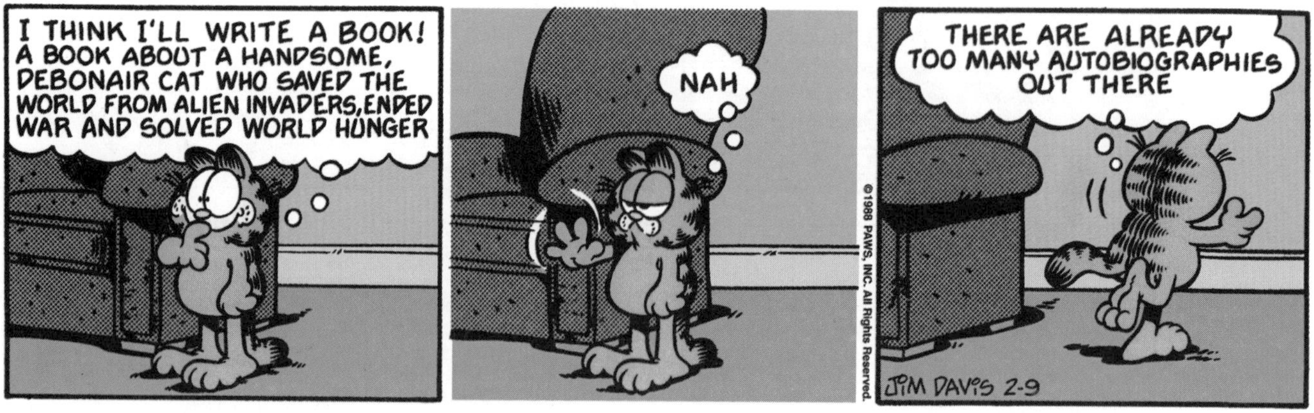
I THINK I'LL WRITE A BOOK! A BOOK ABOUT A HANDSOME, DEBONAIR CAT WHO SAVED THE WORLD FROM ALIEN INVADERS, ENDED WAR AND SOLVED WORLD HUNGER
NAH
THERE ARE ALREADY TOO MANY AUTOBIOGRAPHIES OUT THERE
JIM DAVIS 2-9
© 1988 PAWS, INC. All Rights Reserved.

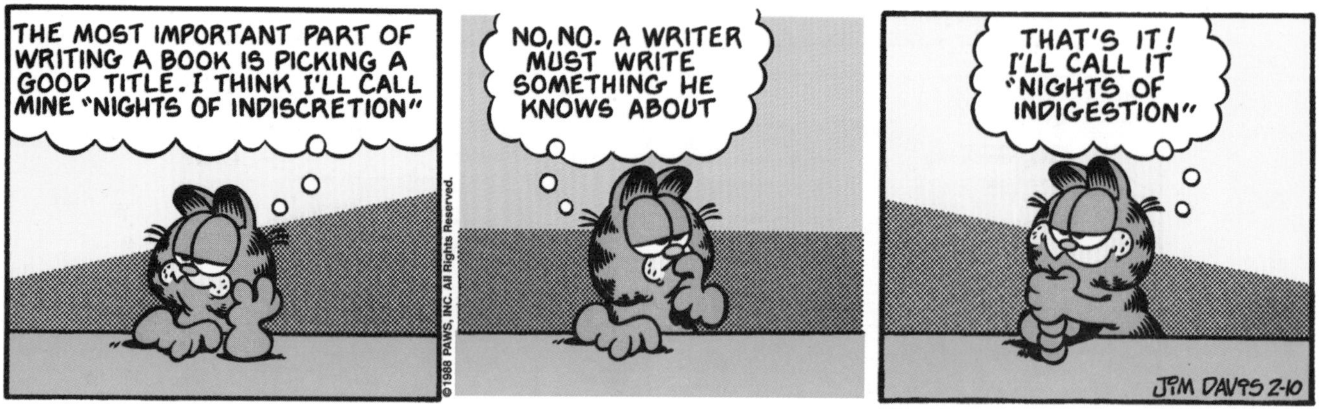
THE MOST IMPORTANT PART OF WRITING A BOOK IS PICKING A GOOD TITLE. I THINK I'LL CALL MINE "NIGHTS OF INDISCRETION"
NO, NO. A WRITER MUST WRITE SOMETHING HE KNOWS ABOUT
THAT'S IT! I'LL CALL IT "NIGHTS OF INDIGESTION"
JIM DAVIS 2-10
© 1988 PAWS, INC. All Rights Reserved.

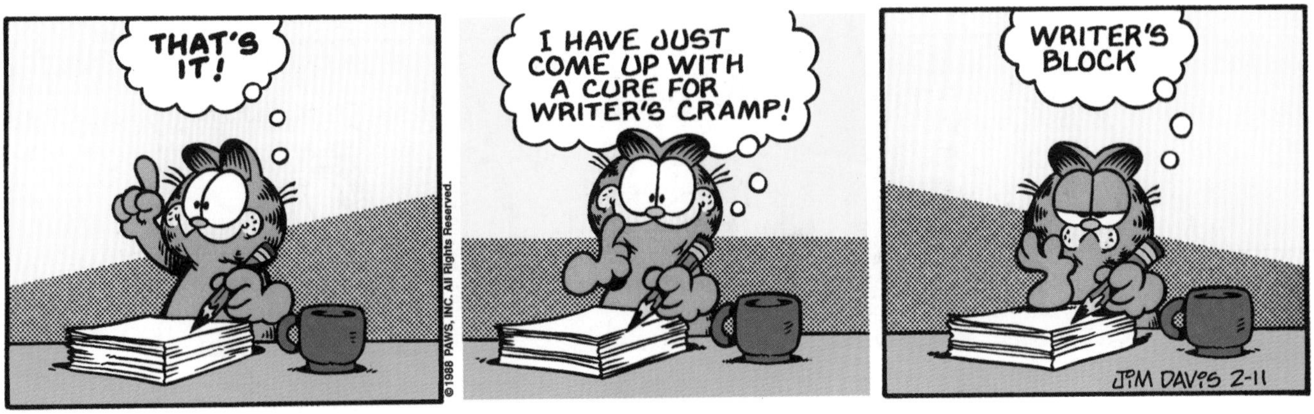
THAT'S IT!
I HAVE JUST COME UP WITH A CURE FOR WRITER'S CRAMP!
WRITER'S BLOCK
© 1988 PAWS, INC. All Rights Reserved.
JIM DAVIS 2-11

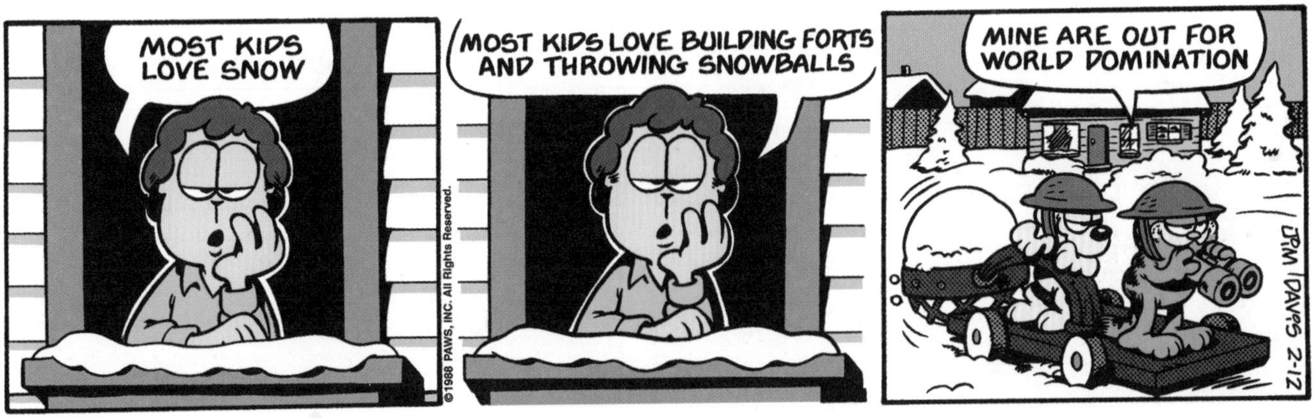
MOST KIDS LOVE SNOW
MOST KIDS LOVE BUILDING FORTS AND THROWING SNOWBALLS
MINE ARE OUT FOR WORLD DOMINATION
© 1988 PAWS, INC. All Rights Reserved.
JIM DAVIS 2-12

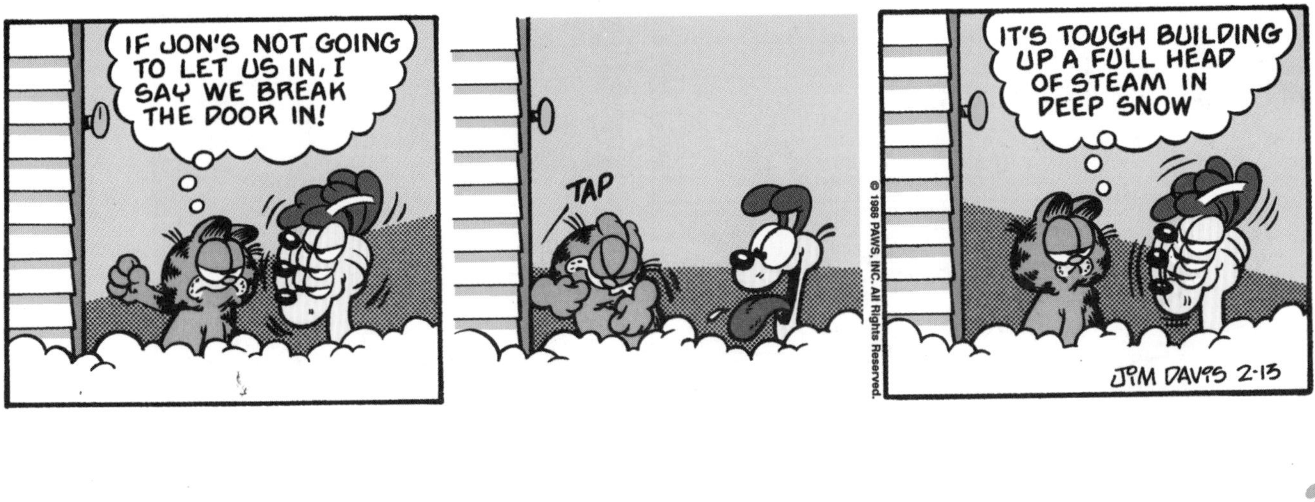
IF JON'S NOT GOING TO LET US IN, I SAY WE BREAK THE DOOR IN!
TAP
IT'S TOUGH BUILDING UP A FULL HEAD OF STEAM IN DEEP SNOW
© 1988 PAWS, INC. All Rights Reserved.
JIM DAVIS 2-13

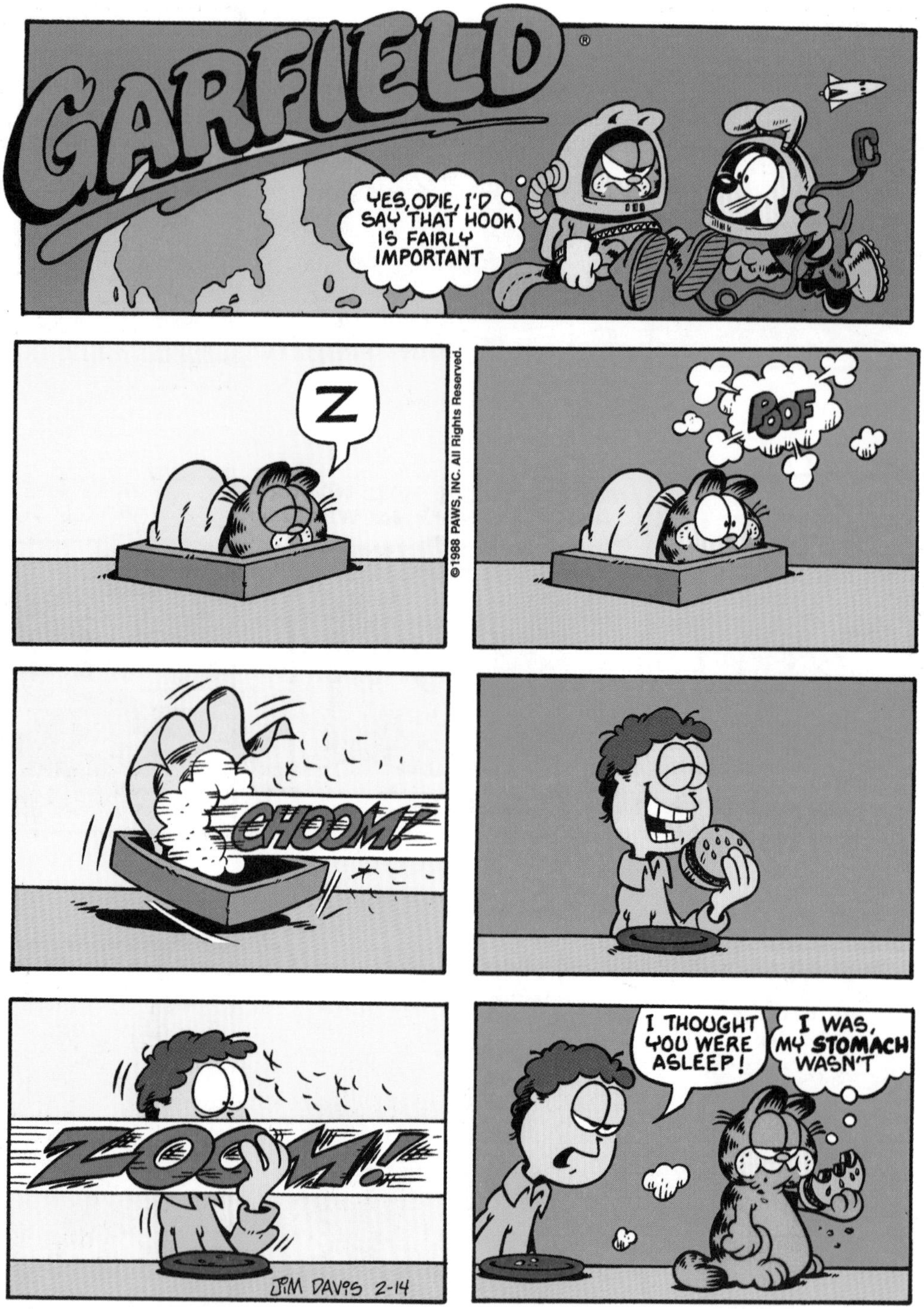
GARFIELD®
YES, ODIE, I'D SAY THAT HOOK IS FAIRLY IMPORTANT
©1988 PAWS, INC. All Rights Reserved.
Z
POOF
CHOOM!
ZOOM!
JIM DAVIS 2-14
I THOUGHT YOU WERE ASLEEP!
I WAS, MY STOMACH WASN'T

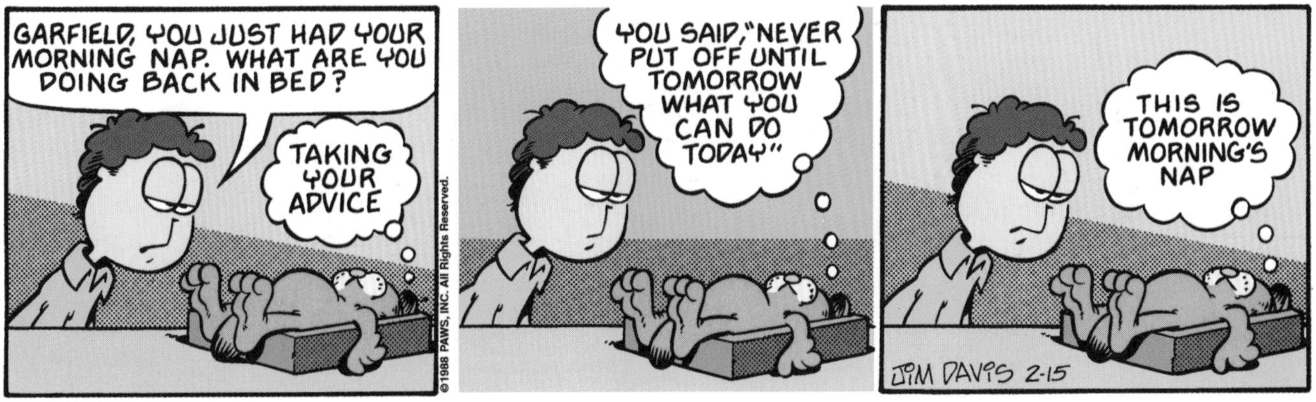
GARFIELD, YOU JUST HAD YOUR MORNING NAP. WHAT ARE YOU DOING BACK IN BED?
TAKING YOUR ADVICE
YOU SAID, "NEVER PUT OFF UNTIL TOMORROW WHAT YOU CAN DO TODAY"
THIS IS TOMORROW MORNING'S NAP
©1988 PAWS, INC. All Rights Reserved.
JIM DAVIS 2-15

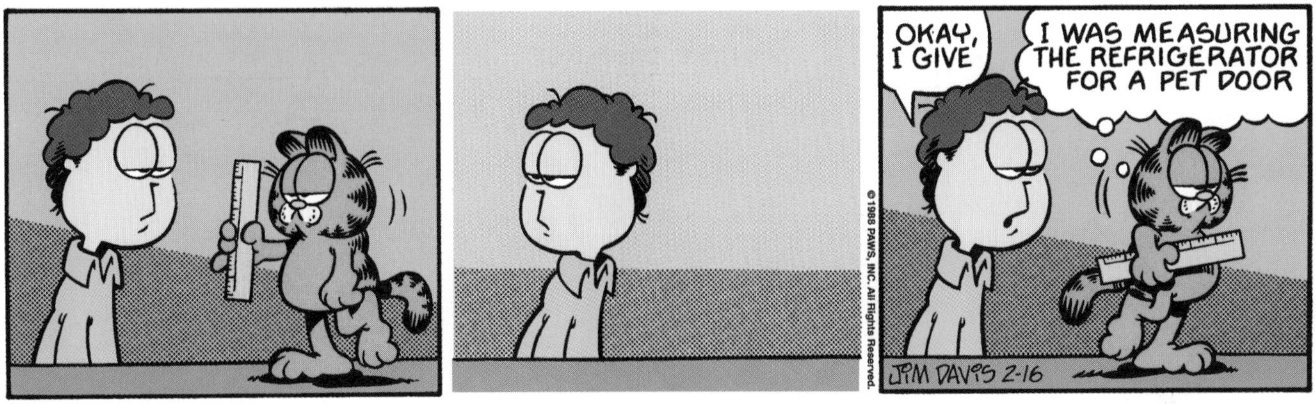
OKAY, I GIVE
I WAS MEASURING THE REFRIGERATOR FOR A PET DOOR
© 1988 PAWS, INC. All Rights Reserved.
JIM DAVIS 2-16

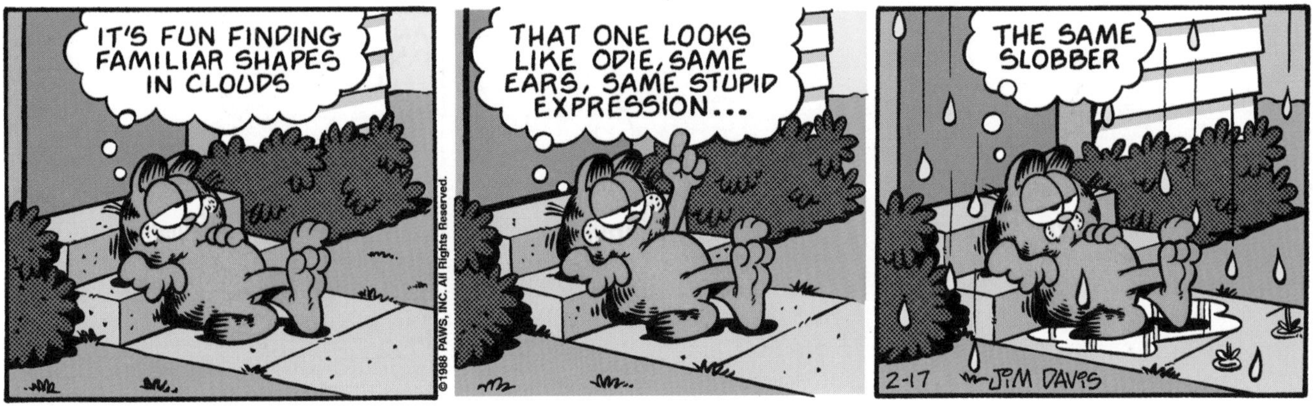
IT'S FUN FINDING FAMILIAR SHAPES IN CLOUDS
THAT ONE LOOKS LIKE ODIE, SAME EARS, SAME STUPID EXPRESSION...
THE SAME SLOBBER
©1988 PAWS, INC. All Rights Reserved.
2-17 JIM DAVIS

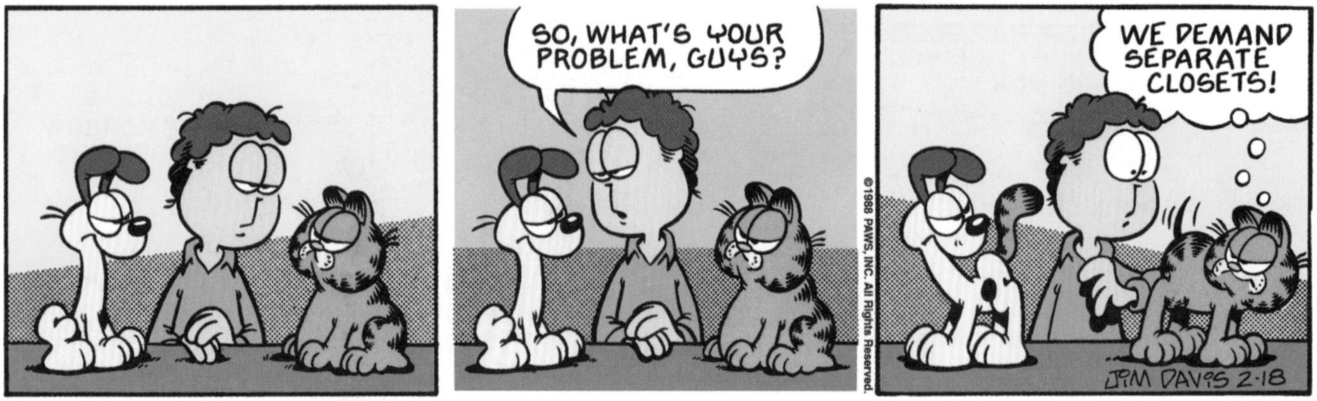
SO, WHAT'S YOUR PROBLEM, GUYS?
WE DEMAND SEPARATE CLOSETS!
©1988 PAWS, INC. All Rights Reserved.
JIM DAVIS 2-18

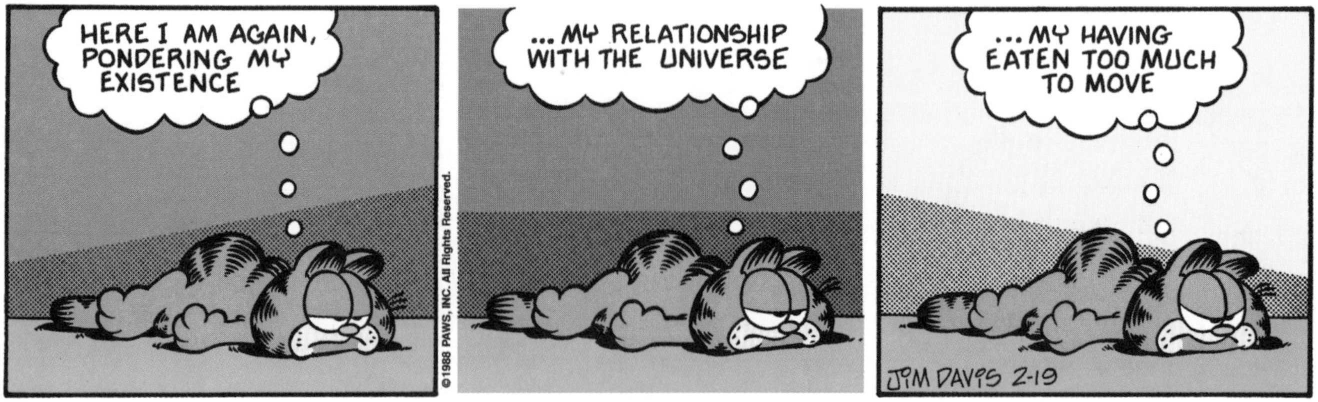
HERE I AM AGAIN, PONDERING MY EXISTENCE
... MY RELATIONSHIP WITH THE UNIVERSE
... MY HAVING EATEN TOO MUCH TO MOVE
©1988 PAWS, INC. All Rights Reserved.
JIM DAVIS 2-19

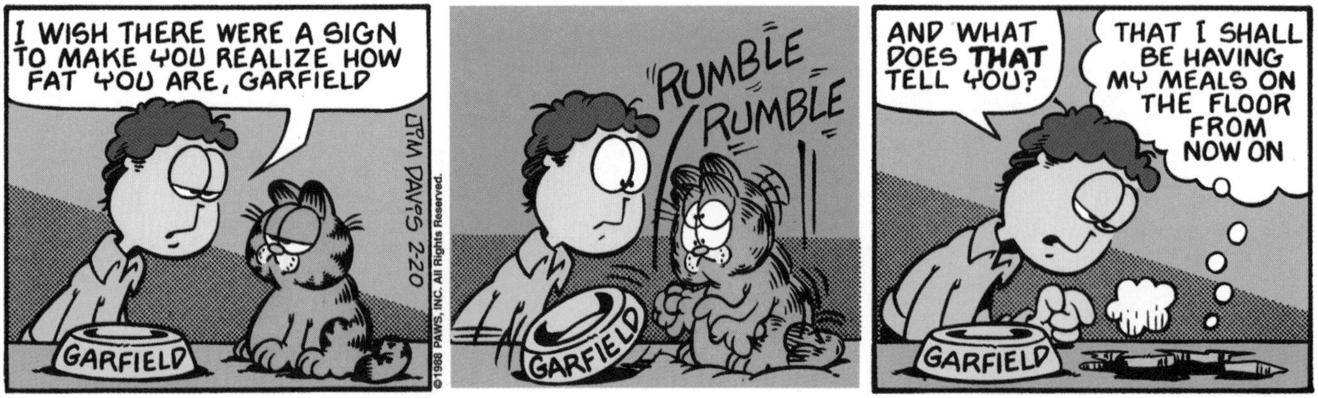
I WISH THERE WERE A SIGN TO MAKE YOU REALIZE HOW FAT YOU ARE, GARFIELD
GARFIELD
JIM DAVIS 2-20
©1988 PAWS, INC. All Rights Reserved.
RUMBLE RUMBLE
GARFIELD
AND WHAT DOES THAT TELL YOU?
THAT I SHALL BE HAVING MY MEALS ON THE FLOOR FROM NOW ON
GARFIELD

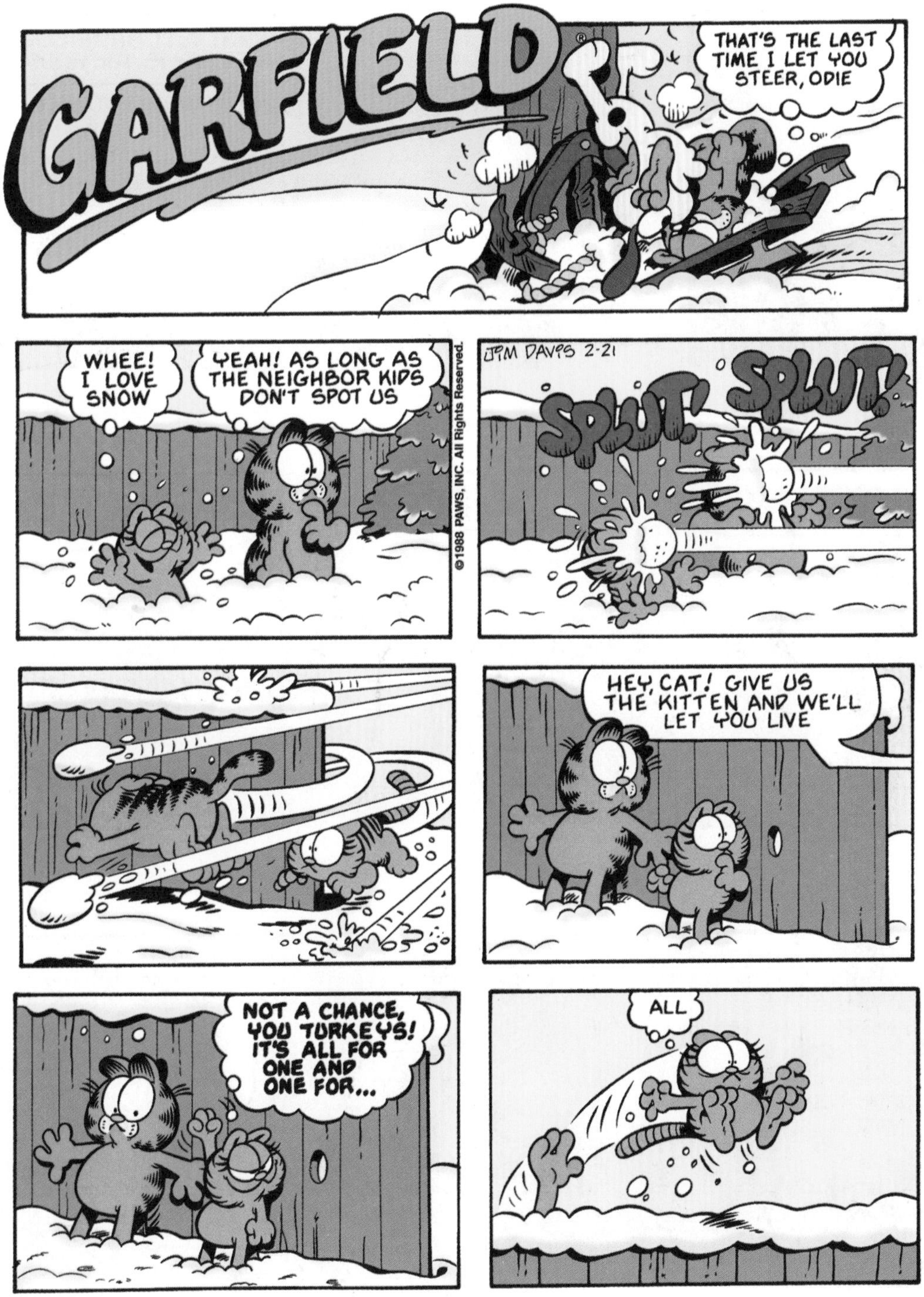
GARFIELD
THAT'S THE LAST TIME I LET YOU STEER, ODIE
WHEE! I LOVE SNOW
YEAH! AS LONG AS THE NEIGHBOR KIDS DON'T SPOT US
©1988 PAWS, INC. All Rights Reserved.
JIM DAVIS 2-21
SPLUT! SPLUT!
HEY, CAT! GIVE US THE KITTEN AND WE'LL LET YOU LIVE
NOT A CHANCE, YOU TURKEYS! IT'S ALL FOR ONE AND ONE FOR...
ALL

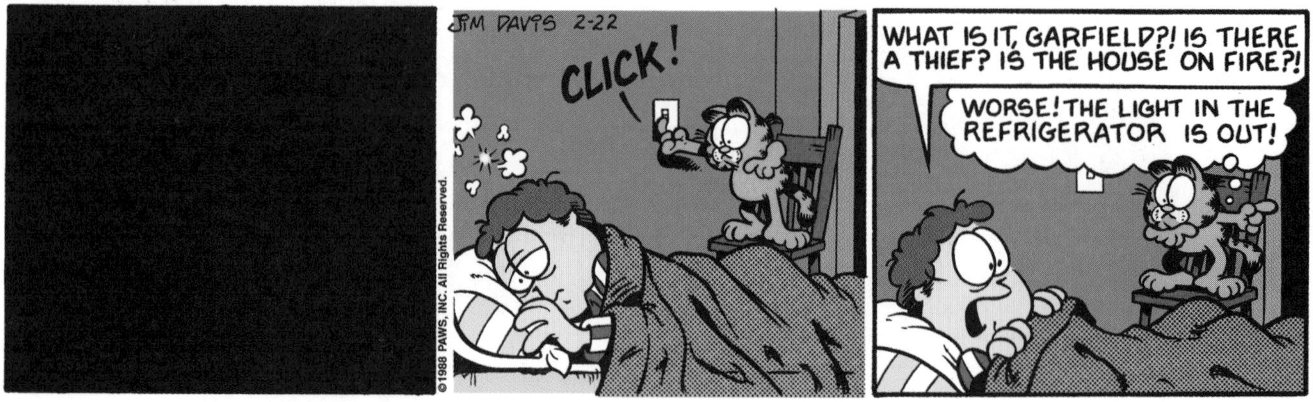
JIM DAVIS 2-22
©1988 PAWS, INC. All Rights Reserved.
CLICK!
WHAT IS IT, GARFIELD?! IS THERE A THIEF? IS THE HOUSE ON FIRE?!
WORSE! THE LIGHT IN THE REFRIGERATOR IS OUT!

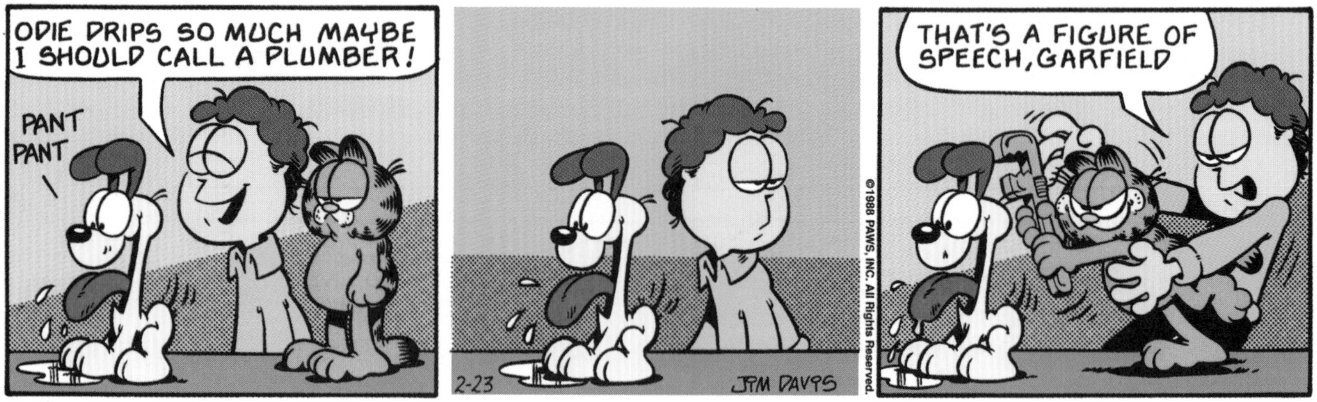
ODIE DRIPS SO MUCH MAYBE I SHOULD CALL A PLUMBER!
PANT PANT
2-23
JIM DAVIS
©1988 PAWS, INC. All Rights Reserved.
THAT'S A FIGURE OF SPEECH, GARFIELD

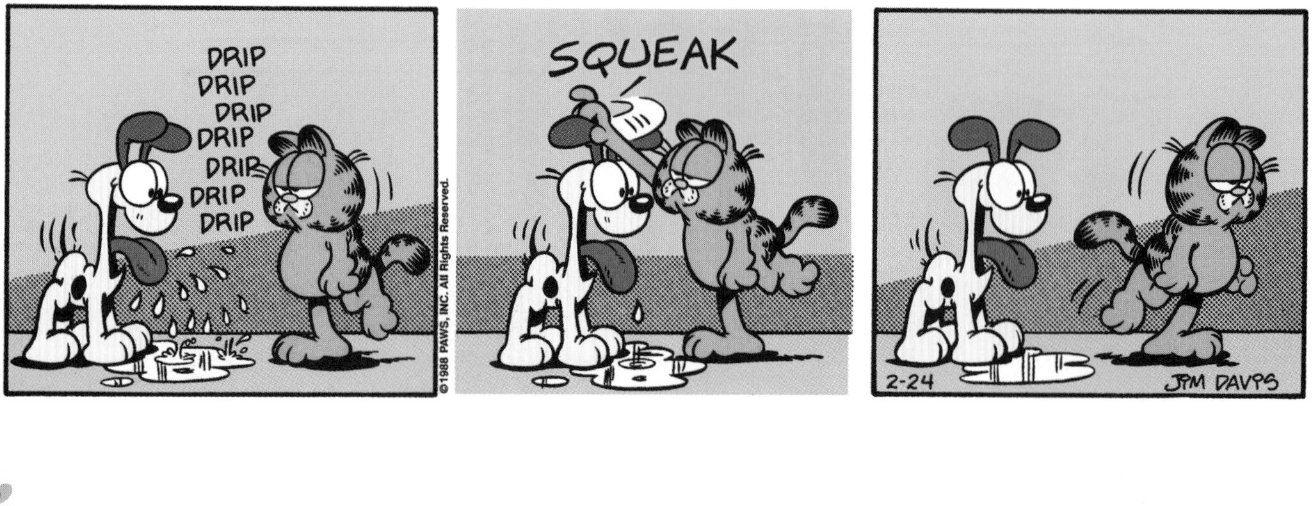
DRIP
DRIP
DRIP
DRIP
DRIP
DRIP
DRIP
©1988 PAWS, INC. All Rights Reserved.
SQUEAK
2-24
JIM DAVIS

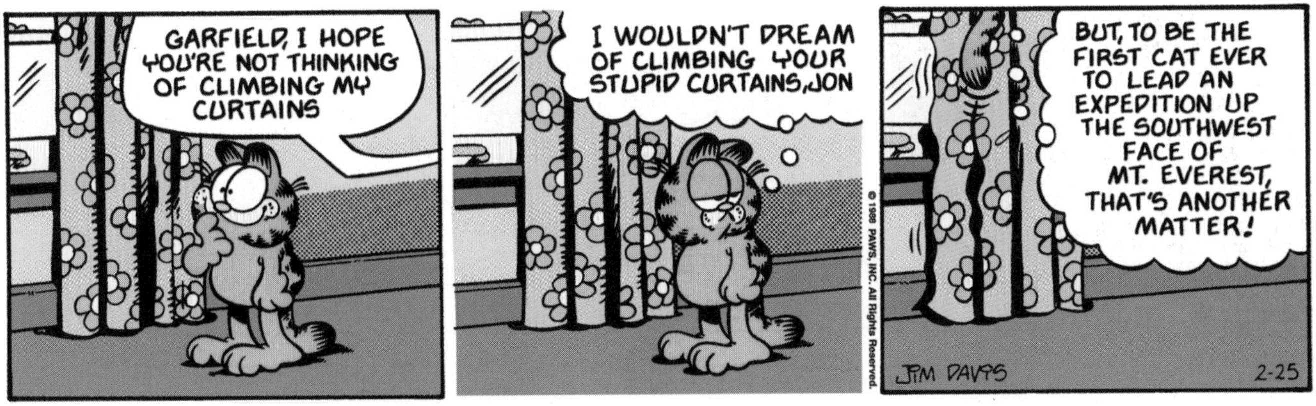
GARFIELD, I HOPE YOU'RE NOT THINKING OF CLIMBING MY CURTAINS
I WOULDN'T DREAM OF CLIMBING YOUR STUPID CURTAINS, JON
BUT, TO BE THE FIRST CAT EVER TO LEAD AN EXPEDITION UP THE SOUTHWEST FACE OF MT. EVEREST, THAT'S ANOTHER MATTER!
© 1988 PAWS, INC. All Rights Reserved.
JIM DAVIS
2-25

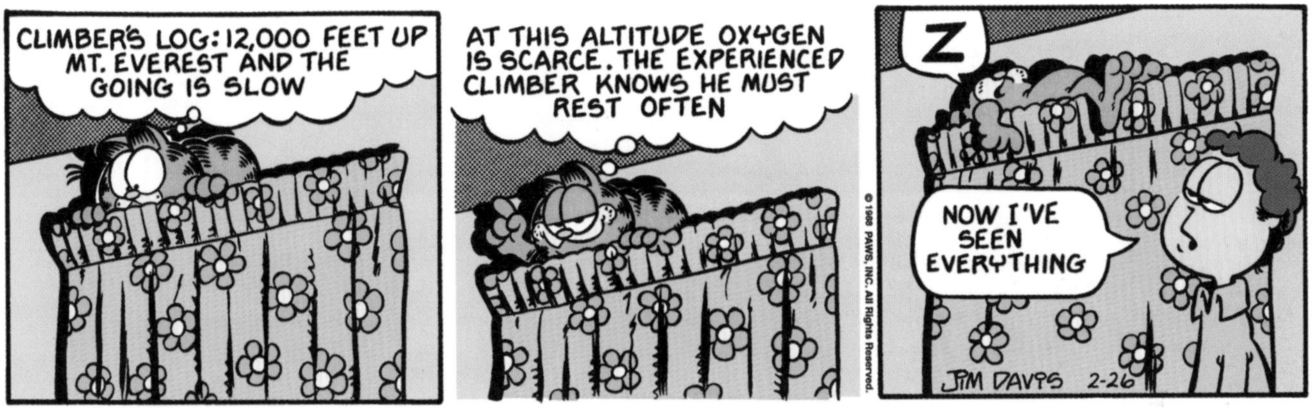
CLIMBER'S LOG: 12,000 FEET UP MT. EVEREST AND THE GOING IS SLOW
AT THIS ALTITUDE OXYGEN IS SCARCE. THE EXPERIENCED CLIMBER KNOWS HE MUST REST OFTEN
Z
NOW I'VE SEEN EVERYTHING
© 1988 PAWS, INC. All Rights Reserved.
JIM DAVIS
2-26

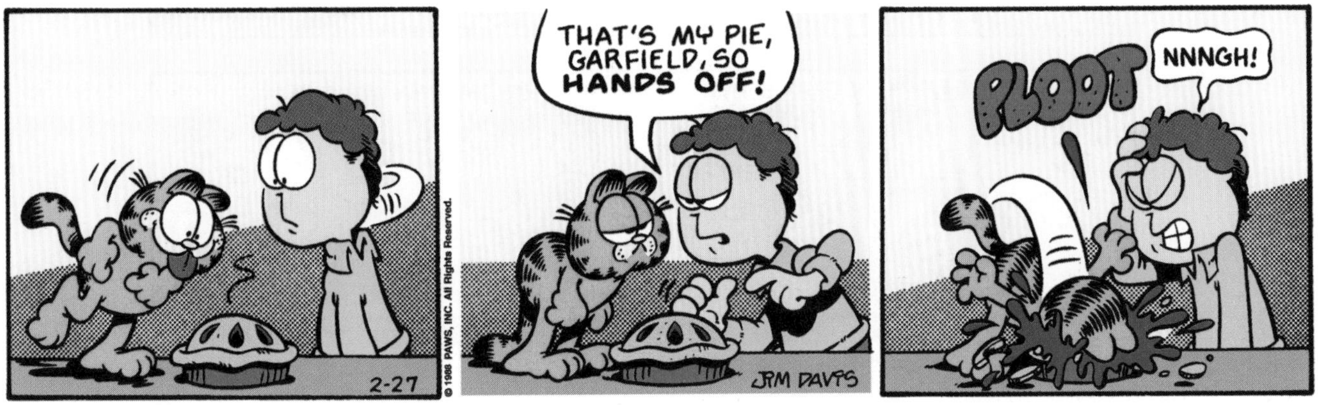
2-27
© 1988 PAWS, INC. All Rights Reserved.
THAT'S MY PIE, GARFIELD, SO **HANDS OFF!**
JIM DAVIS
PLOOT
NNNGH!

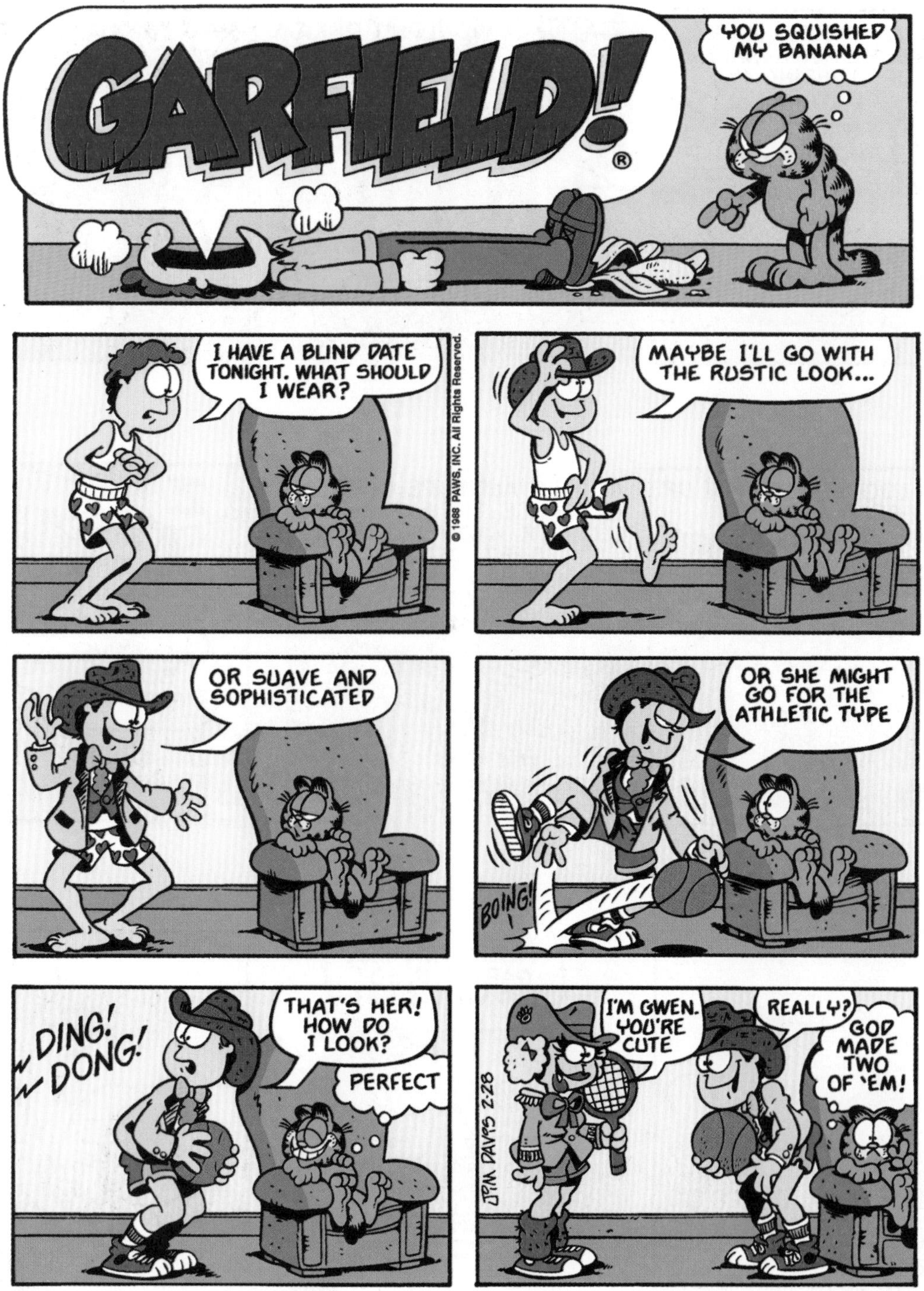
GARFIELD!
YOU SQUISHED MY BANANA
I HAVE A BLIND DATE TONIGHT. WHAT SHOULD I WEAR?
© 1988 PAWS, INC. All Rights Reserved.
MAYBE I'LL GO WITH THE RUSTIC LOOK...
OR SUAVE AND SOPHISTICATED
OR SHE MIGHT GO FOR THE ATHLETIC TYPE
BOING!
DING!
DONG!
THAT'S HER! HOW DO I LOOK?
PERFECT
JIM DAVIS 2-28
I'M GWEN. YOU'RE CUTE
REALLY?
GOD MADE TWO OF 'EM!

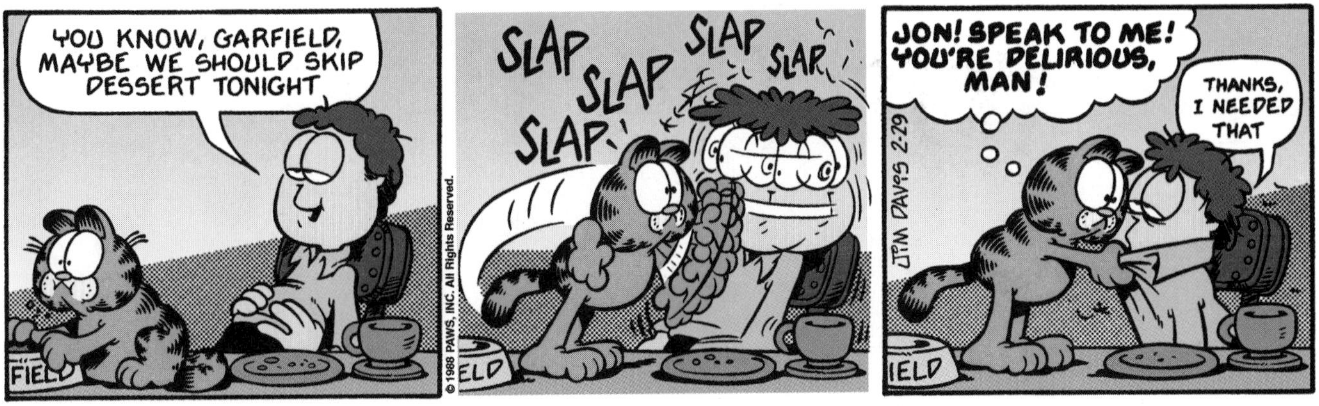
YOU KNOW, GARFIELD, MAYBE WE SHOULD SKIP DESSERT TONIGHT
FIELD
© 1988 PAWS, INC. All Rights Reserved.
SLAP SLAP SLAP SLAP SLAP
ELD
JON! SPEAK TO ME! YOU'RE DELIRIOUS, MAN!
THANKS, I NEEDED THAT
JIM DAVIS 2-29
IELD

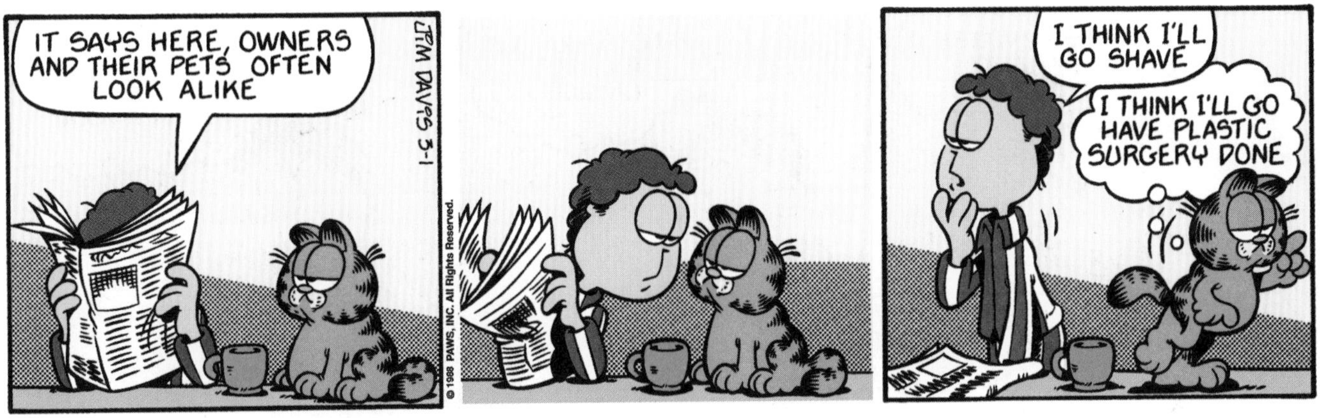
IT SAYS HERE, OWNERS AND THEIR PETS OFTEN LOOK ALIKE
JIM DAVIS 3-1
© 1988 PAWS, INC. All Rights Reserved.
I THINK I'LL GO SHAVE
I THINK I'LL GO HAVE PLASTIC SURGERY DONE

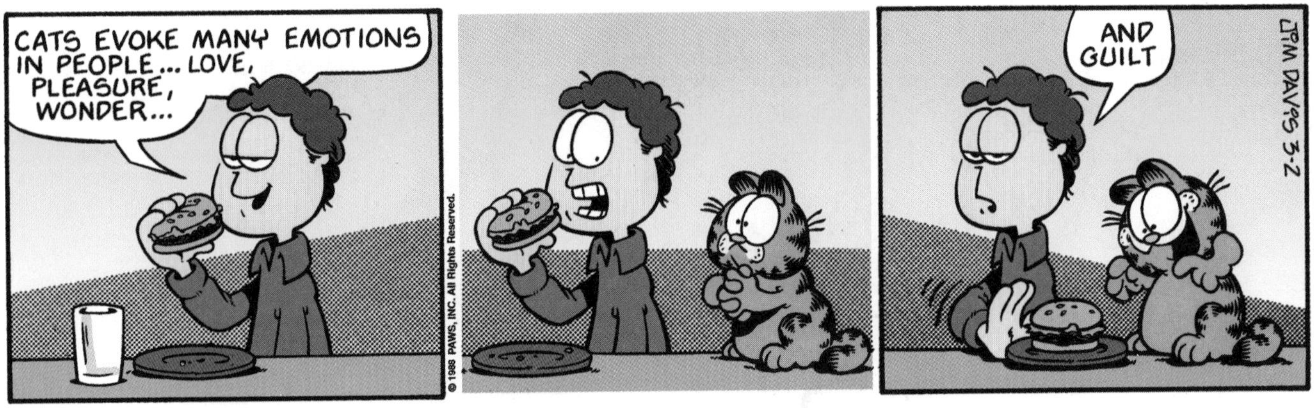
CATS EVOKE MANY EMOTIONS IN PEOPLE... LOVE, PLEASURE, WONDER...
© 1988 PAWS, INC. All Rights Reserved.
AND GUILT
JIM DAVIS 3-2

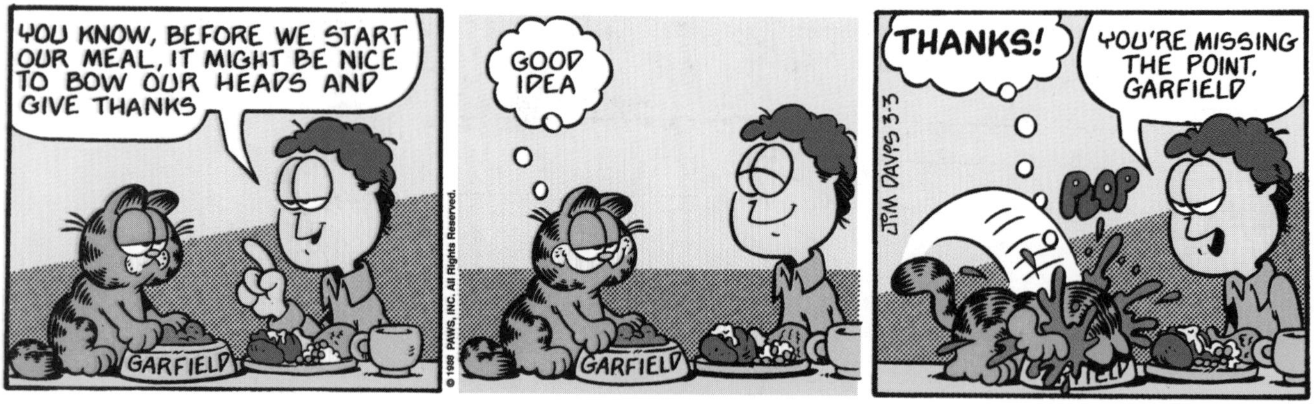
YOU KNOW, BEFORE WE START OUR MEAL, IT MIGHT BE NICE TO BOW OUR HEADS AND GIVE THANKS
© 1988 PAWS, INC. All Rights Reserved.
GOOD IDEA
THANKS!
YOU'RE MISSING THE POINT, GARFIELD
PLOP
JPM DAVIS 3-3

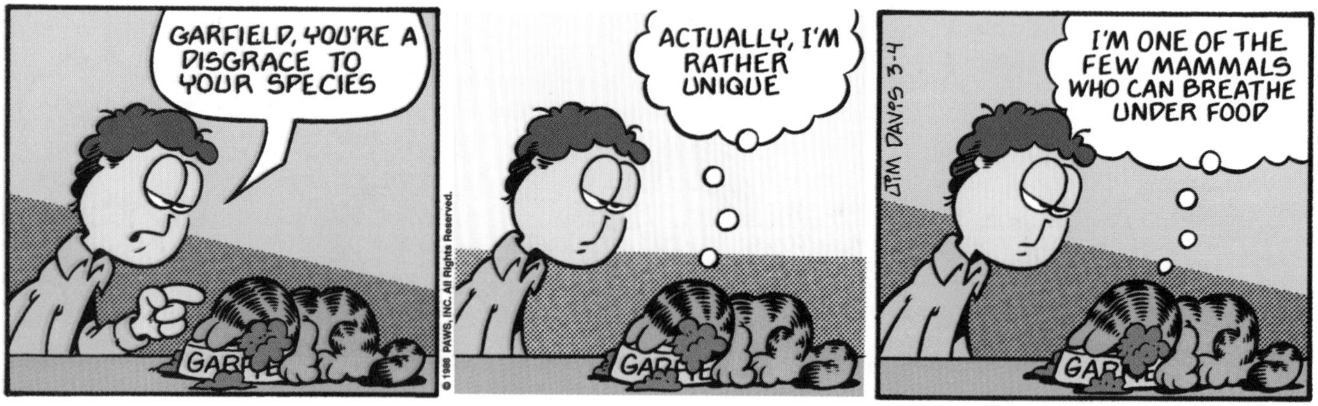
GARFIELD, YOU'RE A DISGRACE TO YOUR SPECIES
© 1988 PAWS, INC. All Rights Reserved.
ACTUALLY, I'M RATHER UNIQUE
I'M ONE OF THE FEW MAMMALS WHO CAN BREATHE UNDER FOOD
JPM DAVIS 3-4

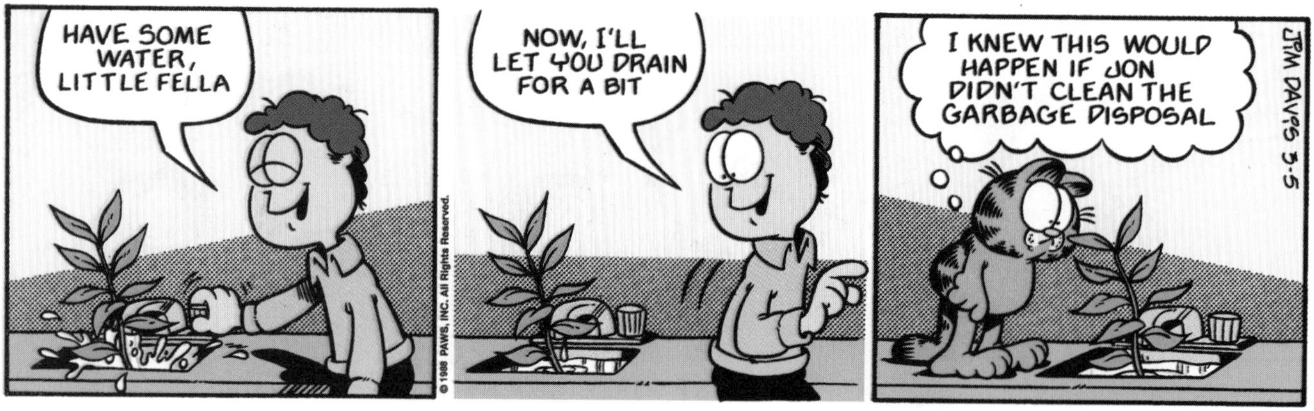
HAVE SOME WATER, LITTLE FELLA
© 1988 PAWS, INC. All Rights Reserved.
NOW, I'LL LET YOU DRAIN FOR A BIT
I KNEW THIS WOULD HAPPEN IF JON DIDN'T CLEAN THE GARBAGE DISPOSAL
JPM DAVIS 3-5

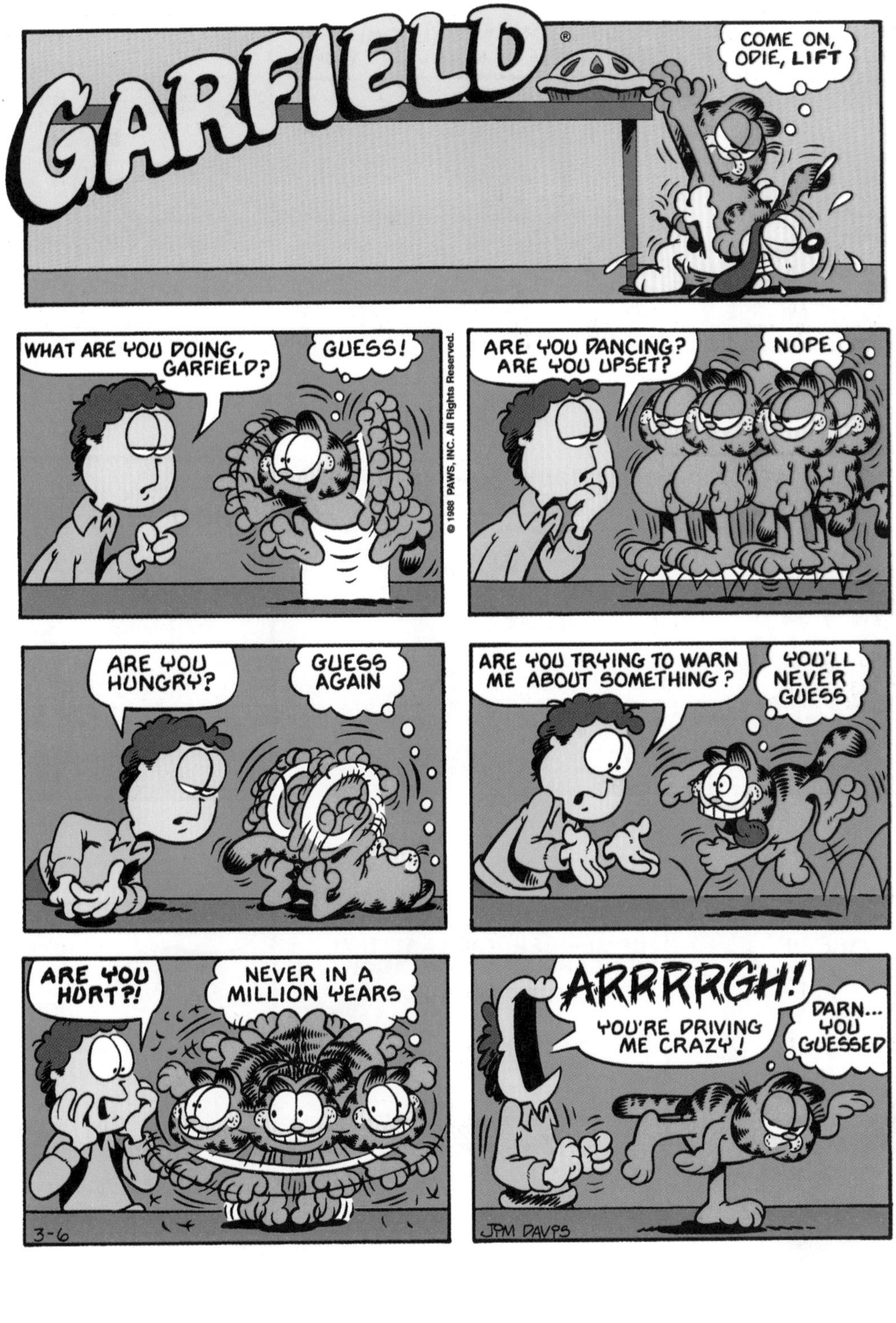
GARFIELD®
COME ON, ODIE, LIFT
WHAT ARE YOU DOING, GARFIELD?
GUESS!
© 1988 PAWS, INC. All Rights Reserved.
ARE YOU DANCING? ARE YOU UPSET?
NOPE
ARE YOU HUNGRY?
GUESS AGAIN
ARE YOU TRYING TO WARN ME ABOUT SOMETHING?
YOU'LL NEVER GUESS
ARE YOU HURT?!
NEVER IN A MILLION YEARS
3-6
ARRRRGH!
YOU'RE DRIVING ME CRAZY!
DARN... YOU GUESSED
JIM DAVIS

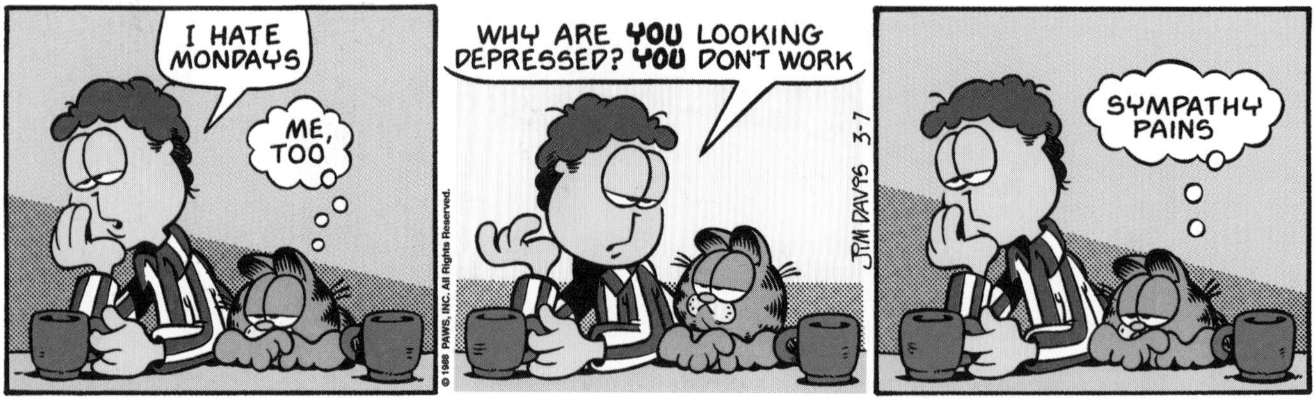
I HATE MONDAYS
ME, TOO
WHY ARE YOU LOOKING DEPRESSED? YOU DON'T WORK
SYMPATHY PAINS
© 1988 PAWS, INC. All Rights Reserved.
JIM DAVIS 3-7

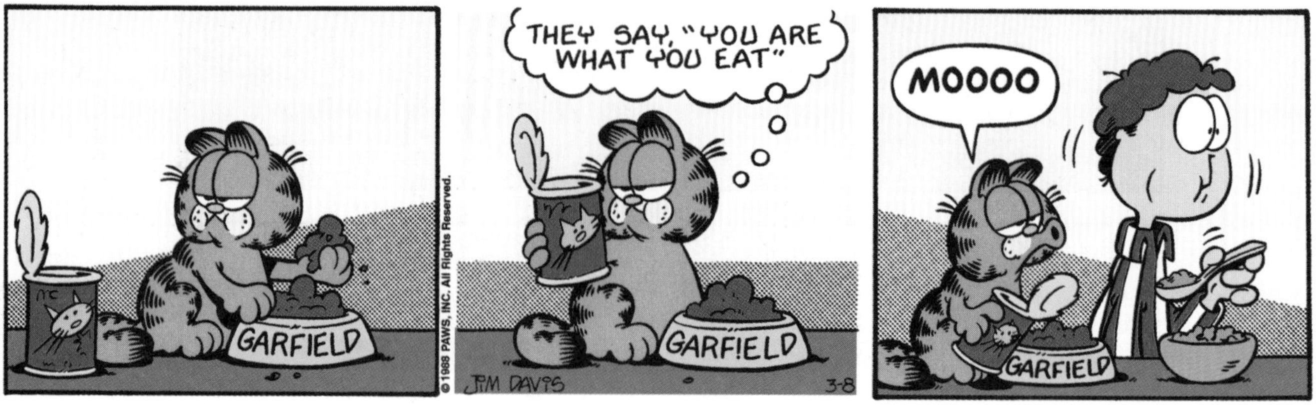
GARFIELD
THEY SAY, "YOU ARE WHAT YOU EAT"
GARFIELD
MOOOO
GARFIELD
© 1988 PAWS, INC. All Rights Reserved.
JIM DAVIS 3-8

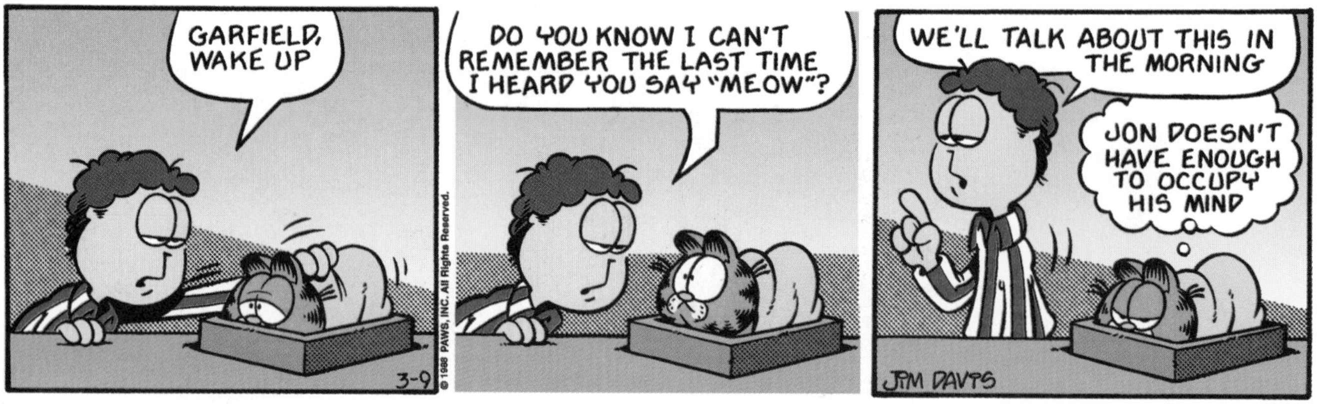
GARFIELD, WAKE UP
DO YOU KNOW I CAN'T REMEMBER THE LAST TIME I HEARD YOU SAY "MEOW"?
WE'LL TALK ABOUT THIS IN THE MORNING
JON DOESN'T HAVE ENOUGH TO OCCUPY HIS MIND
© 1988 PAWS, INC. All Rights Reserved.
3-9
JIM DAVIS

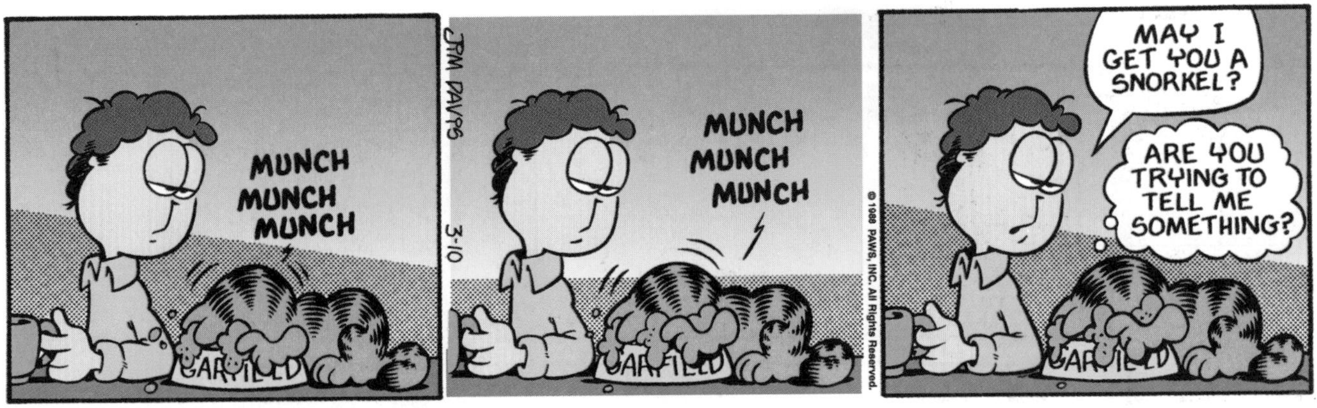
MUNCH
MUNCH
MUNCH
JIM DAVIS
3-10
MUNCH
MUNCH
MUNCH
© 1988 PAWS, INC. All Rights Reserved.
MAY I GET YOU A SNORKEL?
ARE YOU TRYING TO TELL ME SOMETHING?

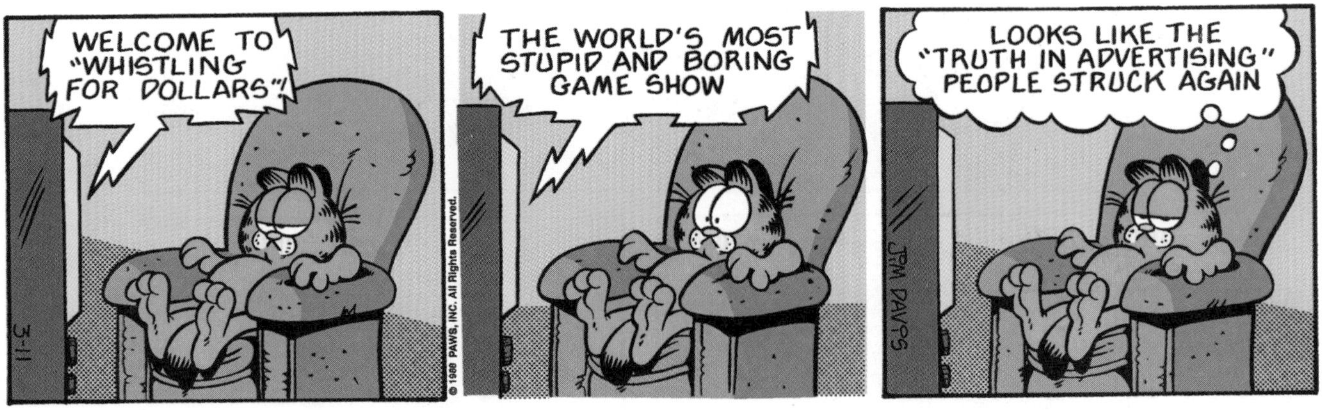
WELCOME TO "WHISTLING FOR DOLLARS"!
3-11
© 1988 PAWS, INC. All Rights Reserved.
THE WORLD'S MOST STUPID AND BORING GAME SHOW
LOOKS LIKE THE "TRUTH IN ADVERTISING" PEOPLE STRUCK AGAIN
JIM DAVIS

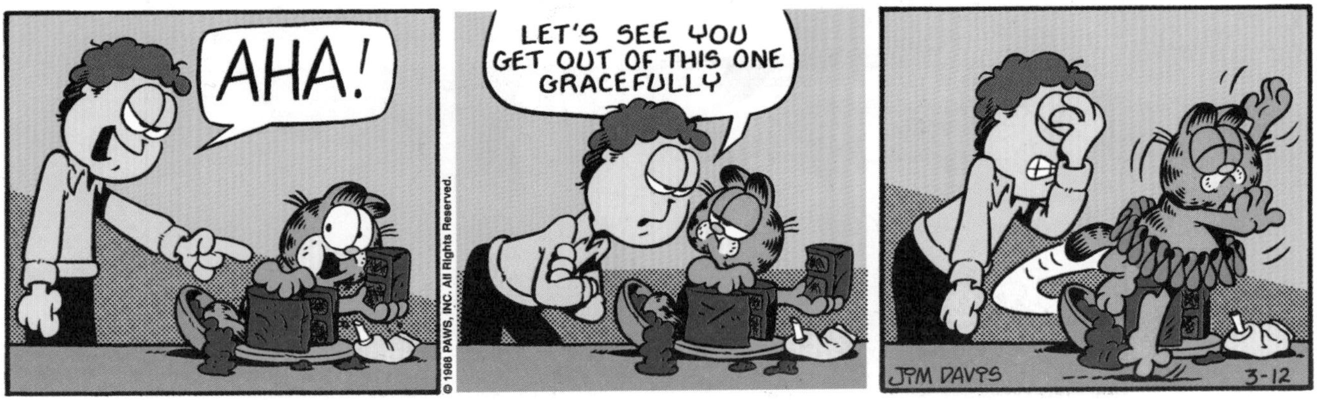
AHA!
© 1988 PAWS, INC. All Rights Reserved.
LET'S SEE YOU GET OUT OF THIS ONE GRACEFULLY
JIM DAVIS
3-12

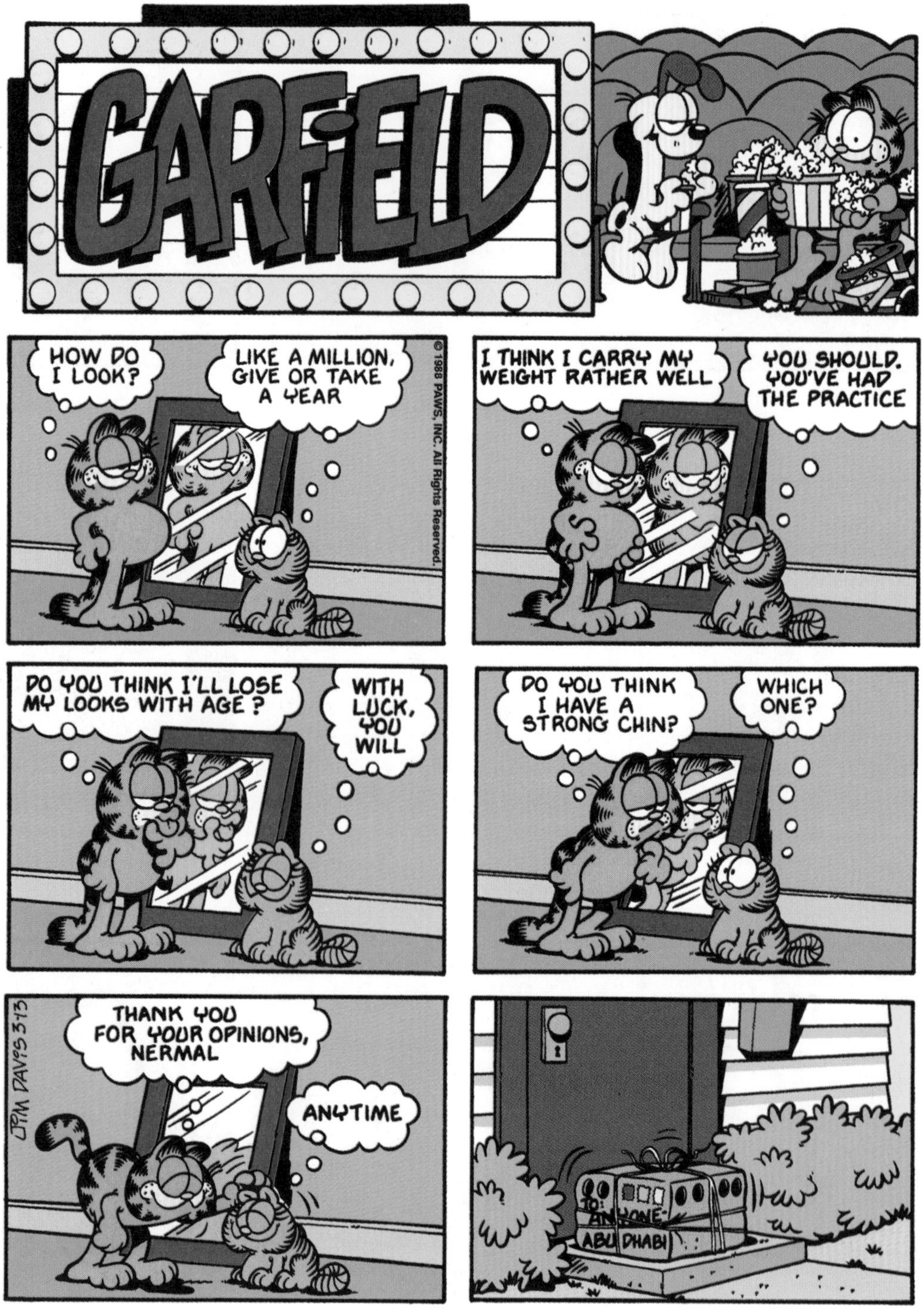
GARFIELD
© 1988 PAWS, INC. All Rights Reserved.
HOW DO I LOOK?
LIKE A MILLION, GIVE OR TAKE A YEAR
I THINK I CARRY MY WEIGHT RATHER WELL
YOU SHOULD. YOU'VE HAD THE PRACTICE
DO YOU THINK I'LL LOSE MY LOOKS WITH AGE ?
WITH LUCK, YOU WILL
DO YOU THINK I HAVE A STRONG CHIN?
WHICH ONE?
JIM DAVIS 3-13
THANK YOU FOR YOUR OPINIONS, NERMAL
ANYTIME
TO:
ABU DHABI

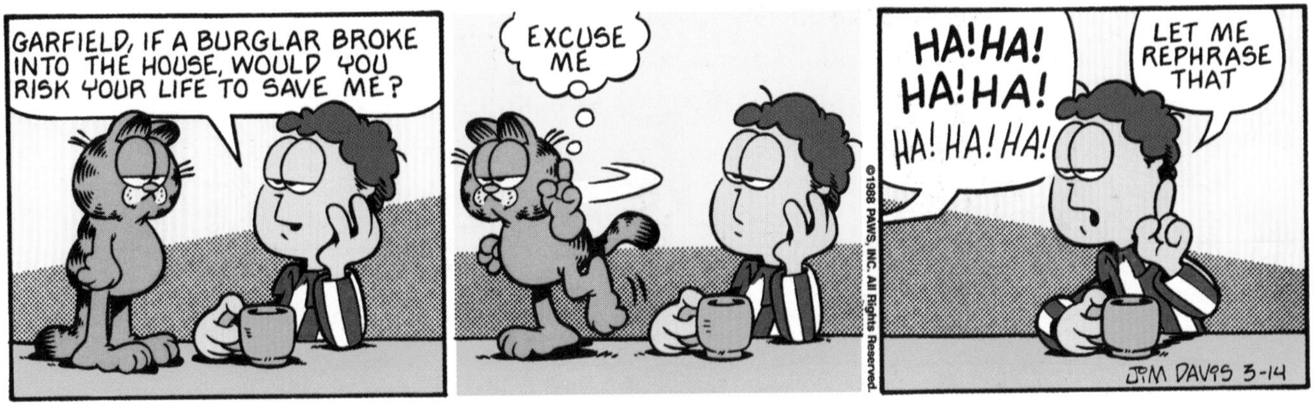
GARFIELD, IF A BURGLAR BROKE INTO THE HOUSE, WOULD YOU RISK YOUR LIFE TO SAVE ME?
EXCUSE ME
©1988 PAWS, INC. All Rights Reserved.
HA! HA! HA! HA! HA! HA! HA!
LET ME REPHRASE THAT
JIM DAVIS 3-14

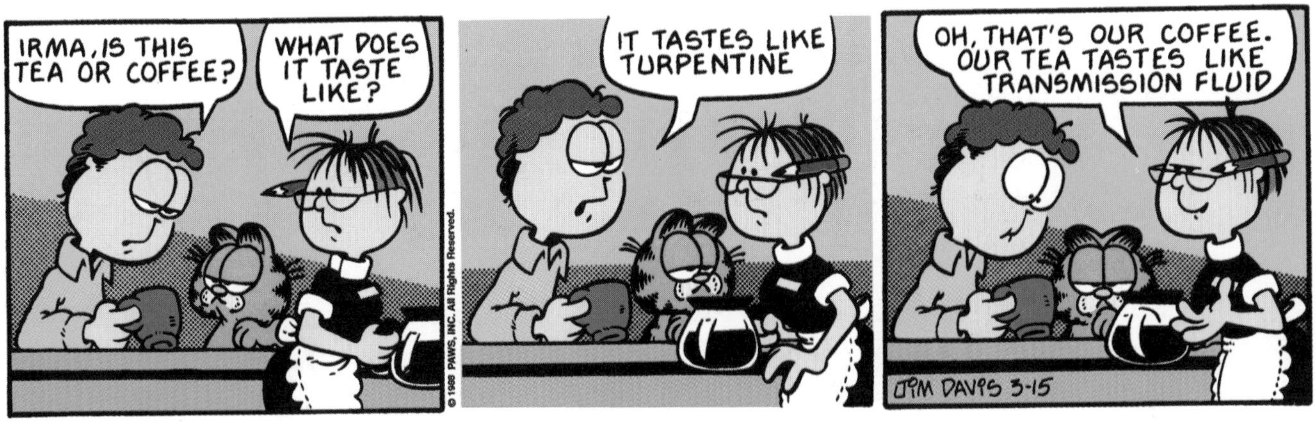
IRMA, IS THIS TEA OR COFFEE?
WHAT DOES IT TASTE LIKE?
© 1988 PAWS, INC. All Rights Reserved.
IT TASTES LIKE TURPENTINE
OH, THAT'S OUR COFFEE. OUR TEA TASTES LIKE TRANSMISSION FLUID
JIM DAVIS 3-15

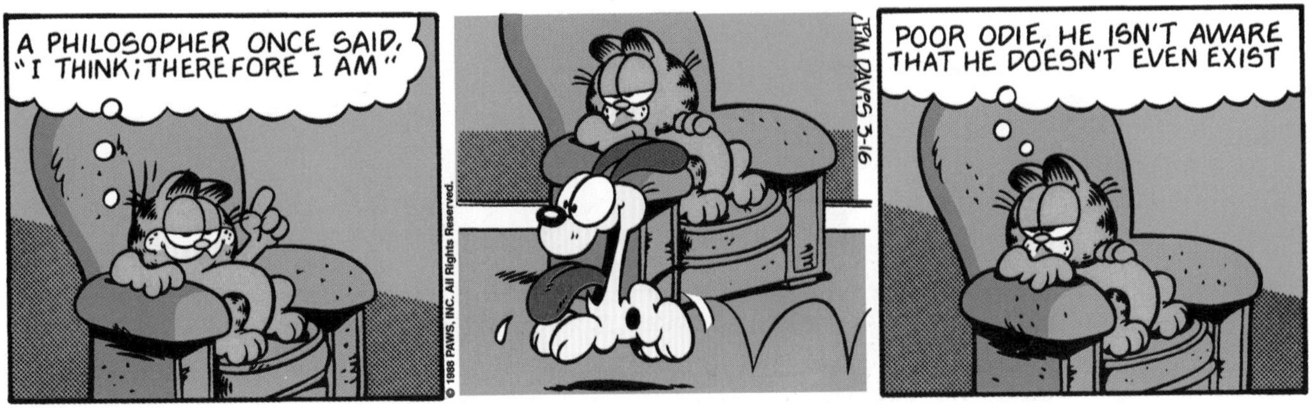
A PHILOSOPHER ONCE SAID, "I THINK; THEREFORE I AM"
© 1988 PAWS, INC. All Rights Reserved.
JIM DAVIS 3-16
POOR ODIE, HE ISN'T AWARE THAT HE DOESN'T EVEN EXIST

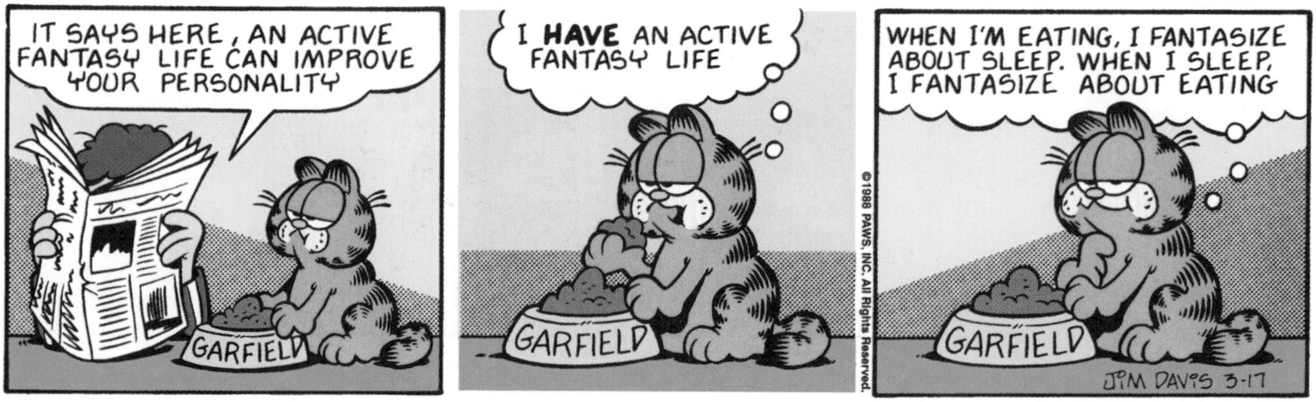
IT SAYS HERE, AN ACTIVE FANTASY LIFE CAN IMPROVE YOUR PERSONALITY
GARFIELD
I **HAVE** AN ACTIVE FANTASY LIFE
GARFIELD
©1988 PAWS, INC. All Rights Reserved.
WHEN I'M EATING, I FANTASIZE ABOUT SLEEP. WHEN I SLEEP, I FANTASIZE ABOUT EATING
GARFIELD
JIM DAVIS 3-17

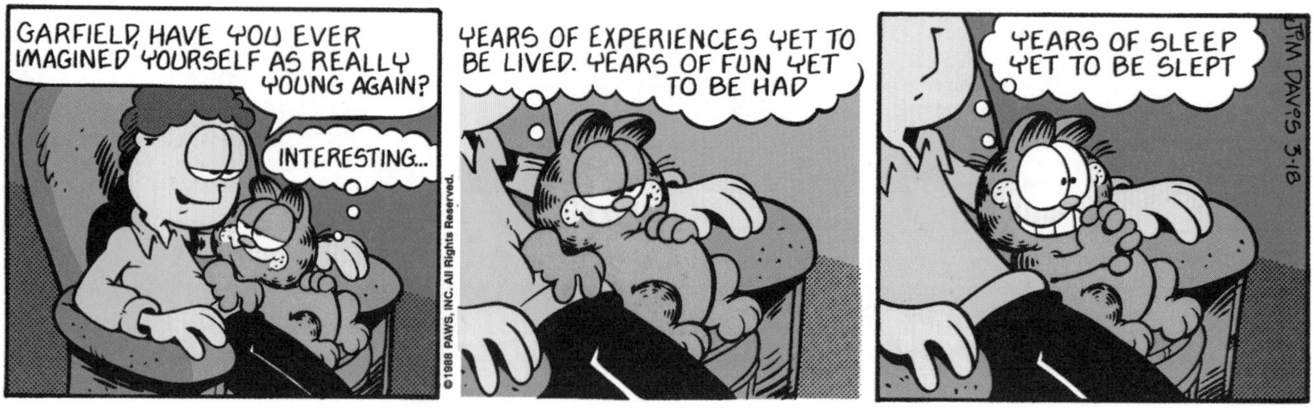
GARFIELD, HAVE YOU EVER IMAGINED YOURSELF AS REALLY YOUNG AGAIN?
INTERESTING...
©1988 PAWS, INC. All Rights Reserved.
YEARS OF EXPERIENCES YET TO BE LIVED. YEARS OF FUN YET TO BE HAD
YEARS OF SLEEP YET TO BE SLEPT
JIM DAVIS 3-18

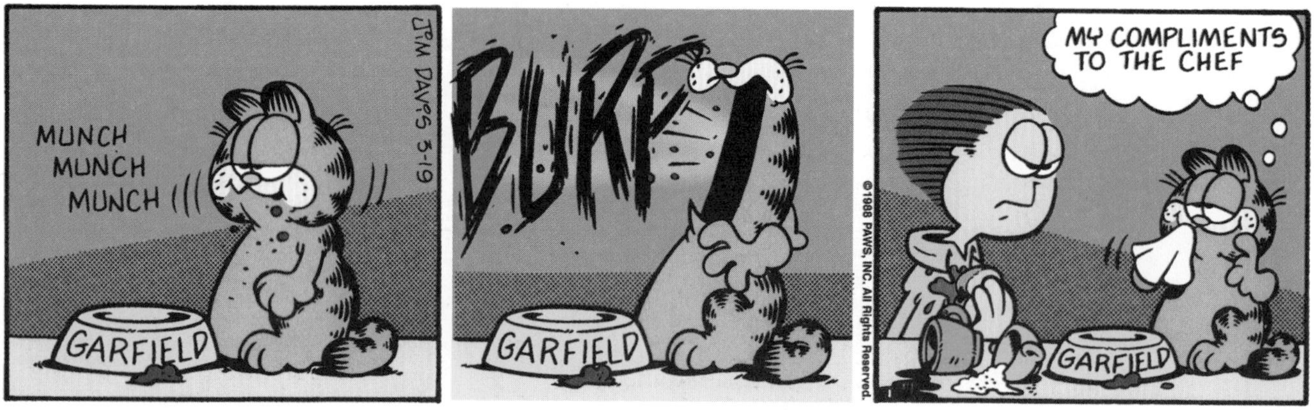
JIM DAVIS 3-19
MUNCH MUNCH MUNCH
GARFIELD
BURP
GARFIELD
©1988 PAWS, INC. All Rights Reserved.
MY COMPLIMENTS TO THE CHEF
GARFIELD

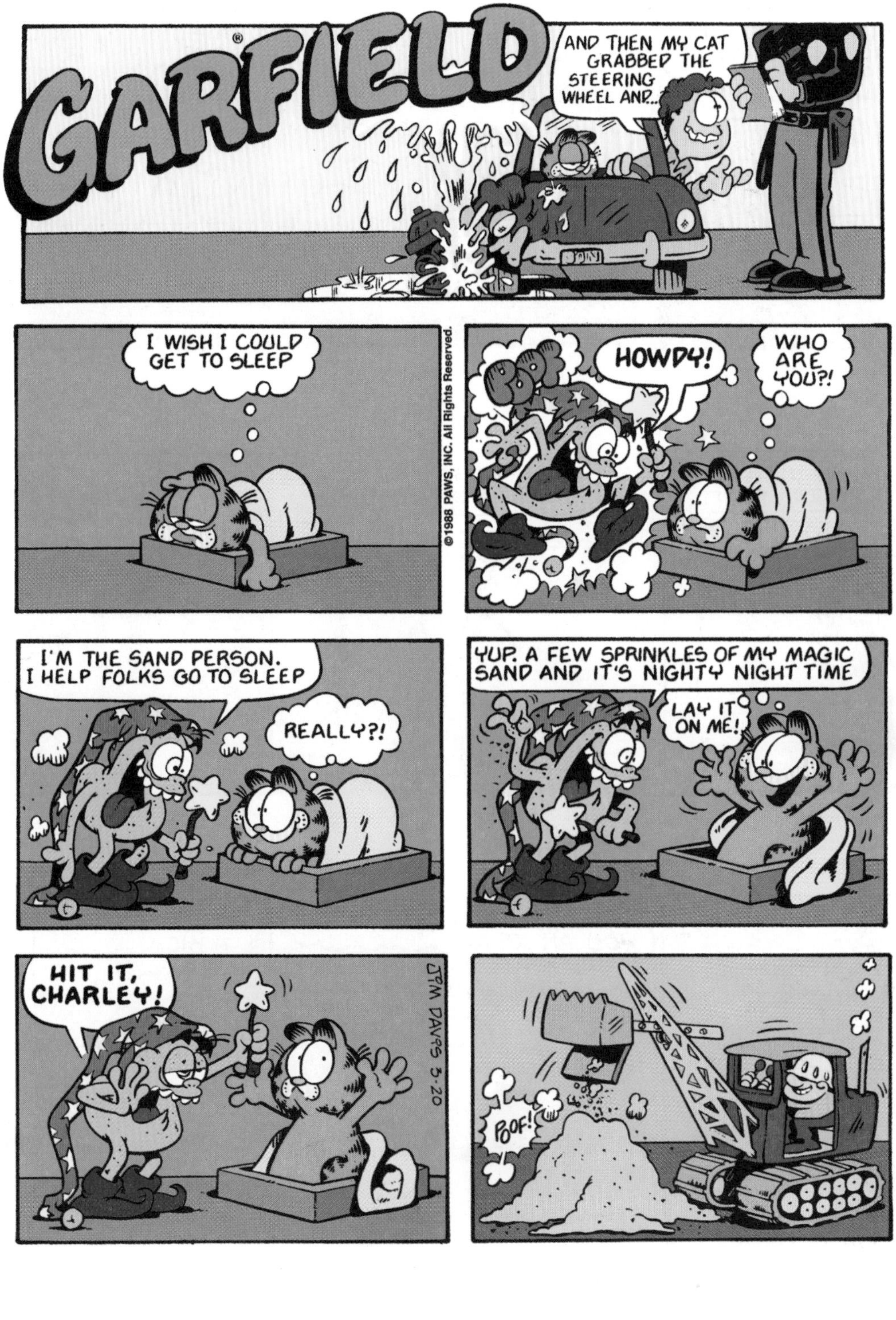
GARFIELD®
AND THEN MY CAT GRABBED THE STEERING WHEEL AND...
JON
I WISH I COULD GET TO SLEEP
©1988 PAWS, INC. All Rights Reserved.
POOF
HOWDY!
WHO ARE YOU?!
I'M THE SAND PERSON. I HELP FOLKS GO TO SLEEP
REALLY?!
YUP. A FEW SPRINKLES OF MY MAGIC SAND AND IT'S NIGHTY NIGHT TIME
LAY IT ON ME!
HIT IT, CHARLEY!
JIM DAVIS 3-20
POOF!

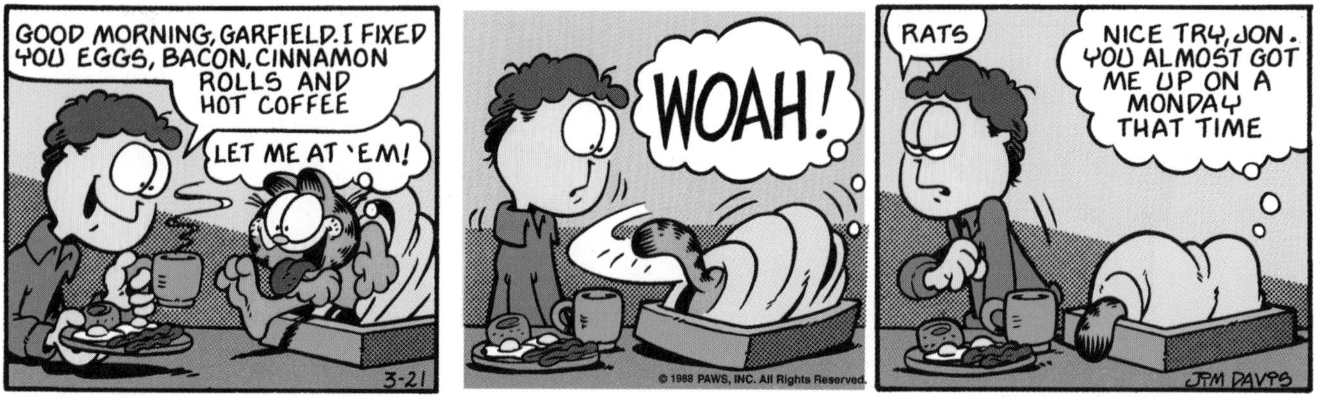
GOOD MORNING, GARFIELD. I FIXED YOU EGGS, BACON, CINNAMON ROLLS AND HOT COFFEE
LET ME AT 'EM!
3-21
WOAH!
© 1988 PAWS, INC. All Rights Reserved.
RATS
NICE TRY, JON. YOU ALMOST GOT ME UP ON A MONDAY THAT TIME
JIM DAVIS

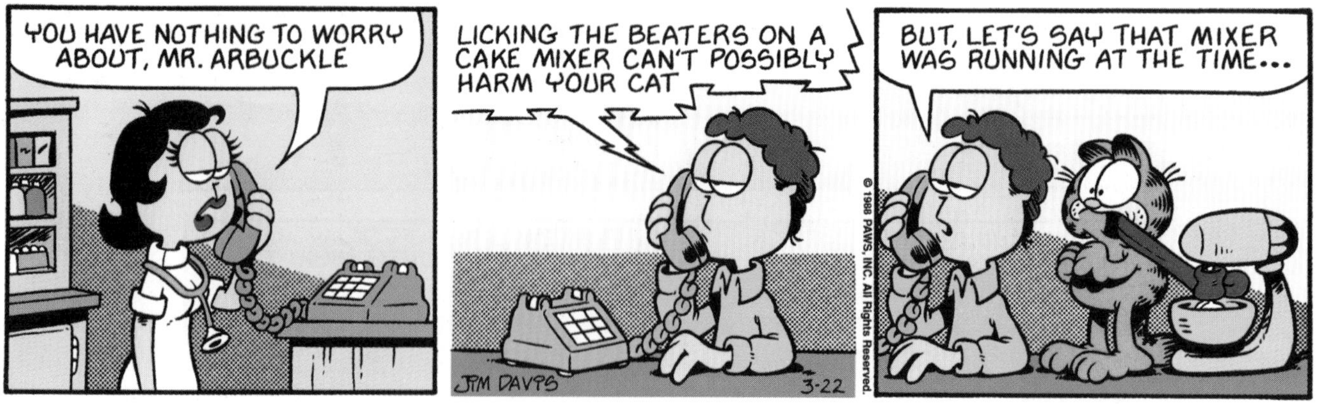
YOU HAVE NOTHING TO WORRY ABOUT, MR. ARBUCKLE
LICKING THE BEATERS ON A CAKE MIXER CAN'T POSSIBLY HARM YOUR CAT
JIM DAVIS
3-22
© 1988 PAWS, INC. All Rights Reserved.
BUT, LET'S SAY THAT MIXER WAS RUNNING AT THE TIME...

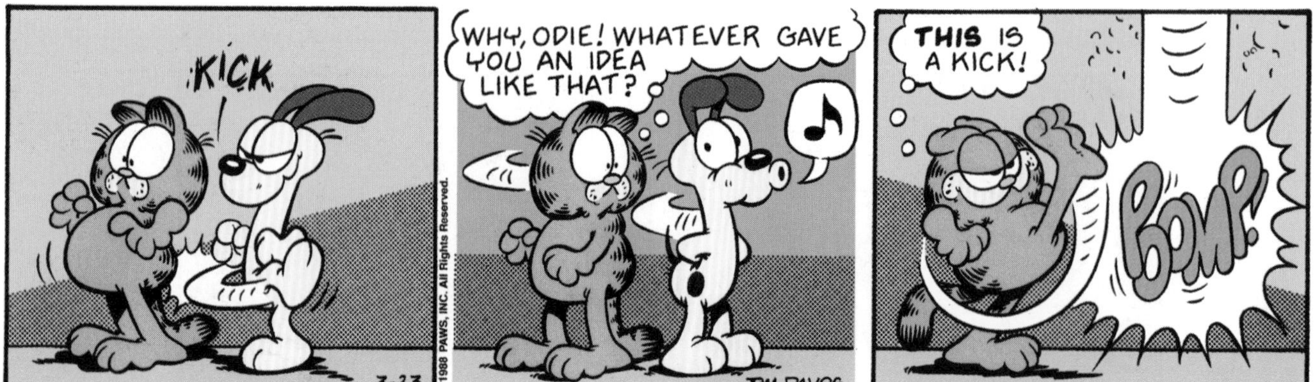
KICK
3-23
© 1988 PAWS, INC. All Rights Reserved.
WHY, ODIE! WHATEVER GAVE YOU AN IDEA LIKE THAT?
JIM DAVIS
THIS IS A KICK!
BOMP!

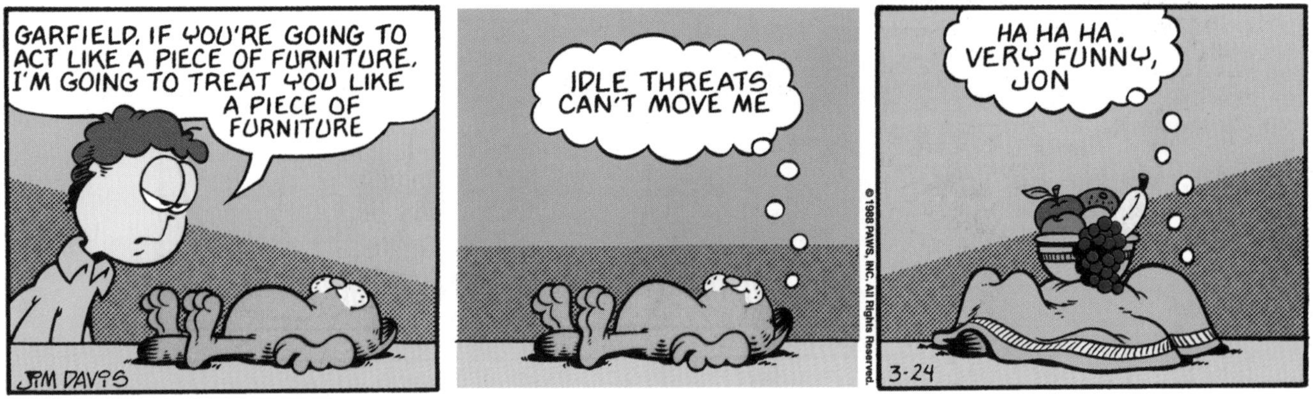
GARFIELD, IF YOU'RE GOING TO ACT LIKE A PIECE OF FURNITURE, I'M GOING TO TREAT YOU LIKE A PIECE OF FURNITURE
JIM DAVIS
IDLE THREATS CAN'T MOVE ME
© 1988 PAWS, INC. All Rights Reserved.
HA HA HA. VERY FUNNY, JON
3-24

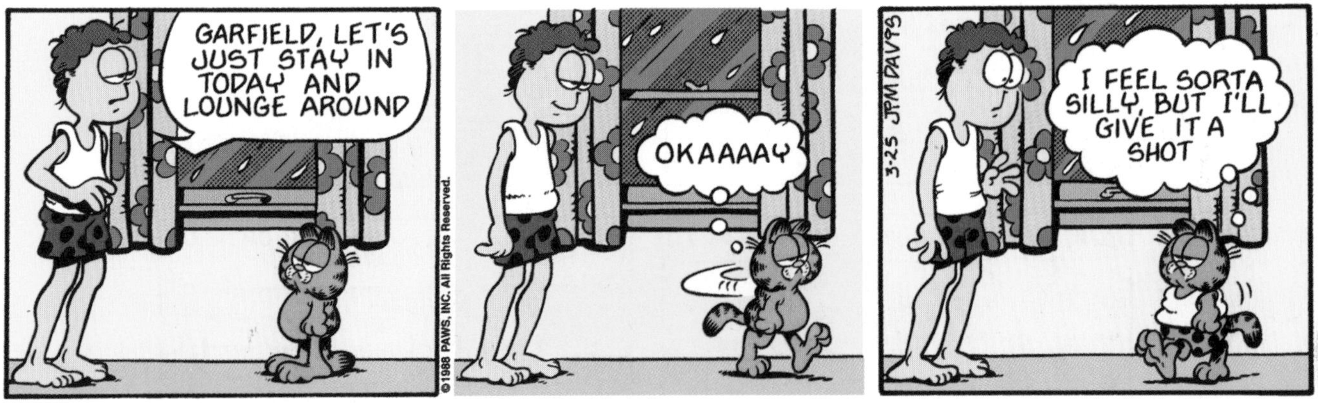
GARFIELD, LET'S JUST STAY IN TODAY AND LOUNGE AROUND
© 1988 PAWS, INC. All Rights Reserved.
OKAAAAY
3-25
JIM DAVIS
I FEEL SORTA SILLY, BUT I'LL GIVE IT A SHOT

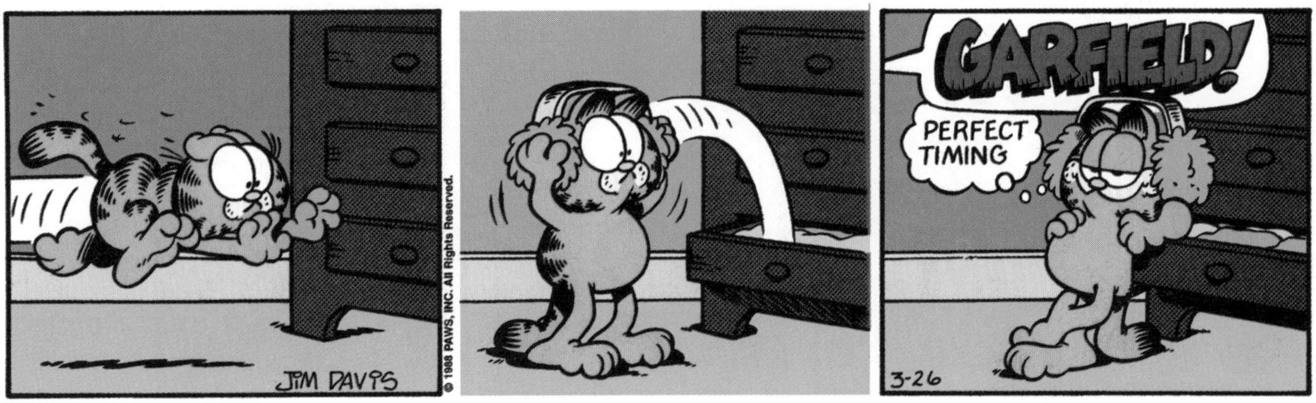
JIM DAVIS
© 1988 PAWS, INC. All Rights Reserved.
GARFIELD!
PERFECT TIMING
3-26

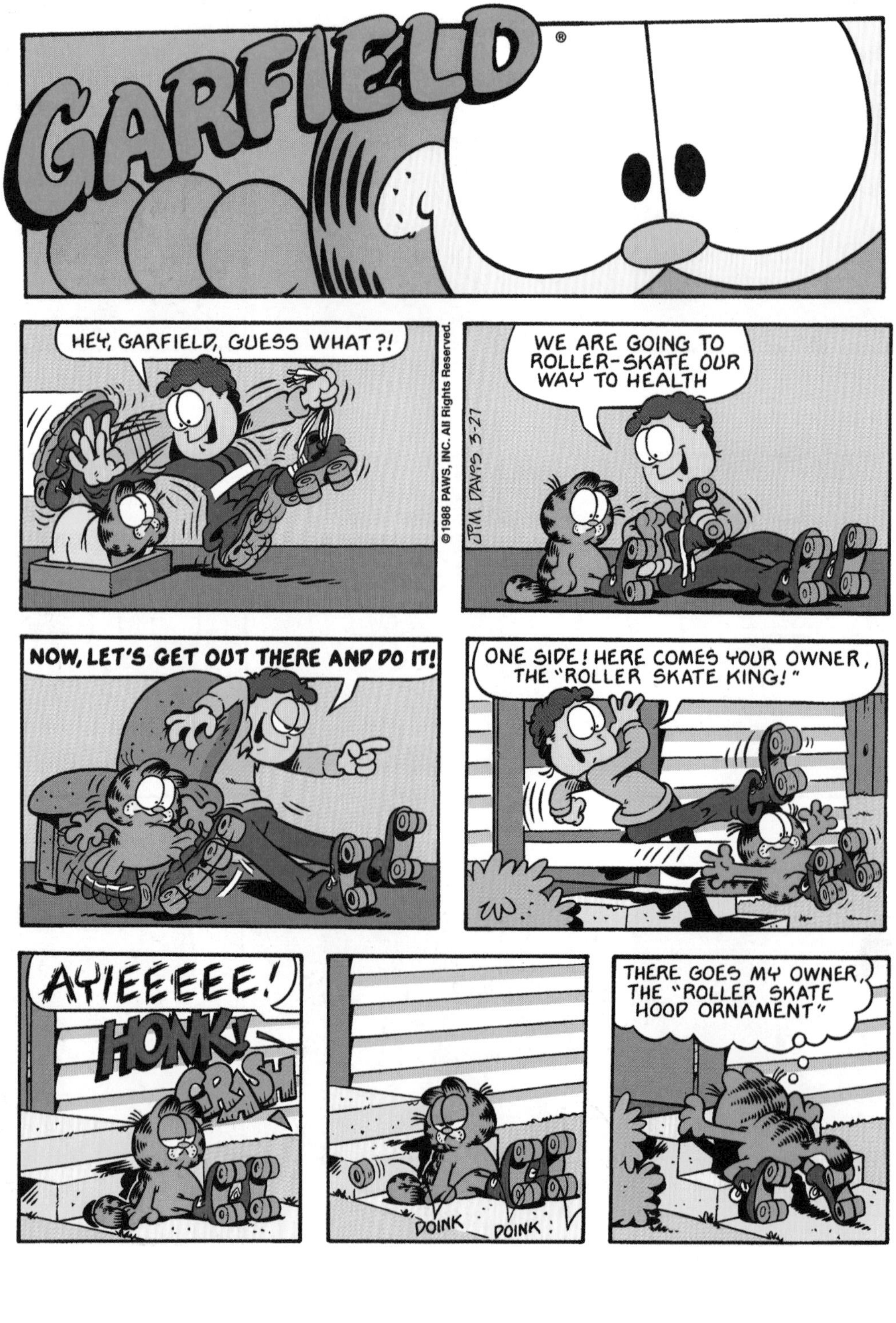
GARFIELD
HEY, GARFIELD, GUESS WHAT?!
©1988 PAWS, INC. All Rights Reserved.
JPM DAVPS 3-27
WE ARE GOING TO ROLLER-SKATE OUR WAY TO HEALTH
NOW, LET'S GET OUT THERE AND DO IT!
ONE SIDE! HERE COMES YOUR OWNER, THE "ROLLER SKATE KING!"
AYIEEEEEE!
HONK!
CRASH
DOINK
DOINK
THERE GOES MY OWNER, THE "ROLLER SKATE HOOD ORNAMENT"

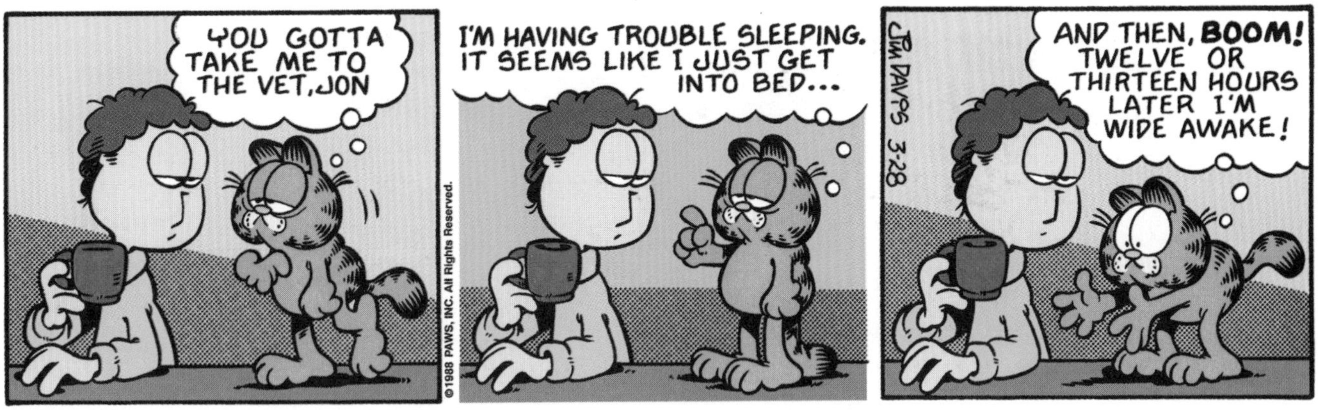
YOU GOTTA TAKE ME TO THE VET, JON
©1988 PAWS, INC. All Rights Reserved.
I'M HAVING TROUBLE SLEEPING. IT SEEMS LIKE I JUST GET INTO BED...
JIM DAVIS 3-28
AND THEN, **BOOM!** TWELVE OR THIRTEEN HOURS LATER I'M WIDE AWAKE!

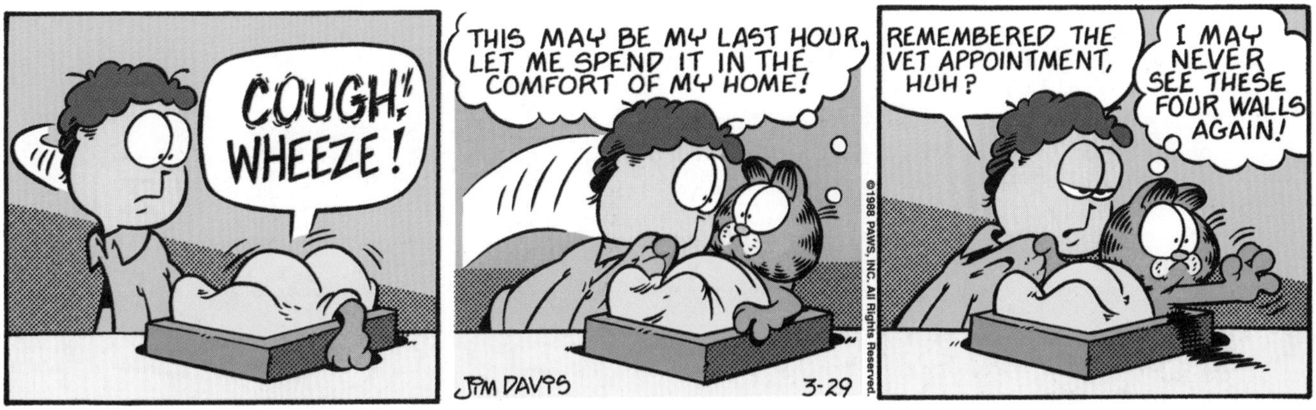
COUGH! WHEEZE!
THIS MAY BE MY LAST HOUR. LET ME SPEND IT IN THE COMFORT OF MY HOME!
JIM DAVIS 3-29
©1988 PAWS, INC. All Rights Reserved.
REMEMBERED THE VET APPOINTMENT, HUH?
I MAY NEVER SEE THESE FOUR WALLS AGAIN!

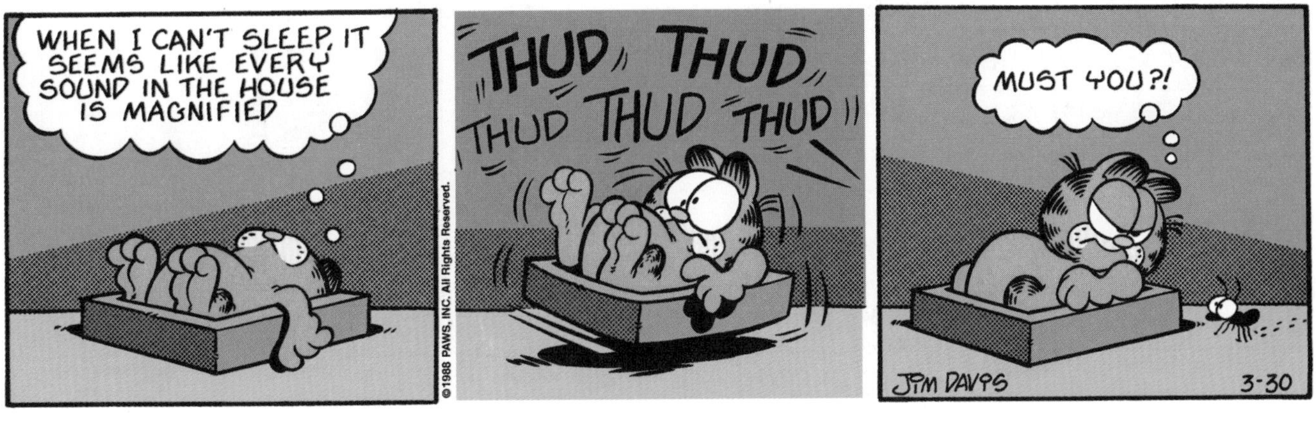
WHEN I CAN'T SLEEP, IT SEEMS LIKE EVERY SOUND IN THE HOUSE IS MAGNIFIED
©1988 PAWS, INC. All Rights Reserved.
THUD THUD THUD THUD THUD
MUST YOU?!
JIM DAVIS 3-30

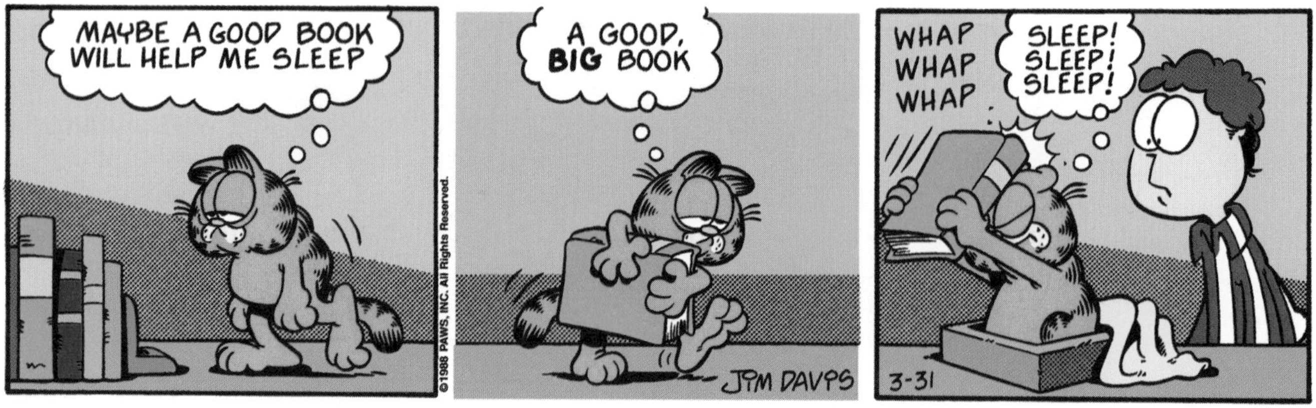
MAYBE A GOOD BOOK WILL HELP ME SLEEP
©1988 PAWS, INC. All Rights Reserved.
A GOOD, **BIG** BOOK
JIM DAVIS
WHAP
WHAP
WHAP
SLEEP! SLEEP! SLEEP!
3-31

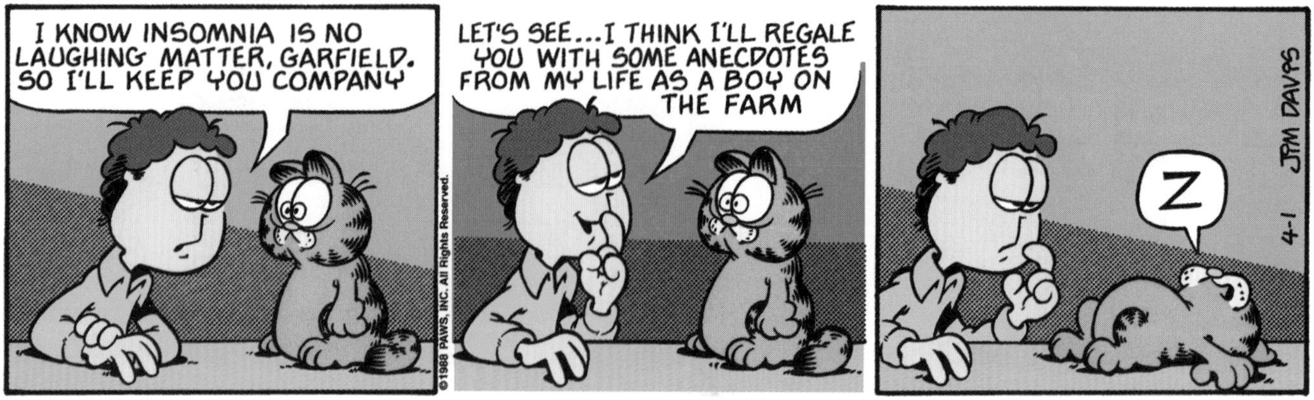
I KNOW INSOMNIA IS NO LAUGHING MATTER, GARFIELD. SO I'LL KEEP YOU COMPANY
©1988 PAWS, INC. All Rights Reserved.
LET'S SEE...I THINK I'LL REGALE YOU WITH SOME ANECDOTES FROM MY LIFE AS A BOY ON THE FARM
JIM DAVIS
4-1
Z

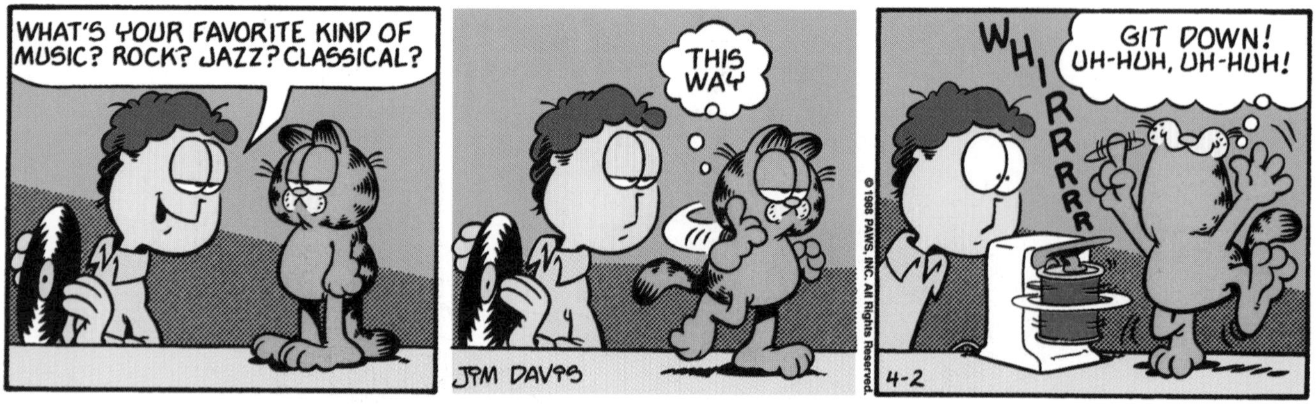
WHAT'S YOUR FAVORITE KIND OF MUSIC? ROCK? JAZZ? CLASSICAL?
THIS WAY
JIM DAVIS
©1988 PAWS, INC. All Rights Reserved.
WHIRRRRR
GIT DOWN! UH-HUH, UH-HUH!
4-2

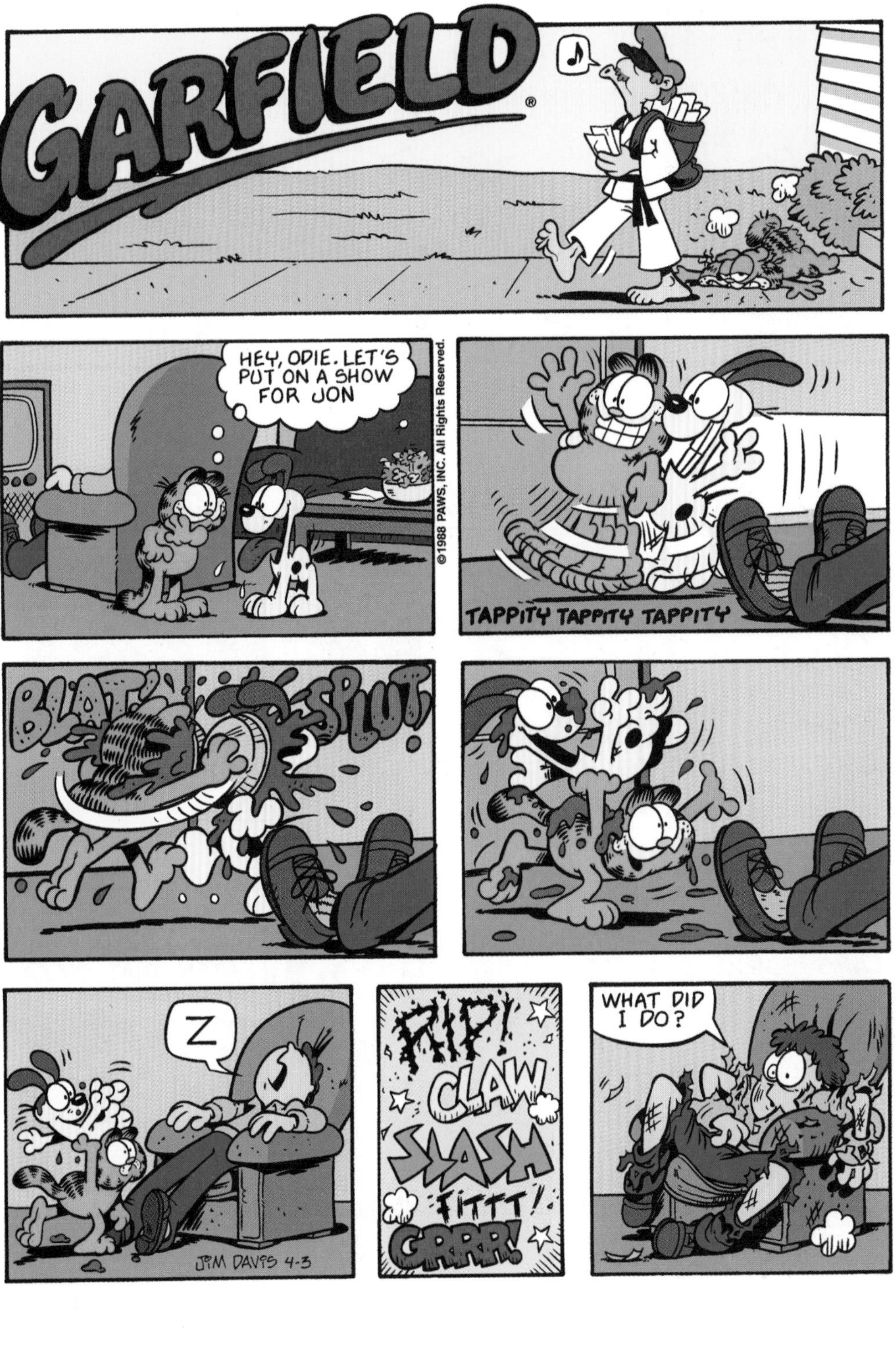
GARFIELD®
HEY, ODIE. LET'S PUT ON A SHOW FOR JON
©1988 PAWS, INC. All Rights Reserved.
TAPPITY TAPPITY TAPPITY
BLAT!
SPLUT!
Z
JIM DAVIS 4-3
RIP!
CLAW
SLASH
FTTTT!
GRRR!
WHAT DID I DO?

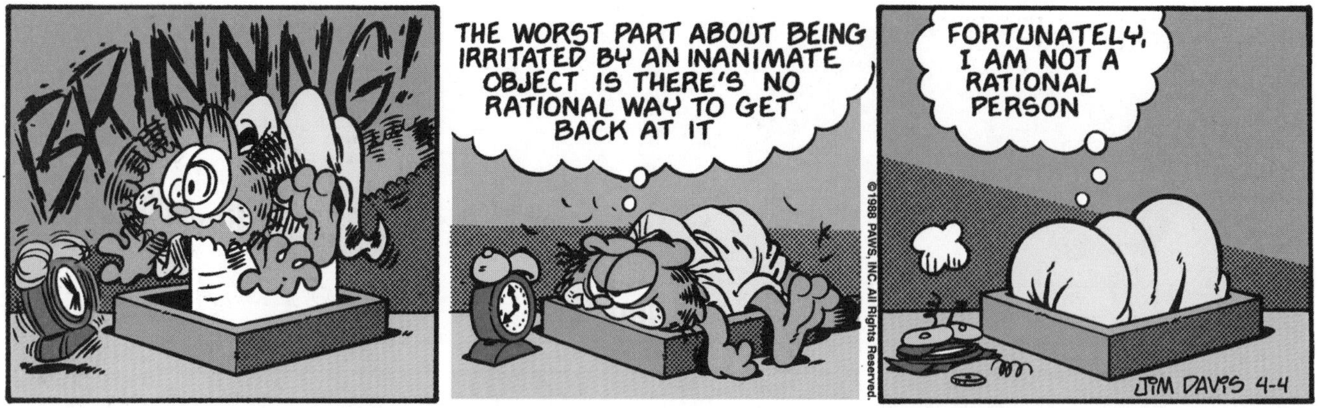
BRINNNG!
THE WORST PART ABOUT BEING IRRITATED BY AN INANIMATE OBJECT IS THERE'S NO RATIONAL WAY TO GET BACK AT IT
FORTUNATELY, I AM NOT A RATIONAL PERSON
JIM DAVIS 4-4
© 1988 PAWS, INC. All Rights Reserved.

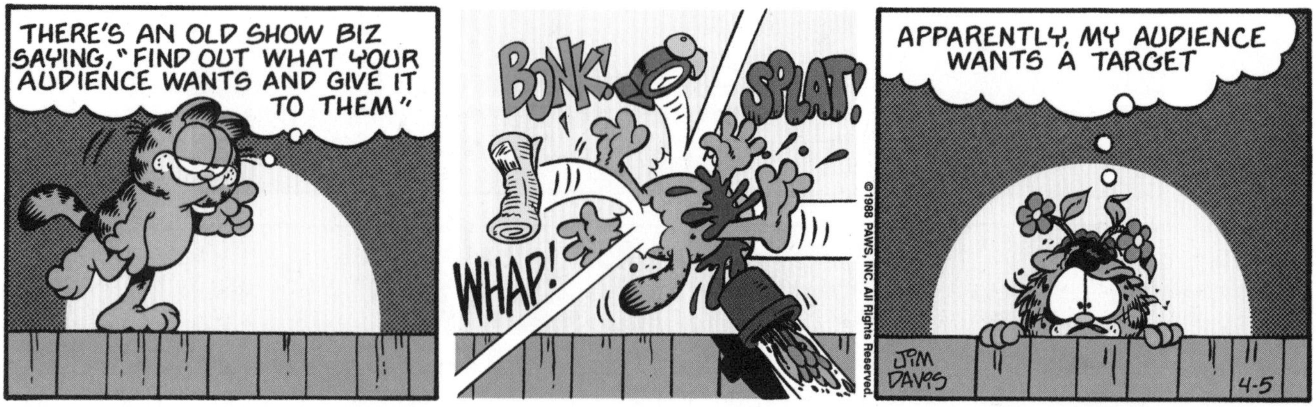
THERE'S AN OLD SHOW BIZ SAYING, "FIND OUT WHAT YOUR AUDIENCE WANTS AND GIVE IT TO THEM"
BONK!
SPLAT!
WHAP!
APPARENTLY, MY AUDIENCE WANTS A TARGET
JIM DAVIS
4-5
© 1988 PAWS, INC. All Rights Reserved.

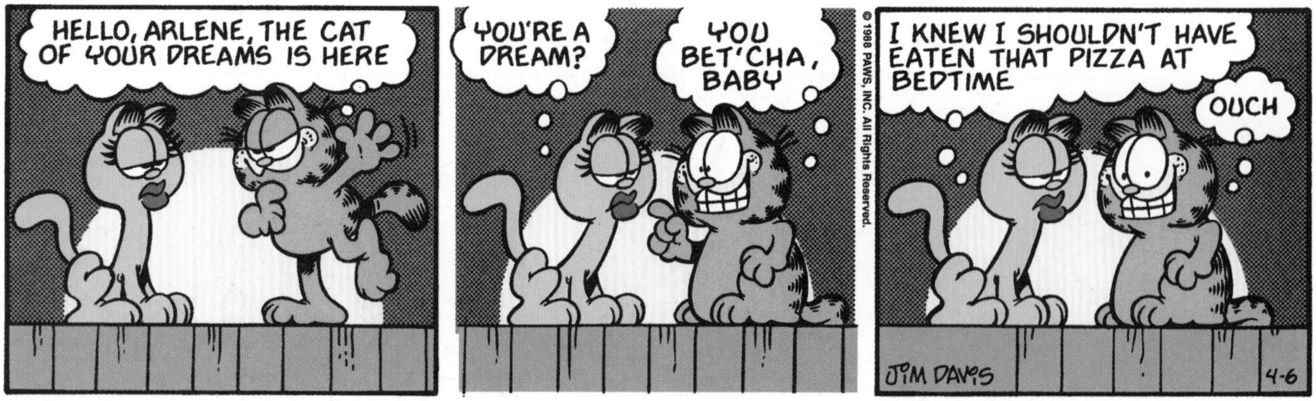
HELLO, ARLENE, THE CAT OF YOUR DREAMS IS HERE
YOU'RE A DREAM?
YOU BET'CHA, BABY
I KNEW I SHOULDN'T HAVE EATEN THAT PIZZA AT BEDTIME
OUCH
JIM DAVIS
4-6
© 1988 PAWS, INC. All Rights Reserved.

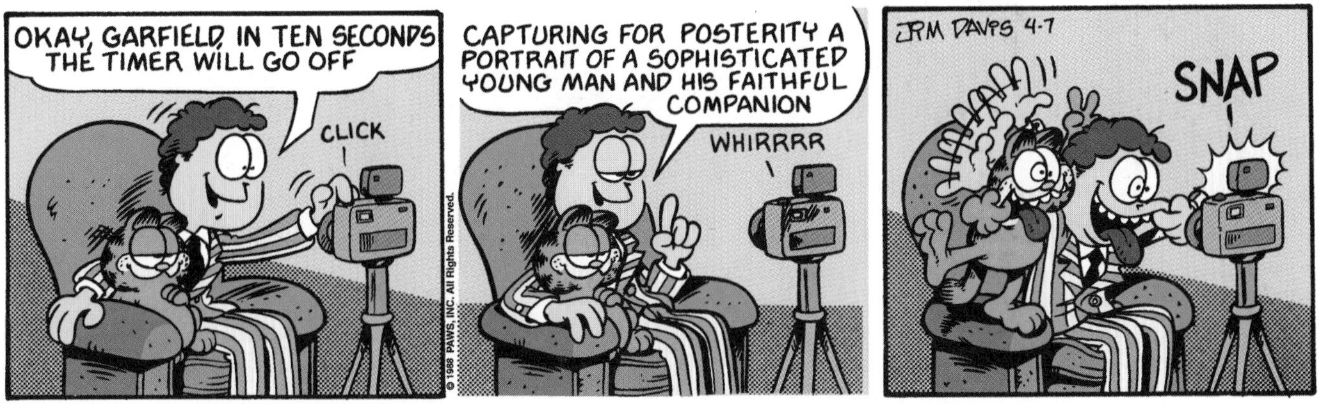
OKAY, GARFIELD, IN TEN SECONDS THE TIMER WILL GO OFF
CLICK
CAPTURING FOR POSTERITY A PORTRAIT OF A SOPHISTICATED YOUNG MAN AND HIS FAITHFUL COMPANION
WHIRRRRR
© 1988 PAWS, INC. All Rights Reserved.
JIM DAVIS 4-7
SNAP

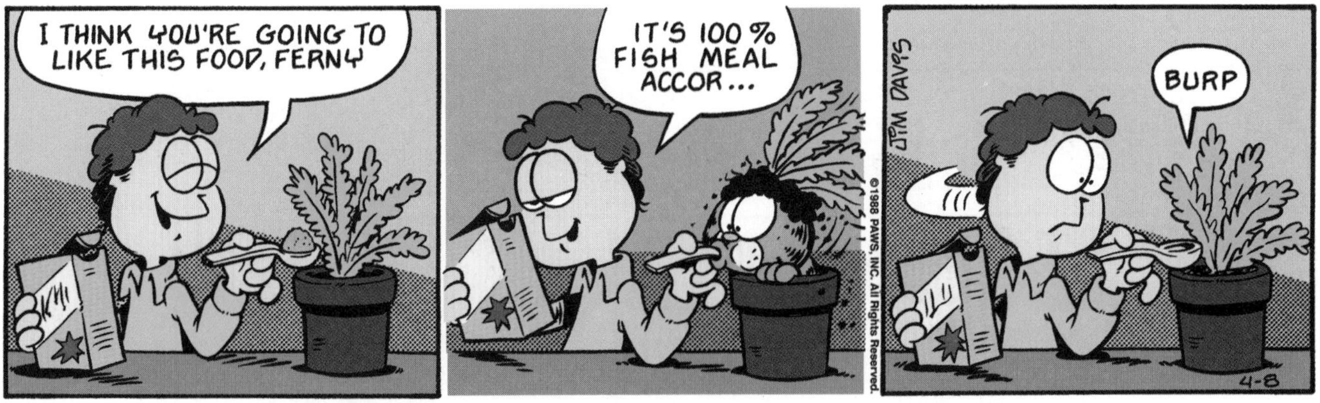
I THINK YOU'RE GOING TO LIKE THIS FOOD, FERNY
IT'S 100 % FISH MEAL ACCOR...
© 1988 PAWS, INC. All Rights Reserved.
JIM DAVIS
BURP
4-8

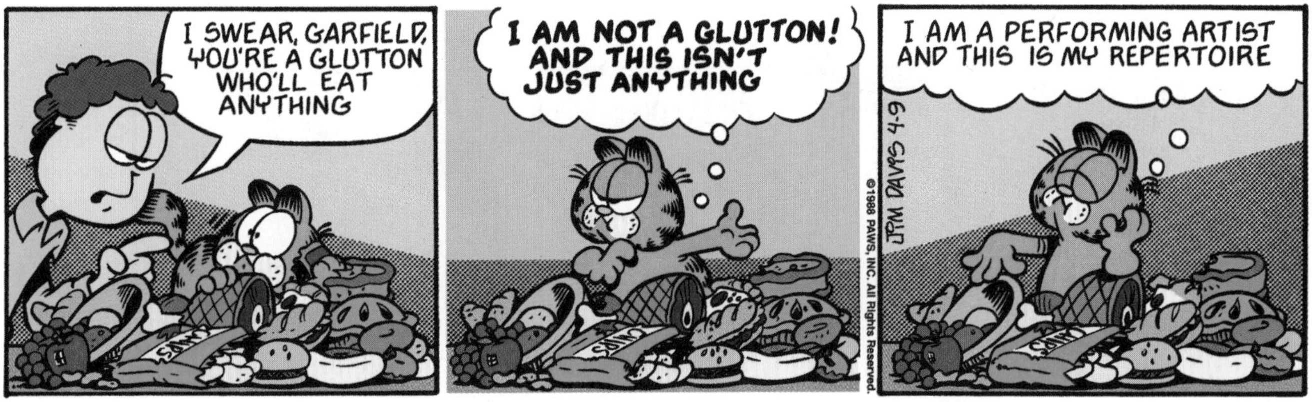
I SWEAR, GARFIELD, YOU'RE A GLUTTON WHO'LL EAT ANYTHING
I AM NOT A GLUTTON! AND THIS ISN'T JUST ANYTHING
JIM DAVIS 4-9
© 1988 PAWS, INC. All Rights Reserved.
I AM A PERFORMING ARTIST AND THIS IS MY REPERTOIRE

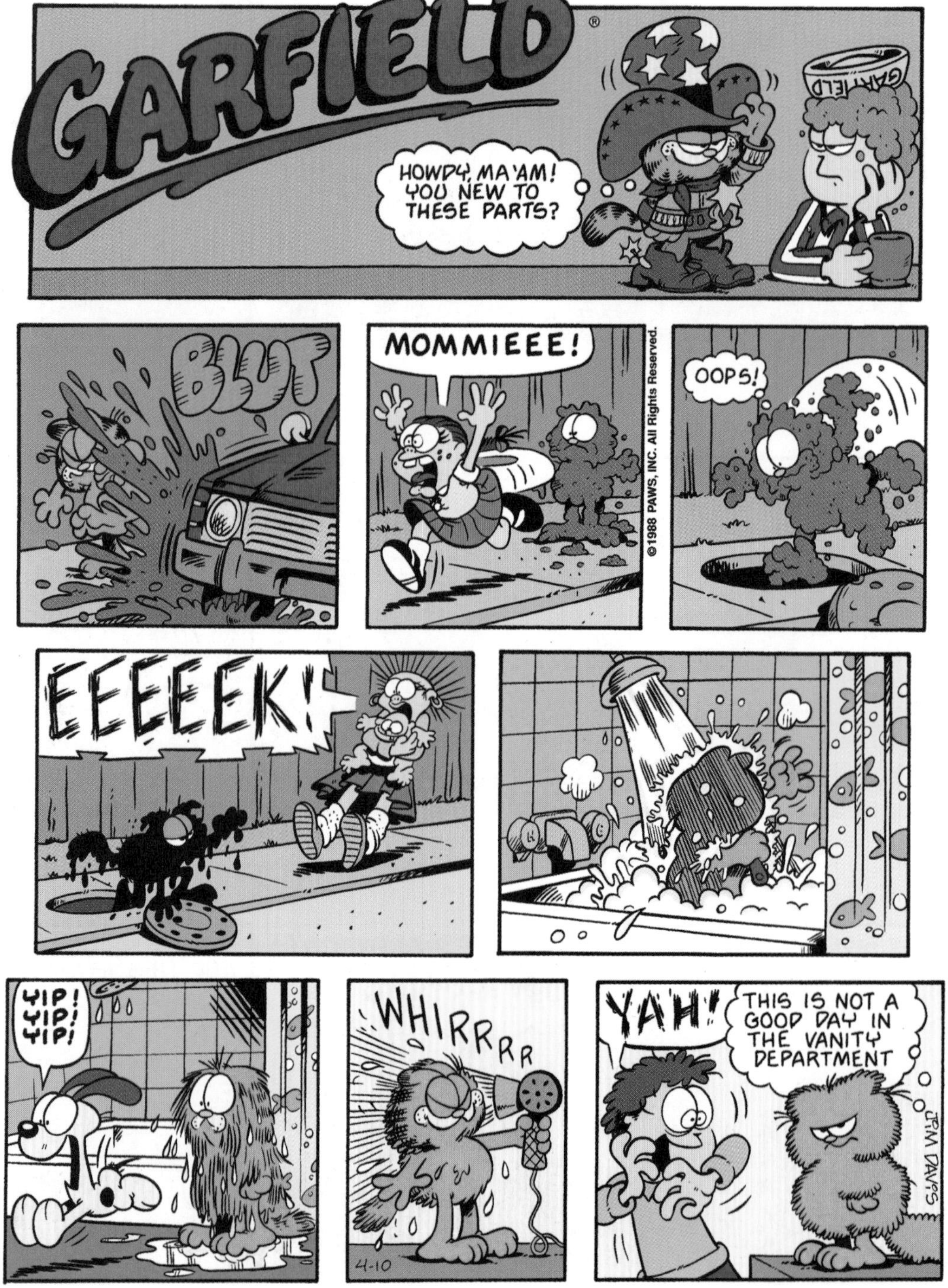
GARFIELD
HOWDY, MA'AM! YOU NEW TO THESE PARTS?
GARFIELD
BLUT
MOMMIEEE!
©1988 PAWS, INC. All Rights Reserved.
OOPS!
EEEEEK!
YIP! YIP! YIP!
WHIRRRR
4-10
YAH!
THIS IS NOT A GOOD DAY IN THE VANITY DEPARTMENT
JPM DAVIS

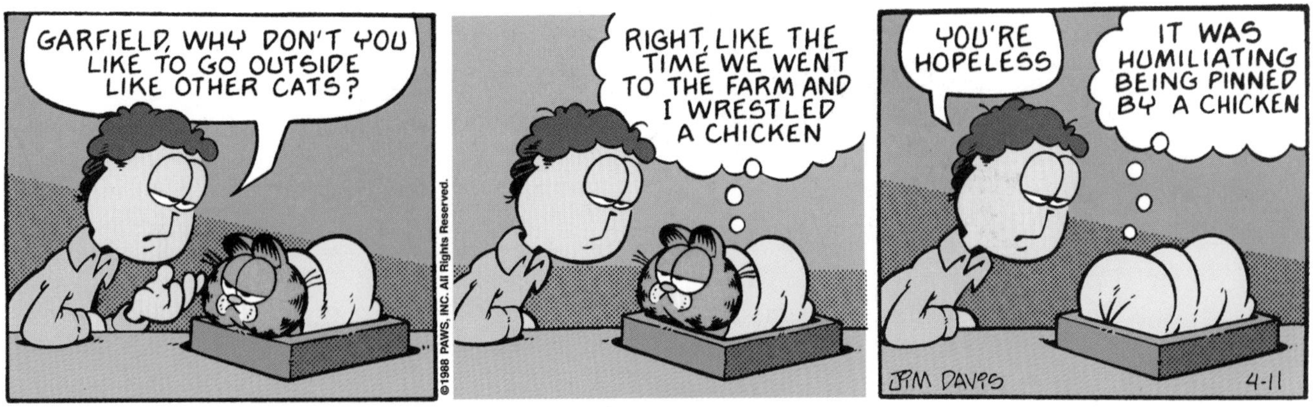
GARFIELD, WHY DON'T YOU LIKE TO GO OUTSIDE LIKE OTHER CATS?
RIGHT, LIKE THE TIME WE WENT TO THE FARM AND I WRESTLED A CHICKEN
YOU'RE HOPELESS
IT WAS HUMILIATING BEING PINNED BY A CHICKEN
©1988 PAWS, INC. All Rights Reserved.
JIM DAVIS
4-11

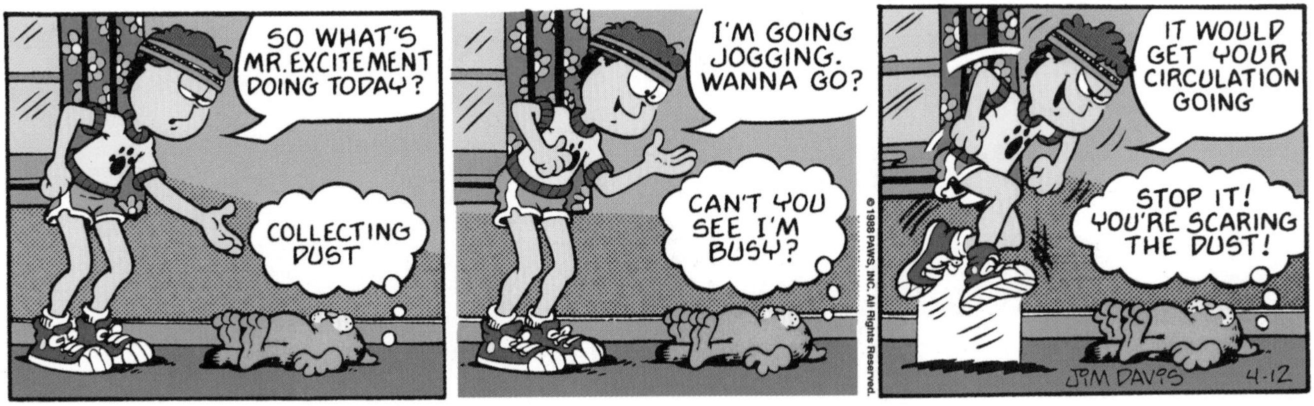
SO WHAT'S MR. EXCITEMENT DOING TODAY?
COLLECTING DUST
I'M GOING JOGGING. WANNA GO?
CAN'T YOU SEE I'M BUSY?
IT WOULD GET YOUR CIRCULATION GOING
STOP IT! YOU'RE SCARING THE DUST!
©1988 PAWS, INC. All Rights Reserved.
JIM DAVIS
4-12

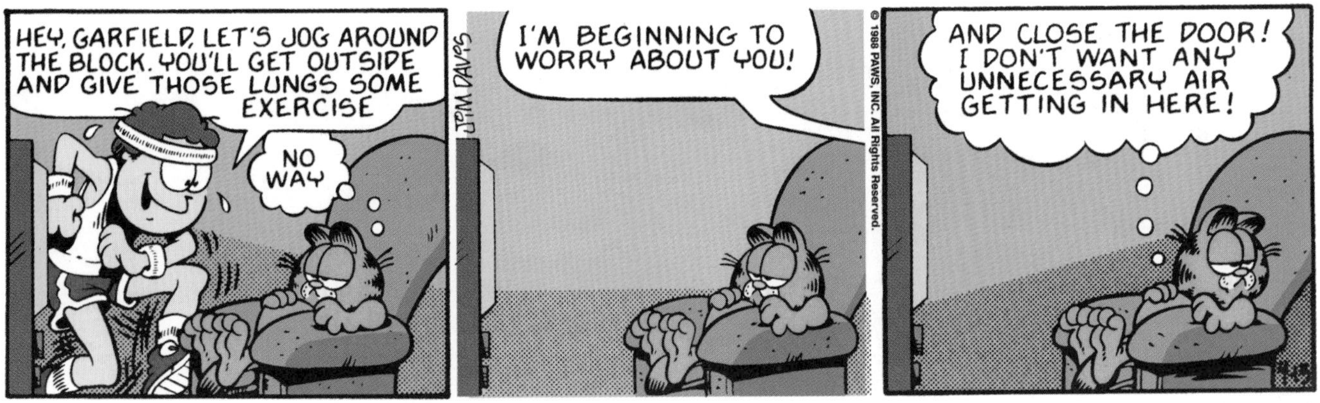
HEY, GARFIELD, LET'S JOG AROUND THE BLOCK. YOU'LL GET OUTSIDE AND GIVE THOSE LUNGS SOME EXERCISE
NO WAY
JIM DAVIS
I'M BEGINNING TO WORRY ABOUT YOU!
©1988 PAWS, INC. All Rights Reserved.
AND CLOSE THE DOOR! I DON'T WANT ANY UNNECESSARY AIR GETTING IN HERE!

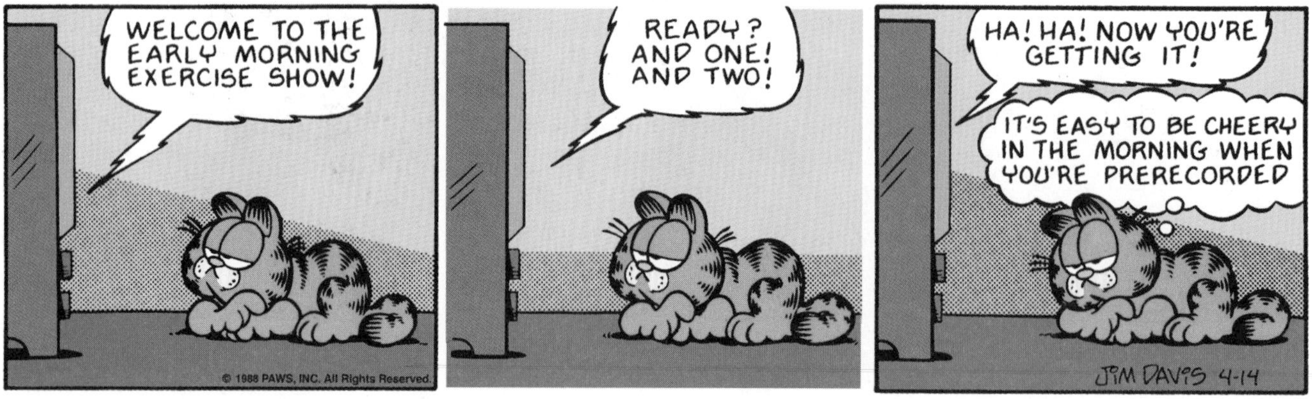
WELCOME TO THE EARLY MORNING EXERCISE SHOW!
READY? AND ONE! AND TWO!
HA! HA! NOW YOU'RE GETTING IT!
IT'S EASY TO BE CHEERY IN THE MORNING WHEN YOU'RE PRERECORDED
© 1988 PAWS, INC. All Rights Reserved.
JIM DAVIS 4-14

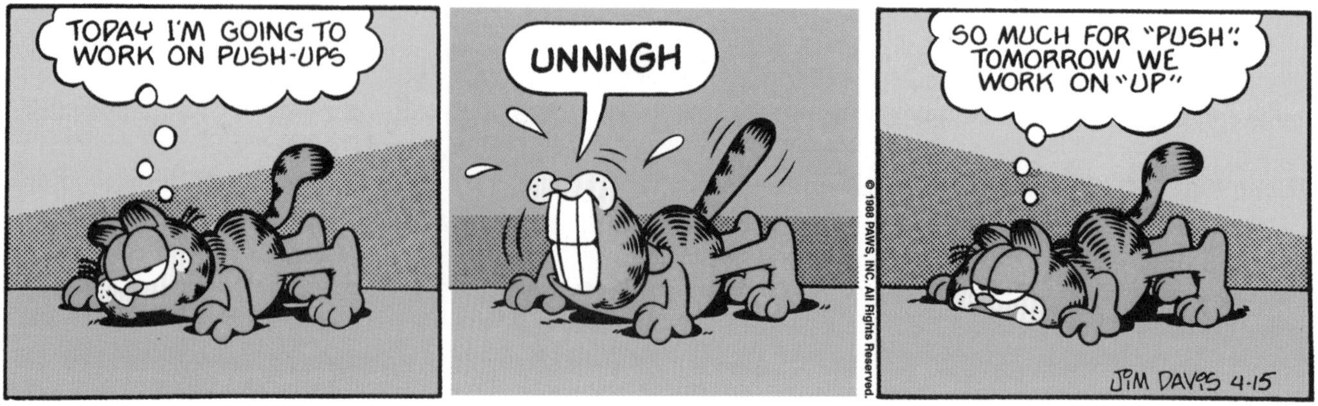
TODAY I'M GOING TO WORK ON PUSH-UPS
UNNNGH
SO MUCH FOR "PUSH". TOMORROW WE WORK ON "UP"
© 1988 PAWS, INC. All Rights Reserved.
JIM DAVIS 4-15

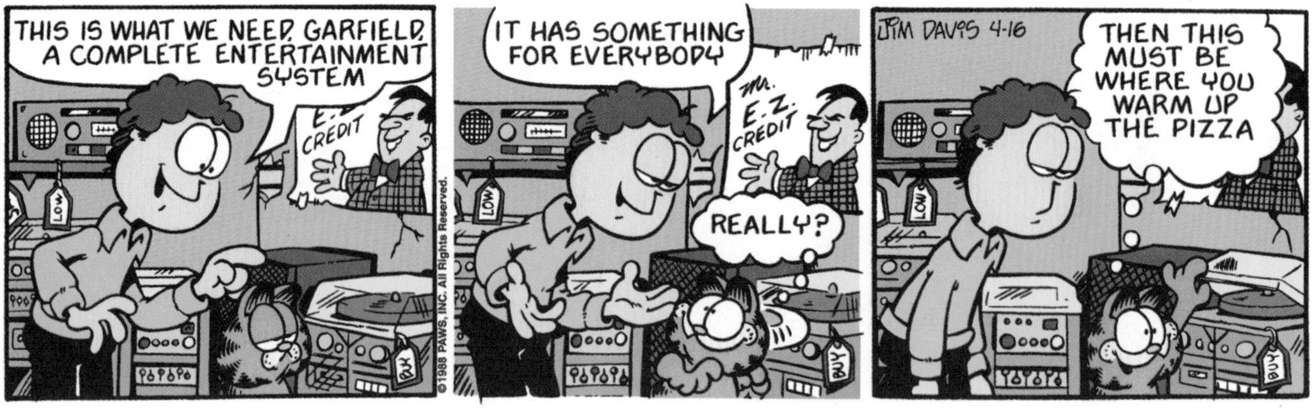
THIS IS WHAT WE NEED, GARFIELD, A COMPLETE ENTERTAINMENT SYSTEM
IT HAS SOMETHING FOR EVERYBODY
REALLY?
THEN THIS MUST BE WHERE YOU WARM UP THE PIZZA
E.Z. CREDIT
LOW
BUY
©1988 PAWS, INC. All Rights Reserved.
JIM DAVIS 4-16

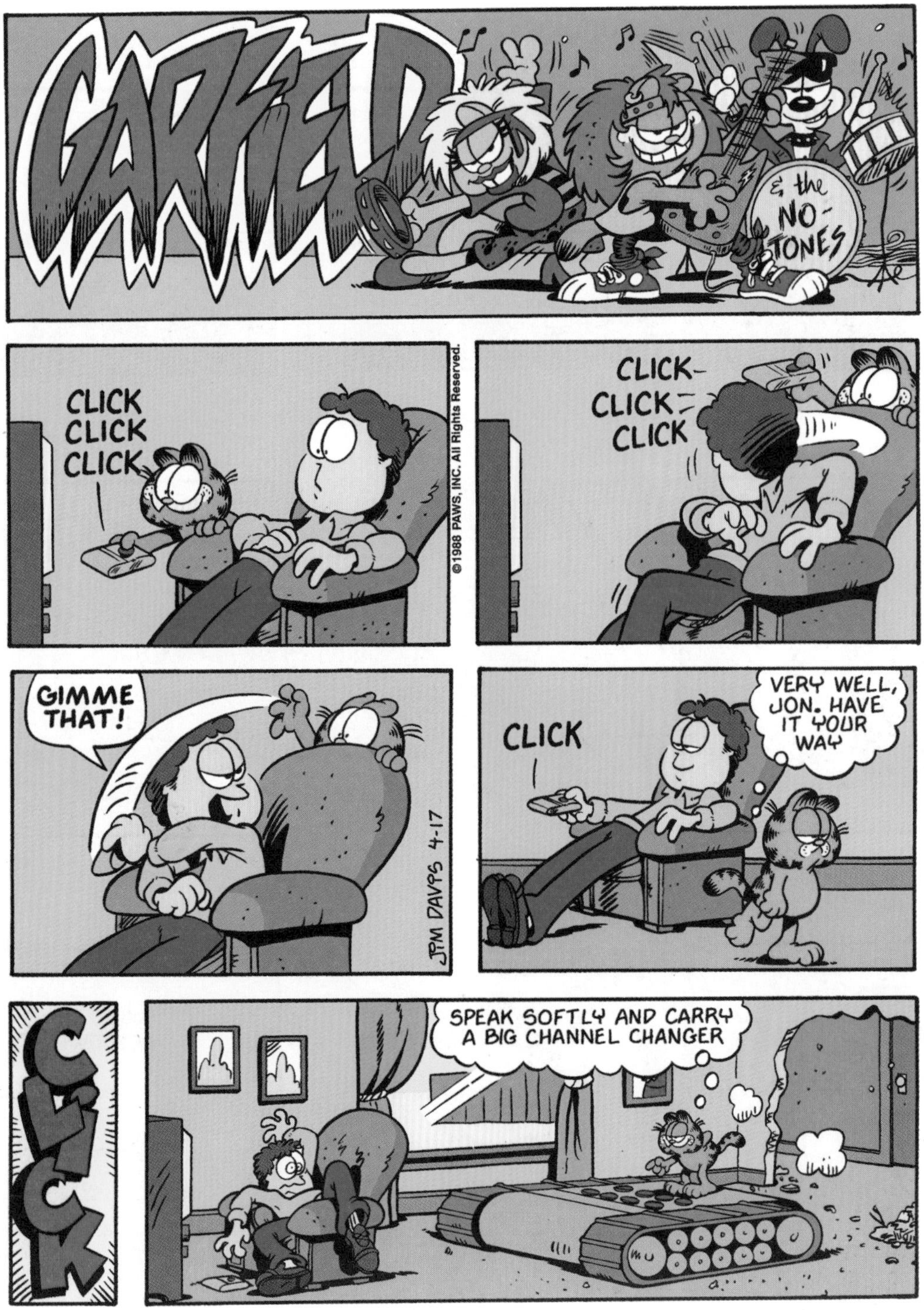
GARFIELD
& the NO-TONES
©1988 PAWS, INC. All Rights Reserved.
CLICK CLICK CLICK
CLICK- CLICK CLICK
GIMME THAT!
JIM DAVIS 4-17
CLICK
VERY WELL, JON. HAVE IT YOUR WAY
CLICK
SPEAK SOFTLY AND CARRY A BIG CHANNEL CHANGER

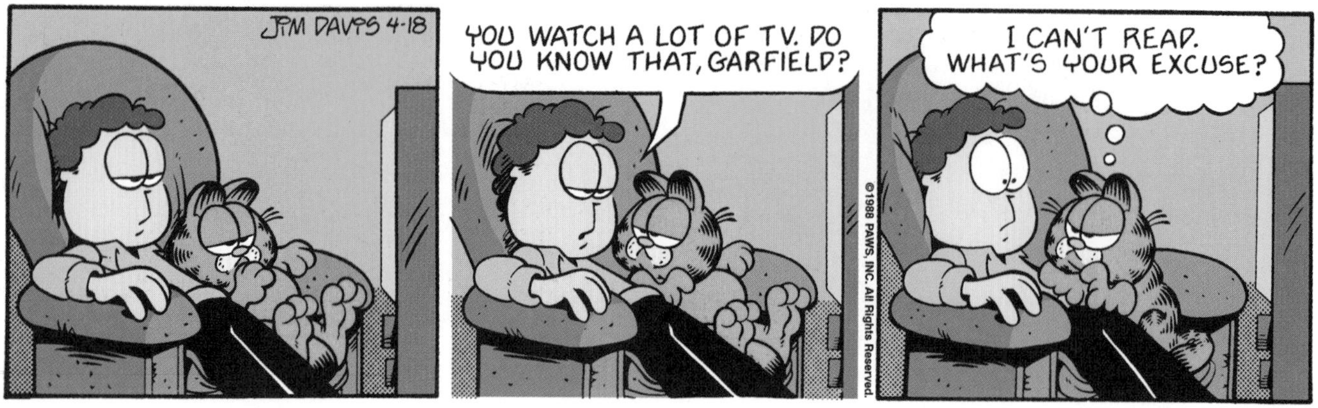
JIM DAVIS 4-18
YOU WATCH A LOT OF T.V. DO YOU KNOW THAT, GARFIELD?
I CAN'T READ. WHAT'S YOUR EXCUSE?
© 1988 PAWS, INC. All Rights Reserved.

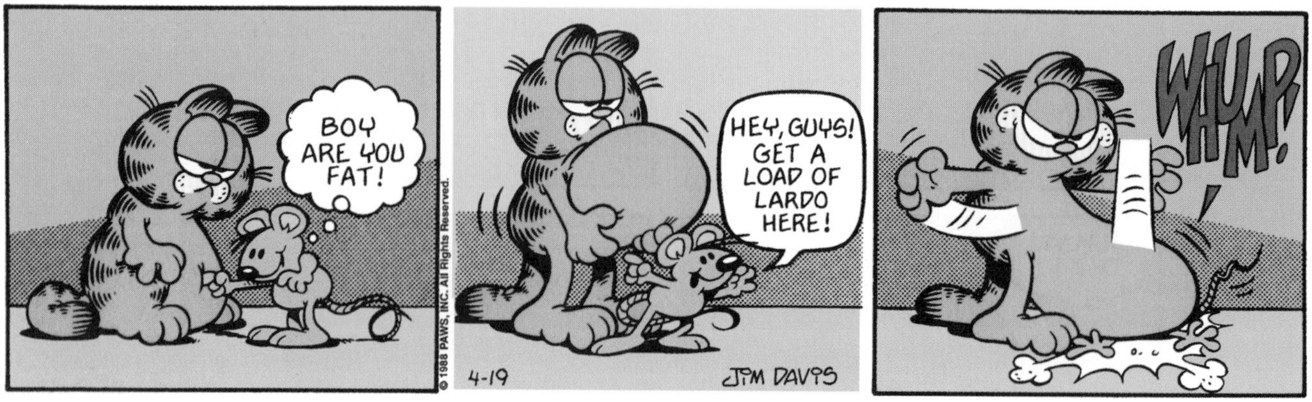
BOY ARE YOU FAT!
© 1988 PAWS, INC. All Rights Reserved.
HEY, GUYS! GET A LOAD OF LARDO HERE!
4-19
JIM DAVIS
WHUMP!

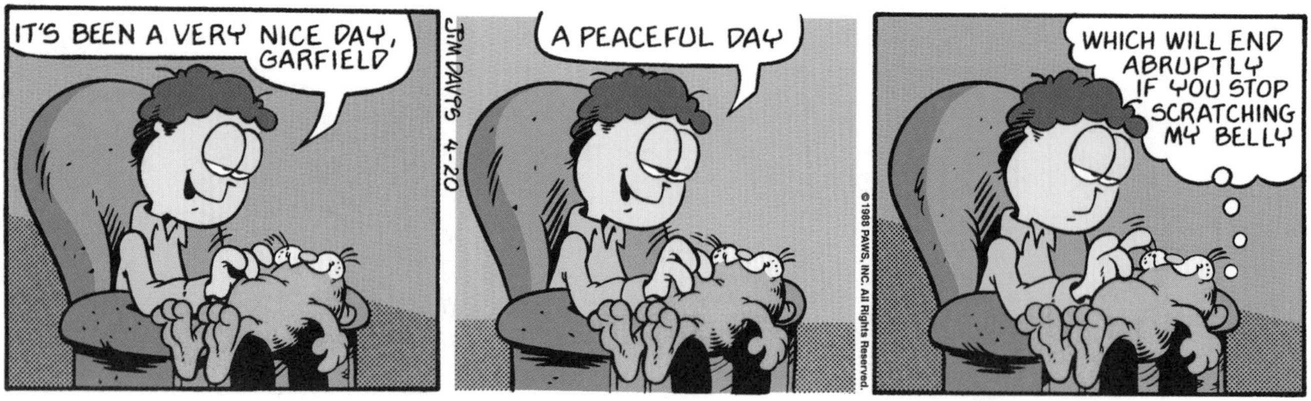
IT'S BEEN A VERY NICE DAY, GARFIELD
JIM DAVIS 4-20
A PEACEFUL DAY
© 1988 PAWS, INC. All Rights Reserved.
WHICH WILL END ABRUPTLY IF YOU STOP SCRATCHING MY BELLY

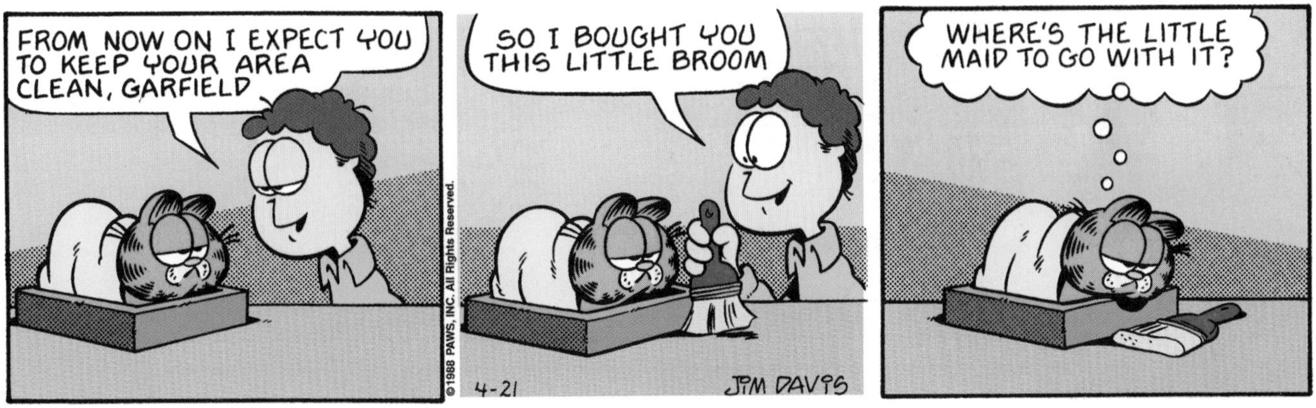
FROM NOW ON I EXPECT YOU TO KEEP YOUR AREA CLEAN, GARFIELD
SO I BOUGHT YOU THIS LITTLE BROOM
WHERE'S THE LITTLE MAID TO GO WITH IT?
©1988 PAWS, INC. All Rights Reserved.
4-21
JIM DAVIS

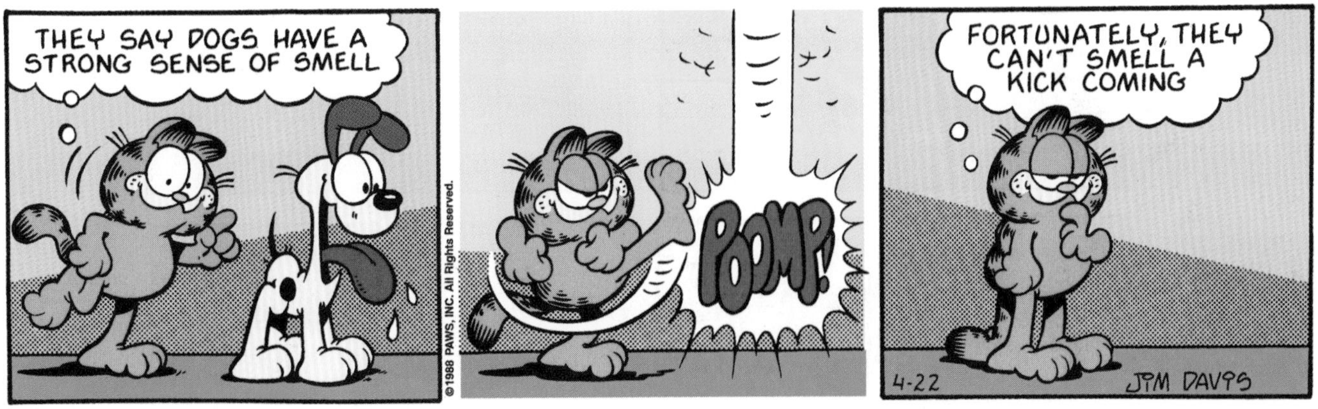
THEY SAY DOGS HAVE A STRONG SENSE OF SMELL
POOMP!
FORTUNATELY, THEY CAN'T SMELL A KICK COMING
©1988 PAWS, INC. All Rights Reserved.
4-22
JIM DAVIS

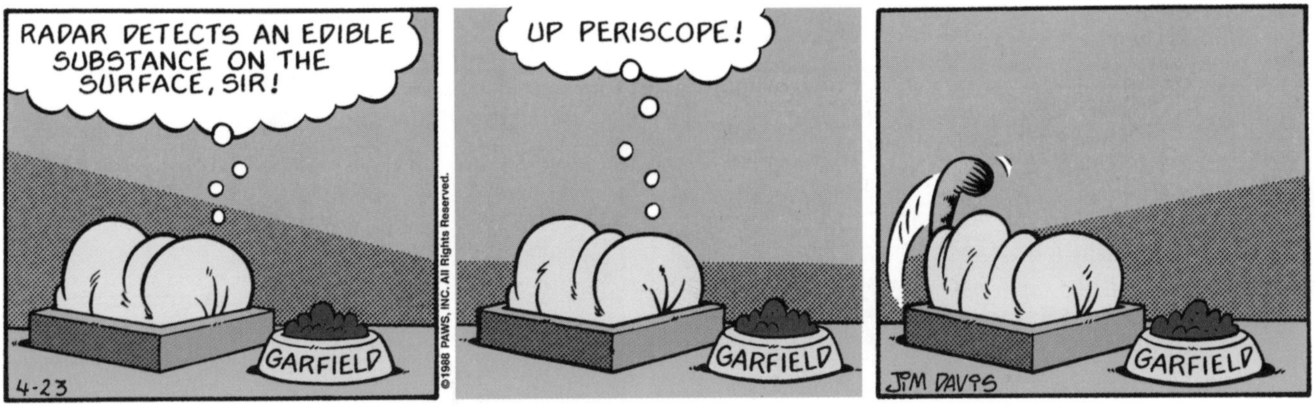
RADAR DETECTS AN EDIBLE SUBSTANCE ON THE SURFACE, SIR!
UP PERISCOPE!
GARFIELD
©1988 PAWS, INC. All Rights Reserved.
4-23
JIM DAVIS

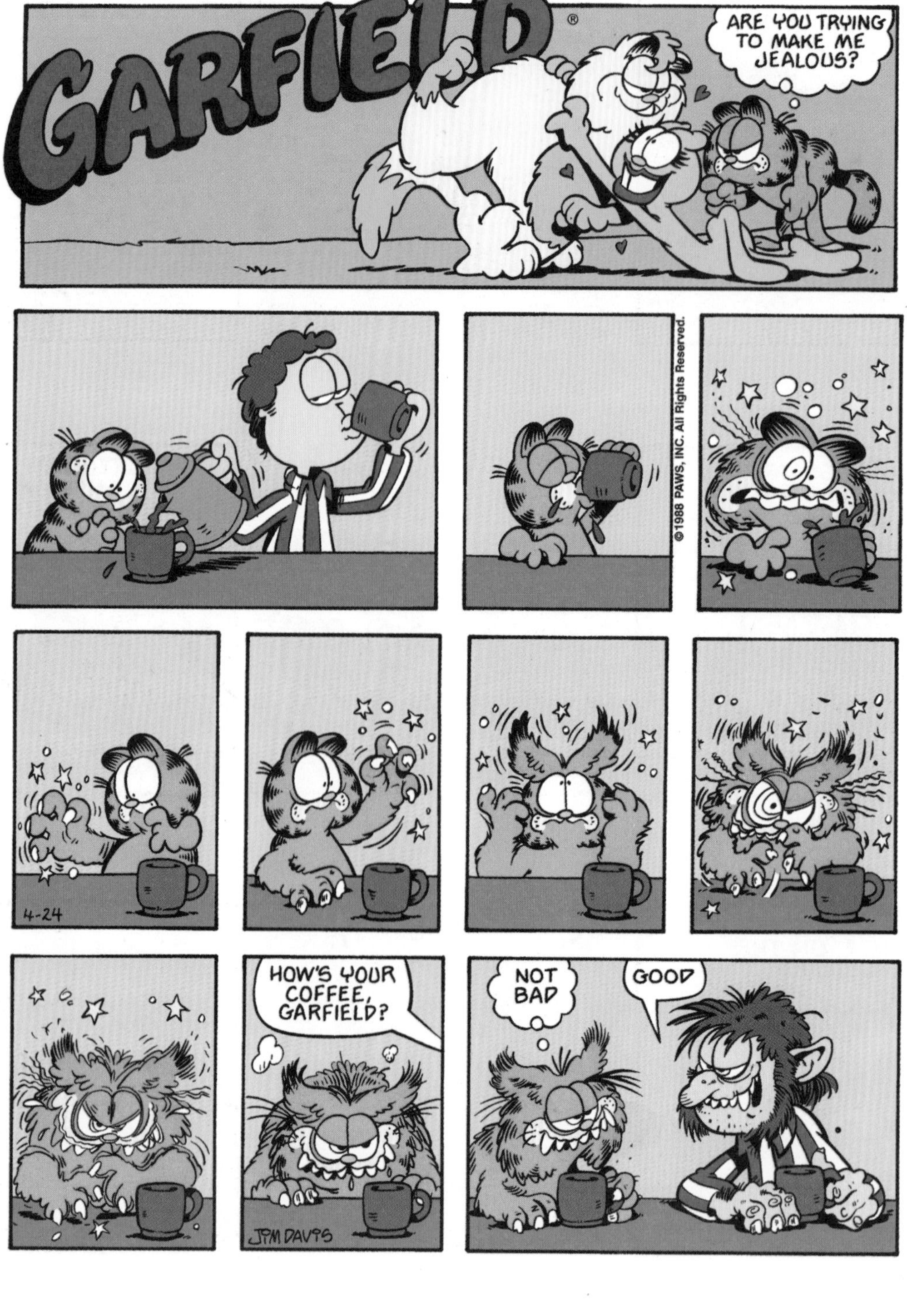
GARFIELD®
ARE YOU TRYING TO MAKE ME JEALOUS?
©1988 PAWS, INC. All Rights Reserved.
4-24
HOW'S YOUR COFFEE, GARFIELD?
NOT BAD
GOOD
JPM DAVIS

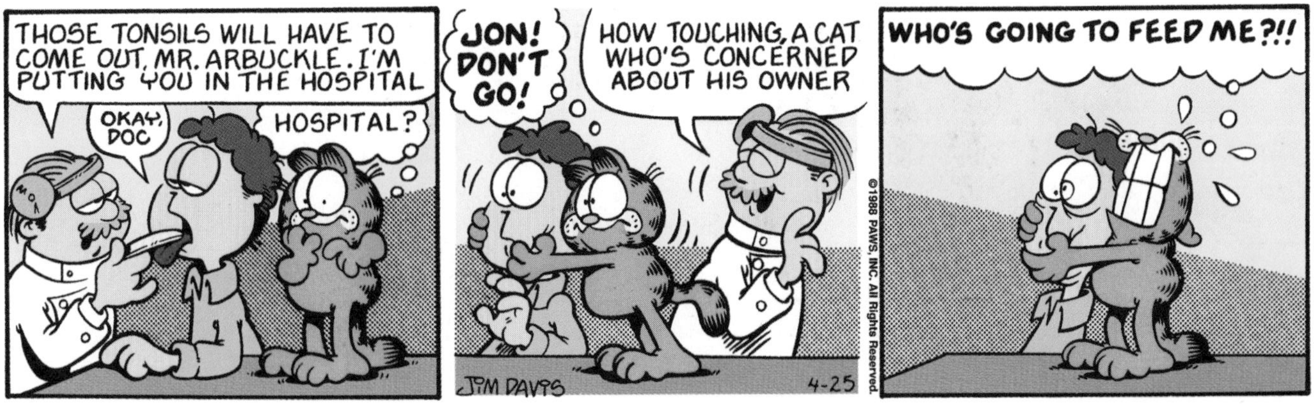
THOSE TONSILS WILL HAVE TO COME OUT, MR. ARBUCKLE. I'M PUTTING YOU IN THE HOSPITAL
OKAY, DOC
HOSPITAL?
JON! DON'T GO!
HOW TOUCHING, A CAT WHO'S CONCERNED ABOUT HIS OWNER
JIM DAVIS 4-25
©1988 PAWS, INC. All Rights Reserved.
WHO'S GOING TO FEED ME?!!

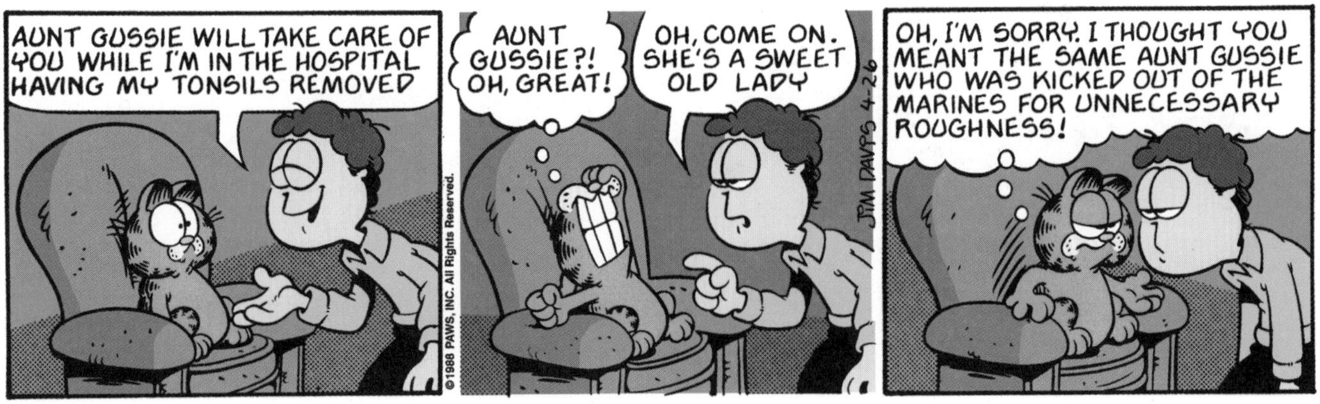
AUNT GUSSIE WILL TAKE CARE OF YOU WHILE I'M IN THE HOSPITAL HAVING MY TONSILS REMOVED
©1988 PAWS, INC. All Rights Reserved.
AUNT GUSSIE?! OH, GREAT!
OH, COME ON. SHE'S A SWEET OLD LADY
JIM DAVIS 4-26
OH, I'M SORRY. I THOUGHT YOU MEANT THE SAME AUNT GUSSIE WHO WAS KICKED OUT OF THE MARINES FOR UNNECESSARY ROUGHNESS!

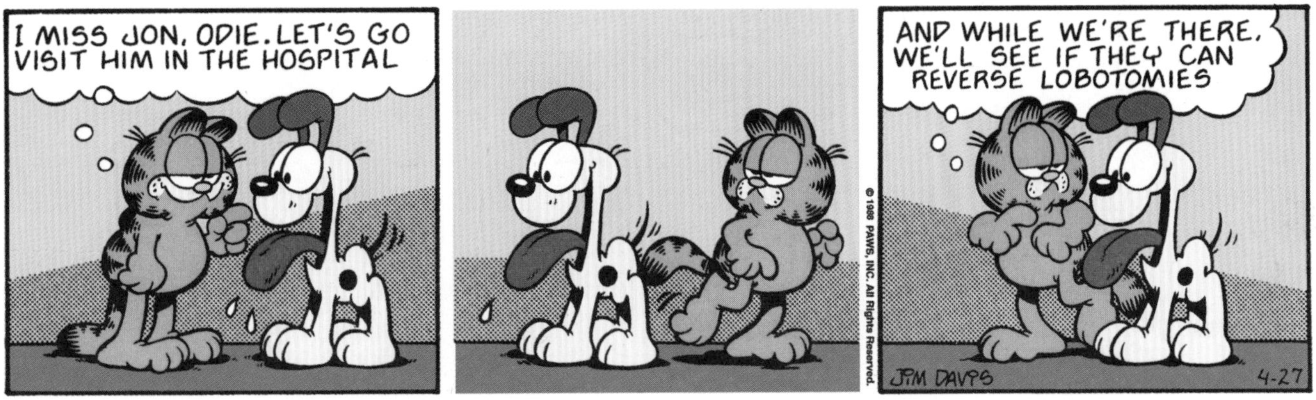
I MISS JON, ODIE. LET'S GO VISIT HIM IN THE HOSPITAL
©1988 PAWS, INC. All Rights Reserved.
AND WHILE WE'RE THERE, WE'LL SEE IF THEY CAN REVERSE LOBOTOMIES
JIM DAVIS 4-27

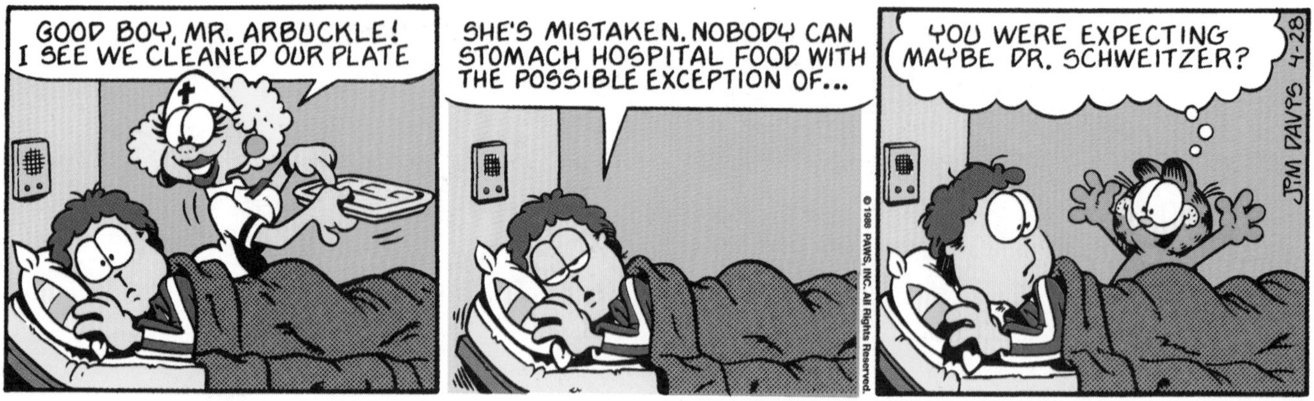
GOOD BOY, MR. ARBUCKLE! I SEE WE CLEANED OUR PLATE
SHE'S MISTAKEN. NOBODY CAN STOMACH HOSPITAL FOOD WITH THE POSSIBLE EXCEPTION OF...
YOU WERE EXPECTING MAYBE DR. SCHWEITZER?
JIM DAVIS 4-28
© 1988 PAWS, INC. All Rights Reserved.

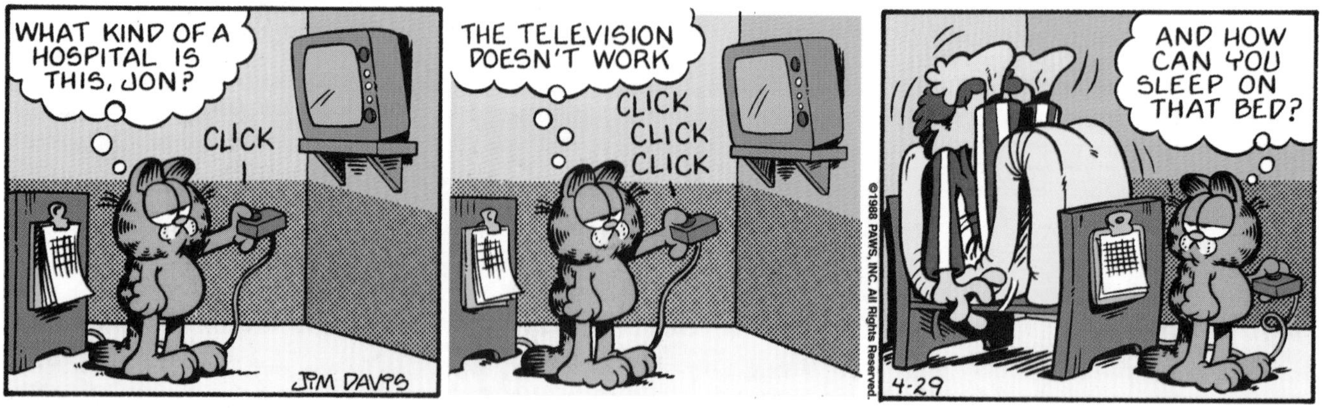
WHAT KIND OF A HOSPITAL IS THIS, JON?
CLICK
JIM DAVIS
THE TELEVISION DOESN'T WORK
CLICK CLICK CLICK
AND HOW CAN YOU SLEEP ON THAT BED?
4-29
© 1988 PAWS, INC. All Rights Reserved.

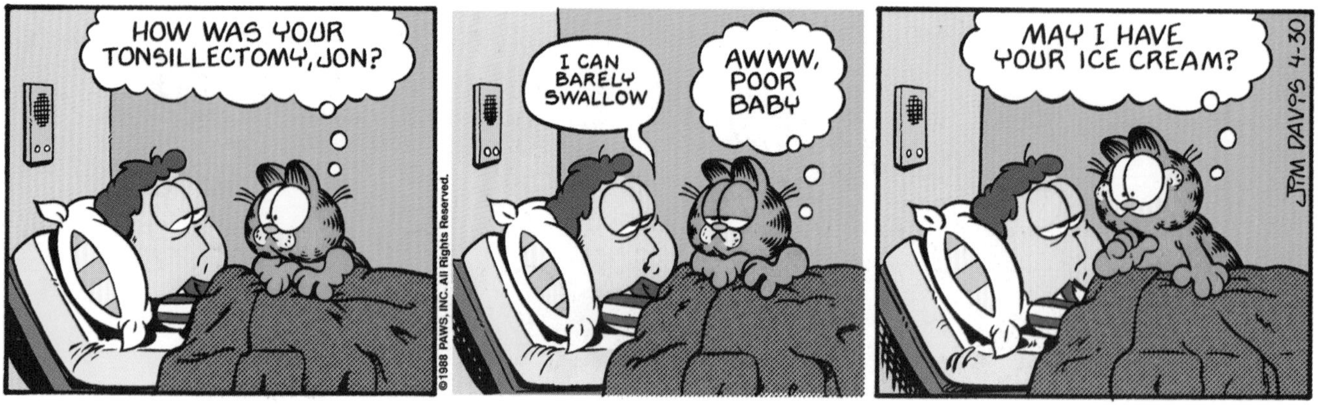
HOW WAS YOUR TONSILLECTOMY, JON?
I CAN BARELY SWALLOW
AWWW, POOR BABY
MAY I HAVE YOUR ICE CREAM?
JIM DAVIS 4-30
© 1988 PAWS, INC. All Rights Reserved.

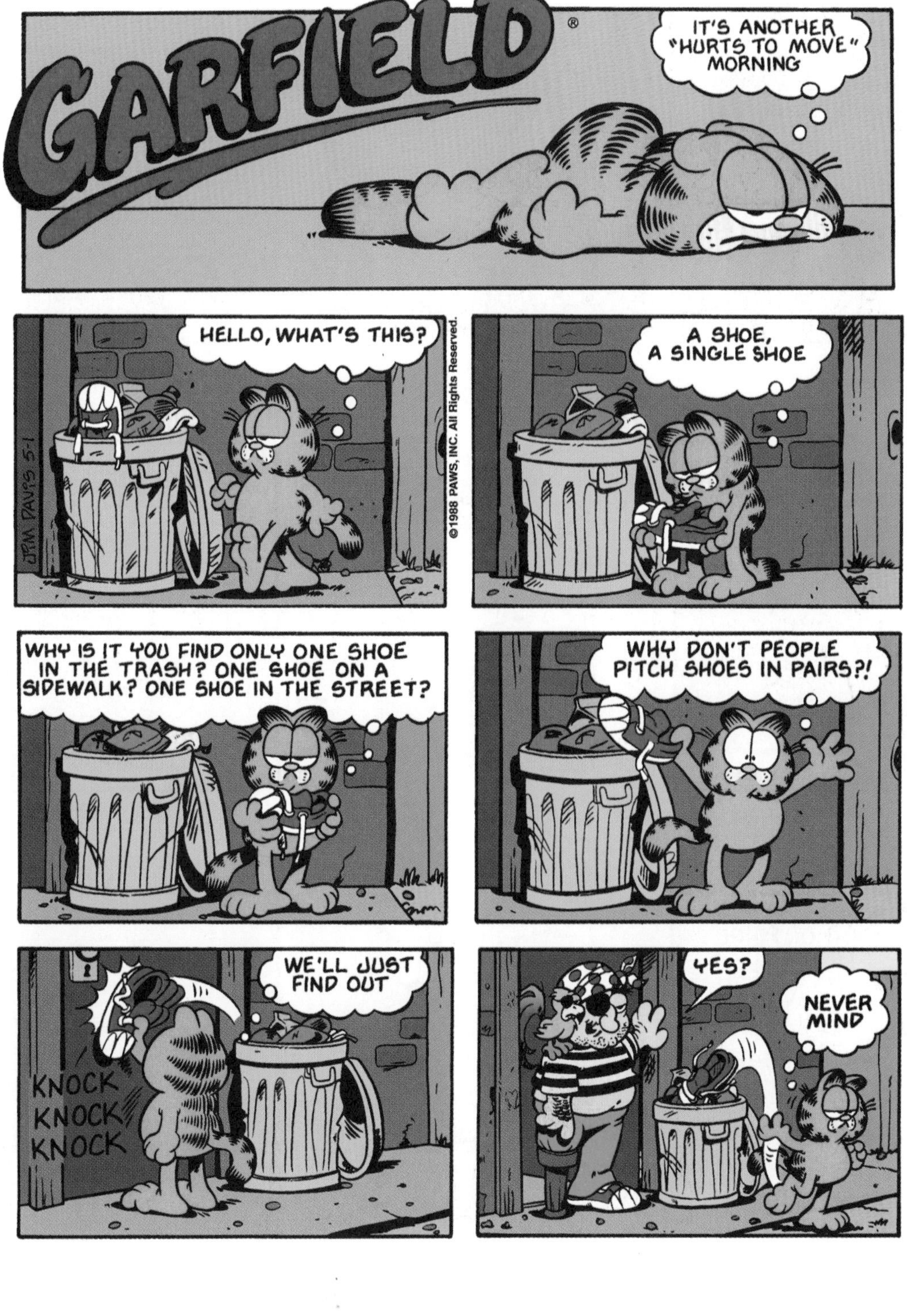
GARFIELD®
IT'S ANOTHER "HURTS TO MOVE" MORNING
JPM DAVIS 5-1
©1988 PAWS, INC. All Rights Reserved.
HELLO, WHAT'S THIS?
A SHOE, A SINGLE SHOE
WHY IS IT YOU FIND ONLY ONE SHOE IN THE TRASH? ONE SHOE ON A SIDEWALK? ONE SHOE IN THE STREET?
WHY DON'T PEOPLE PITCH SHOES IN PAIRS?!
KNOCK KNOCK KNOCK
WE'LL JUST FIND OUT
YES?
NEVER MIND

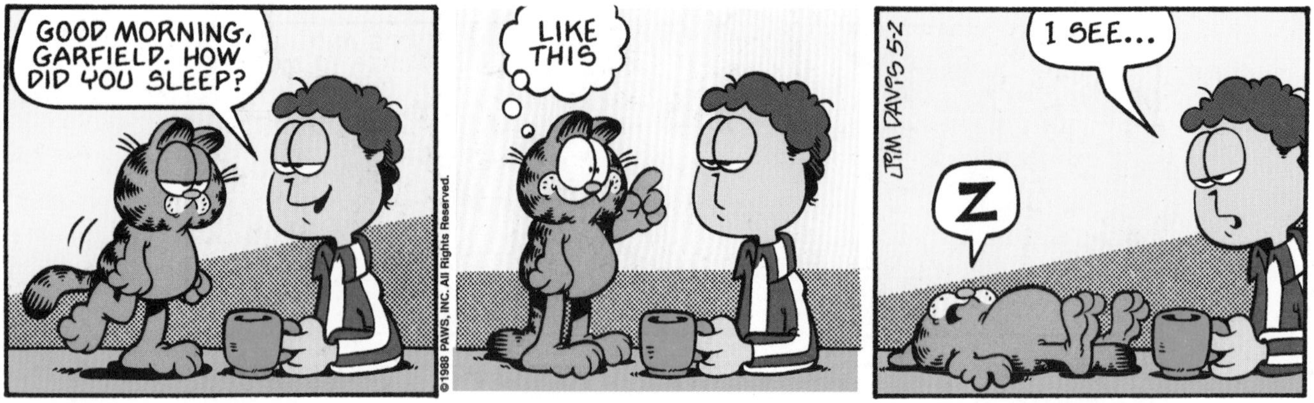
GOOD MORNING, GARFIELD. HOW DID YOU SLEEP?
©1988 PAWS, INC. All Rights Reserved.
LIKE THIS
JIM DAVIS 5-2
I SEE...
Z

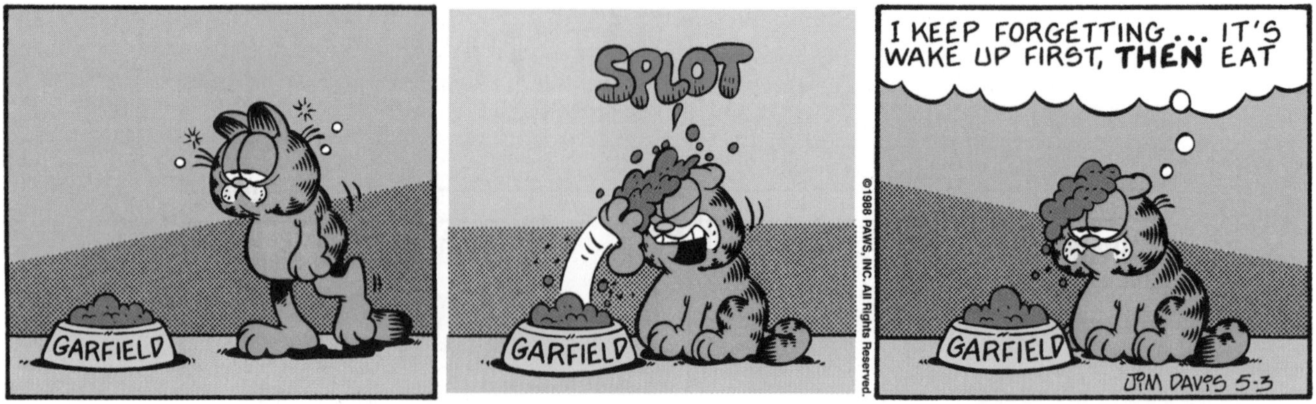
GARFIELD
SPLOT
GARFIELD
©1988 PAWS, INC. All Rights Reserved.
I KEEP FORGETTING... IT'S WAKE UP FIRST, **THEN** EAT
GARFIELD
JIM DAVIS 5-3

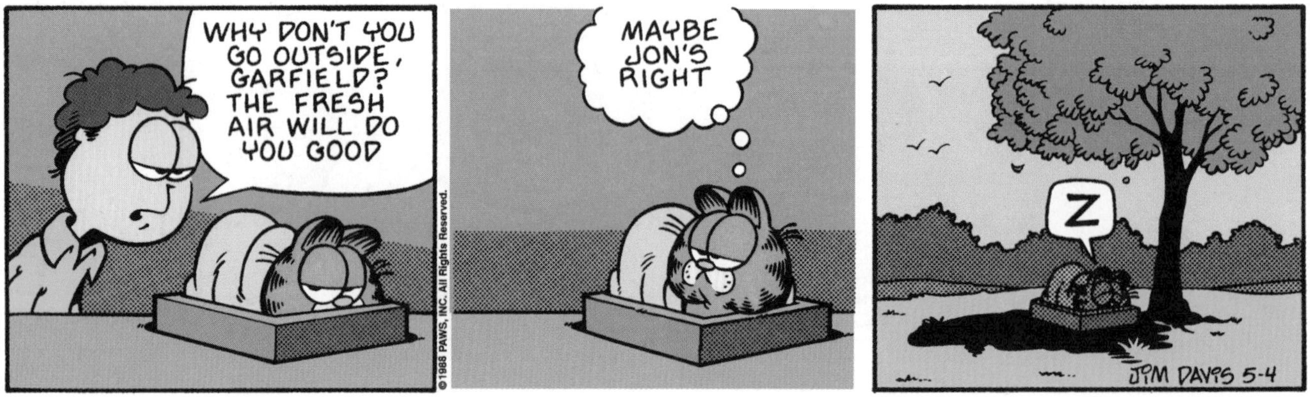
WHY DON'T YOU GO OUTSIDE, GARFIELD? THE FRESH AIR WILL DO YOU GOOD
©1988 PAWS, INC. All Rights Reserved.
MAYBE JON'S RIGHT
Z
JIM DAVIS 5-4

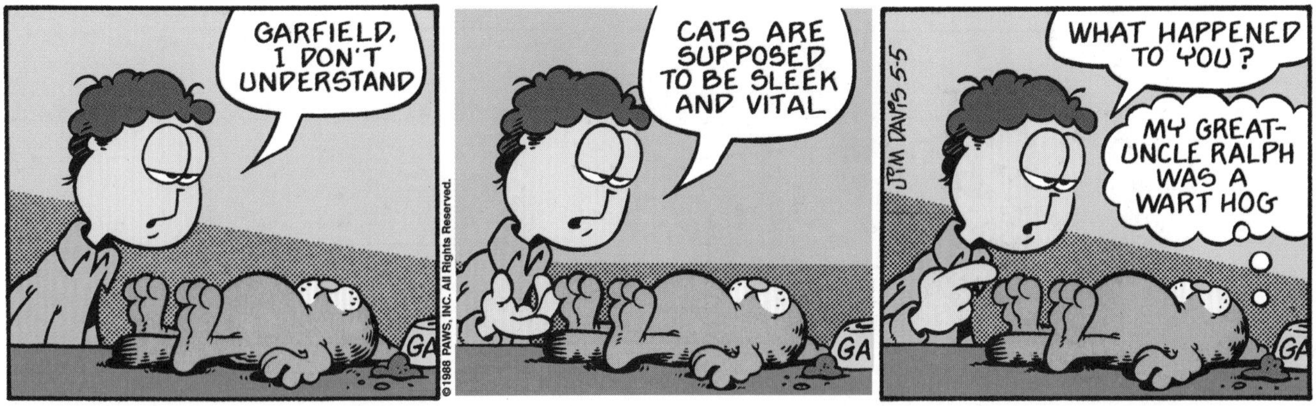
GARFIELD, I DON'T UNDERSTAND
© 1988 PAWS, INC. All Rights Reserved.
CATS ARE SUPPOSED TO BE SLEEK AND VITAL
JIM DAVIS 5-5
WHAT HAPPENED TO YOU?
MY GREAT-UNCLE RALPH WAS A WART HOG

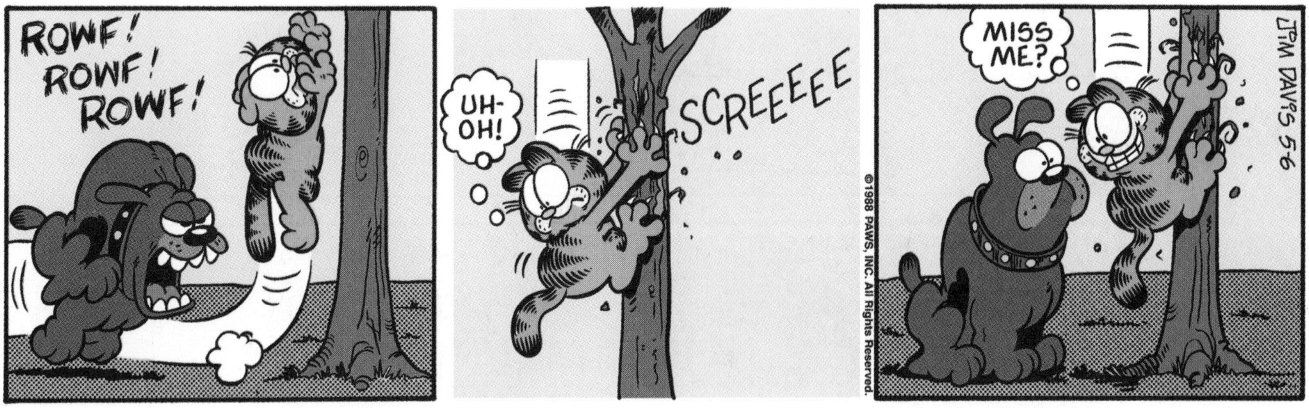
ROWF! ROWF! ROWF!
UH-OH!
SCREEEEEE
© 1988 PAWS, INC. All Rights Reserved.
MISS ME?
JIM DAVIS 5-6

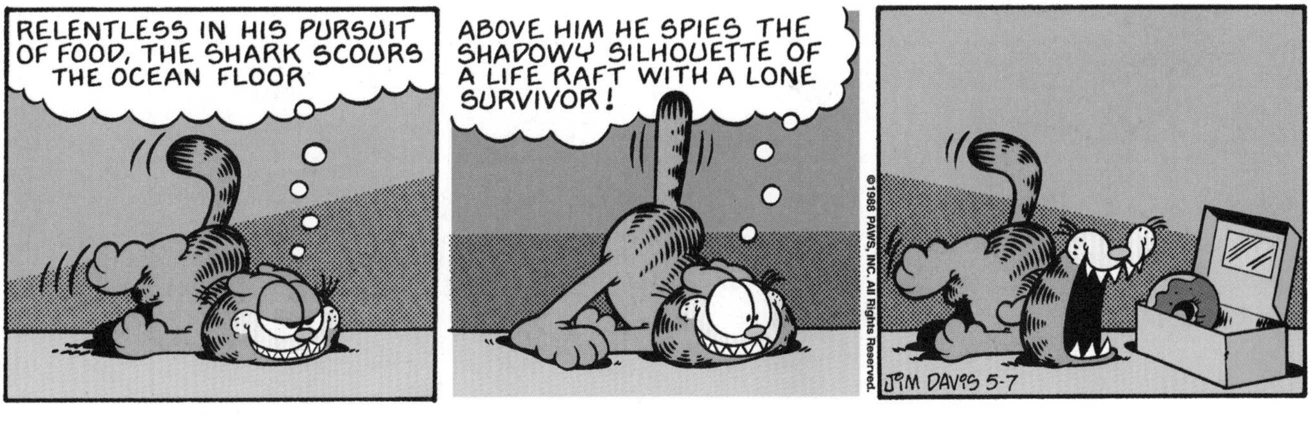
RELENTLESS IN HIS PURSUIT OF FOOD, THE SHARK SCOURS THE OCEAN FLOOR
ABOVE HIM HE SPIES THE SHADOWY SILHOUETTE OF A LIFE RAFT WITH A LONE SURVIVOR!
© 1988 PAWS, INC. All Rights Reserved.
JIM DAVIS 5-7

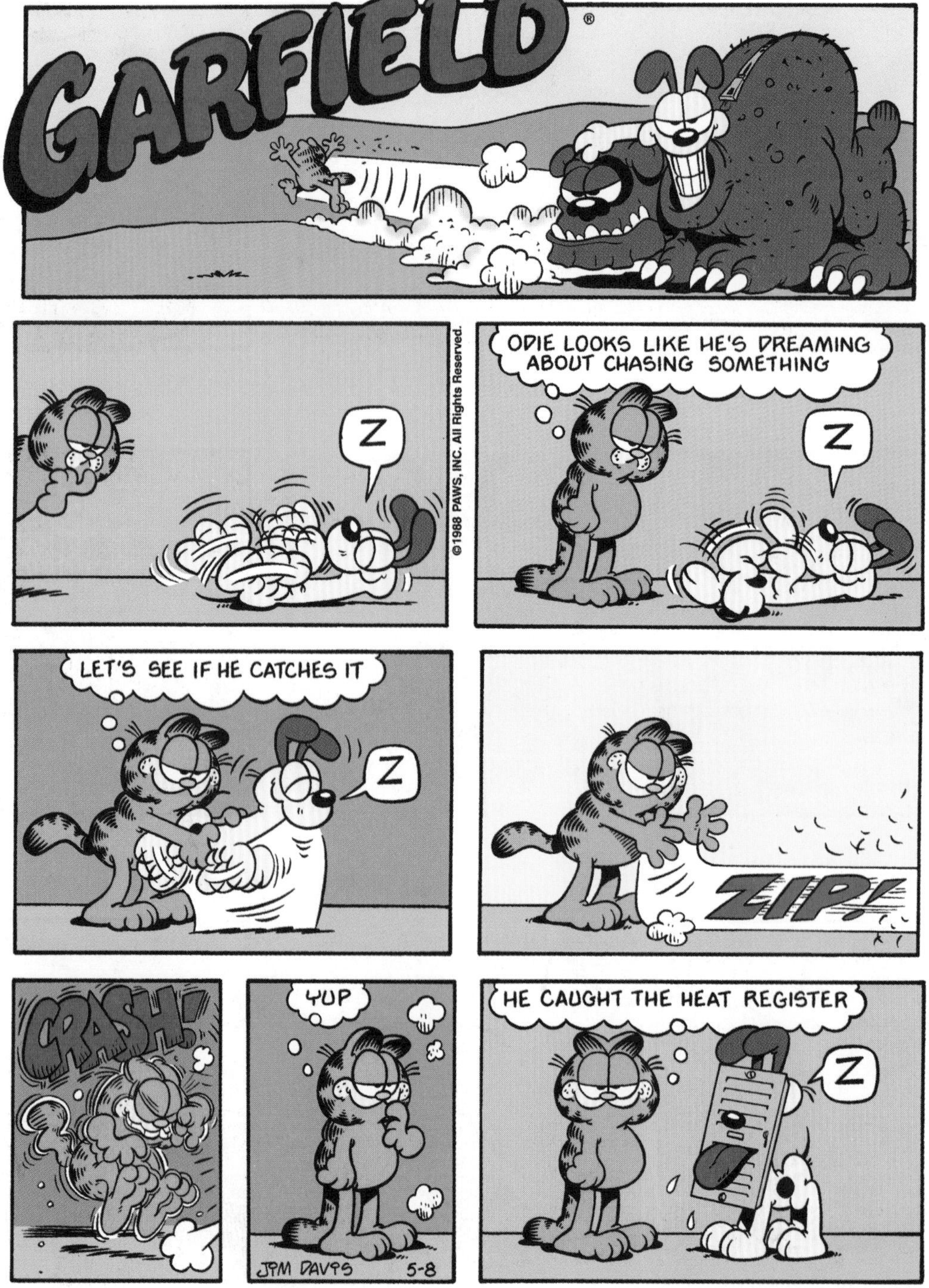
GARFIELD®
©1988 PAWS, INC. All Rights Reserved.
Z
ODIE LOOKS LIKE HE'S DREAMING ABOUT CHASING SOMETHING
Z
LET'S SEE IF HE CATCHES IT
Z
ZIP!
CRASH!
YUP
JIM DAVIS 5-8
HE CAUGHT THE HEAT REGISTER
Z

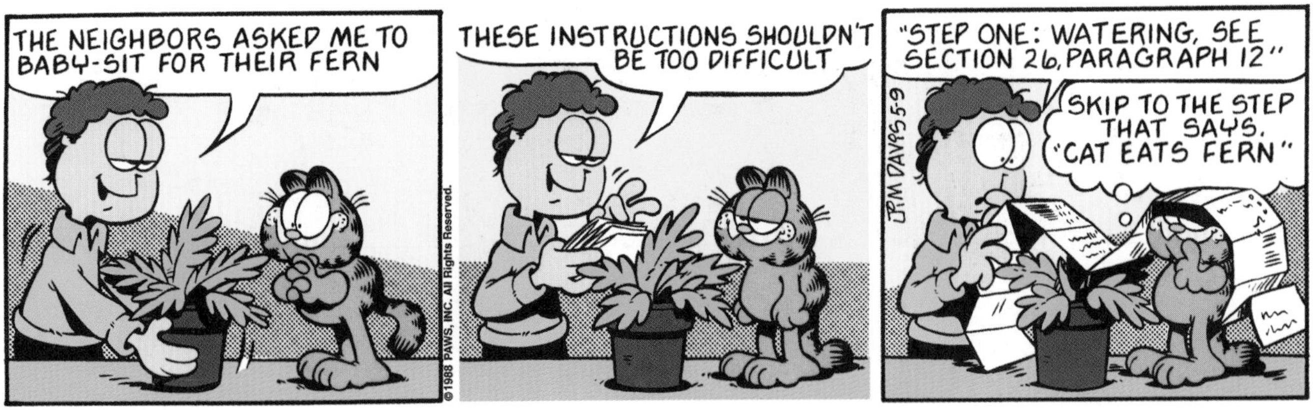
THE NEIGHBORS ASKED ME TO BABY-SIT FOR THEIR FERN
© 1988 PAWS, INC. All Rights Reserved.
THESE INSTRUCTIONS SHOULDN'T BE TOO DIFFICULT
"STEP ONE: WATERING, SEE SECTION 26, PARAGRAPH 12"
SKIP TO THE STEP THAT SAYS, "CAT EATS FERN"
JIM DAVIS 5-9

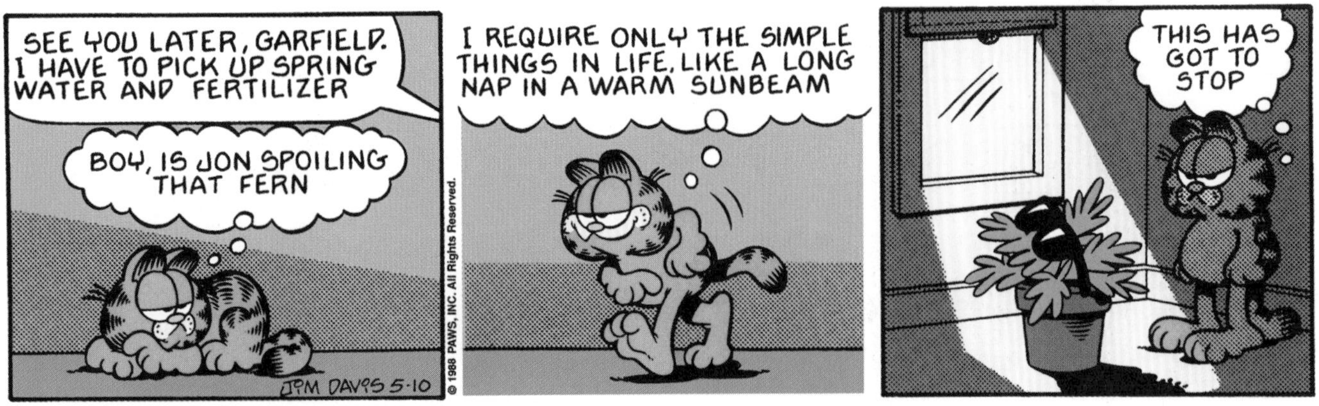
SEE YOU LATER, GARFIELD. I HAVE TO PICK UP SPRING WATER AND FERTILIZER
BOY, IS JON SPOILING THAT FERN
JIM DAVIS 5-10
© 1988 PAWS, INC. All Rights Reserved.
I REQUIRE ONLY THE SIMPLE THINGS IN LIFE, LIKE A LONG NAP IN A WARM SUNBEAM
THIS HAS GOT TO STOP

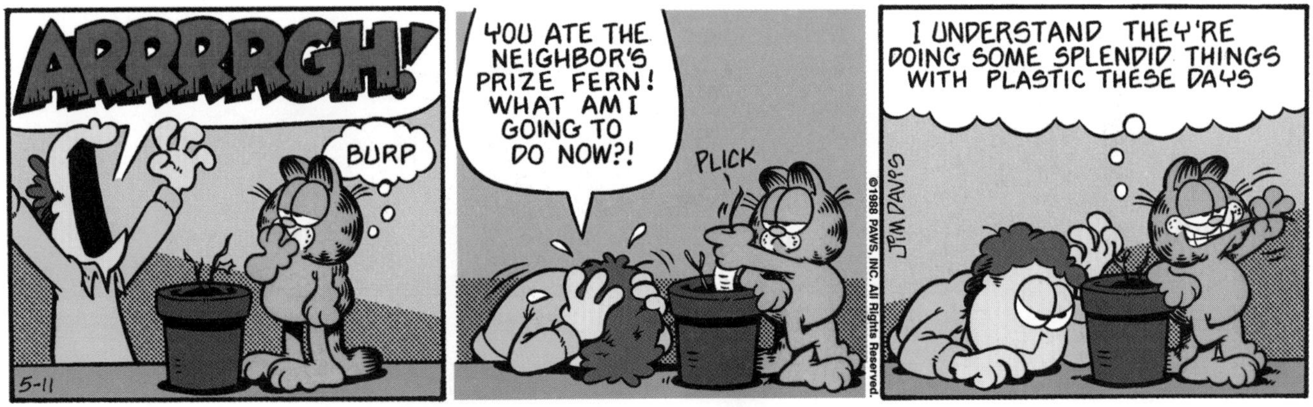
ARRRRGH!
BURP
5-11
YOU ATE THE NEIGHBOR'S PRIZE FERN! WHAT AM I GOING TO DO NOW?!
PLICK
© 1988 PAWS, INC. All Rights Reserved.
JIM DAVIS
I UNDERSTAND THEY'RE DOING SOME SPLENDID THINGS WITH PLASTIC THESE DAYS

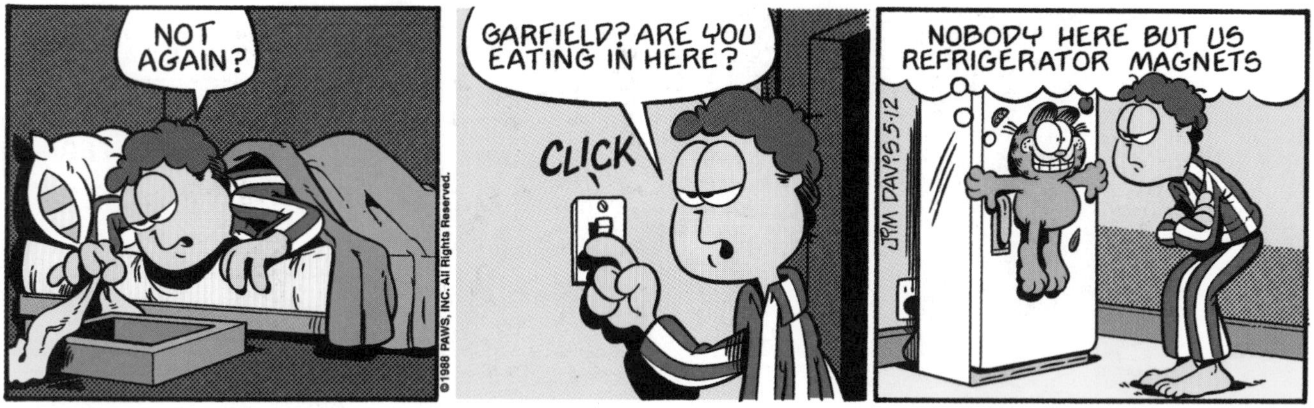
NOT AGAIN?
©1988 PAWS, INC. All Rights Reserved.
GARFIELD? ARE YOU EATING IN HERE?
CLICK
NOBODY HERE BUT US REFRIGERATOR MAGNETS
JIM DAVIS 5-12

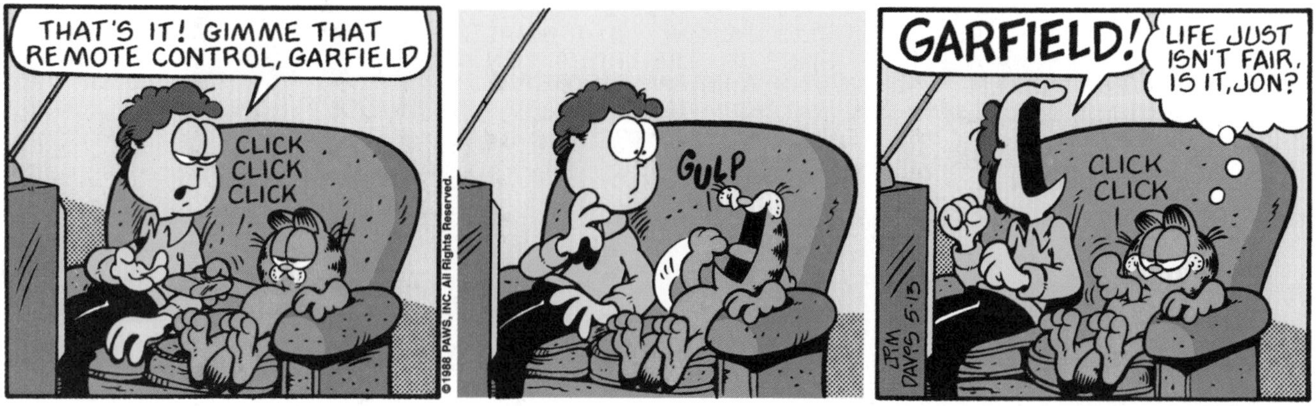
THAT'S IT! GIMME THAT REMOTE CONTROL, GARFIELD
CLICK CLICK CLICK
©1988 PAWS, INC. All Rights Reserved.
GULP
GARFIELD!
LIFE JUST ISN'T FAIR, IS IT, JON?
CLICK CLICK
JIM DAVIS 5-13

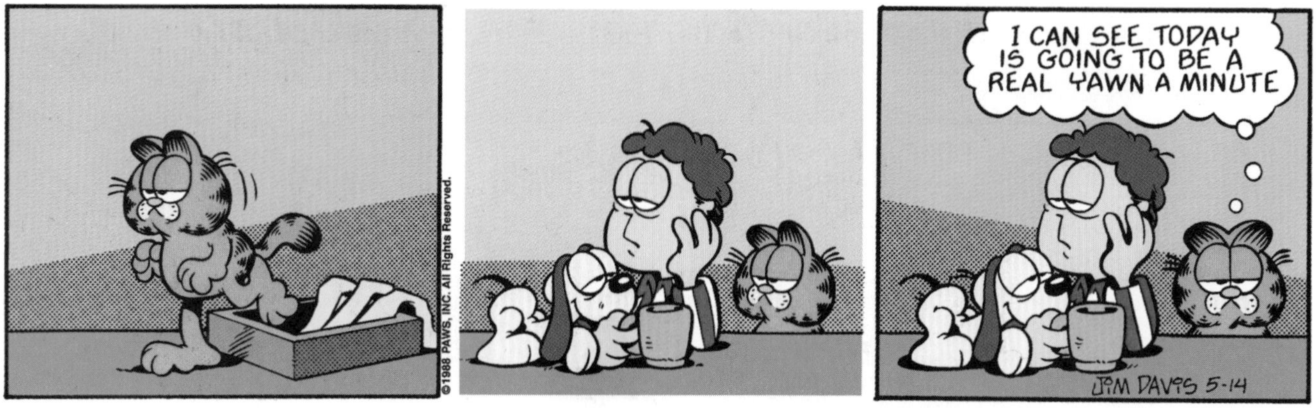
©1988 PAWS, INC. All Rights Reserved.
I CAN SEE TODAY IS GOING TO BE A REAL YAWN A MINUTE
JIM DAVIS 5-14

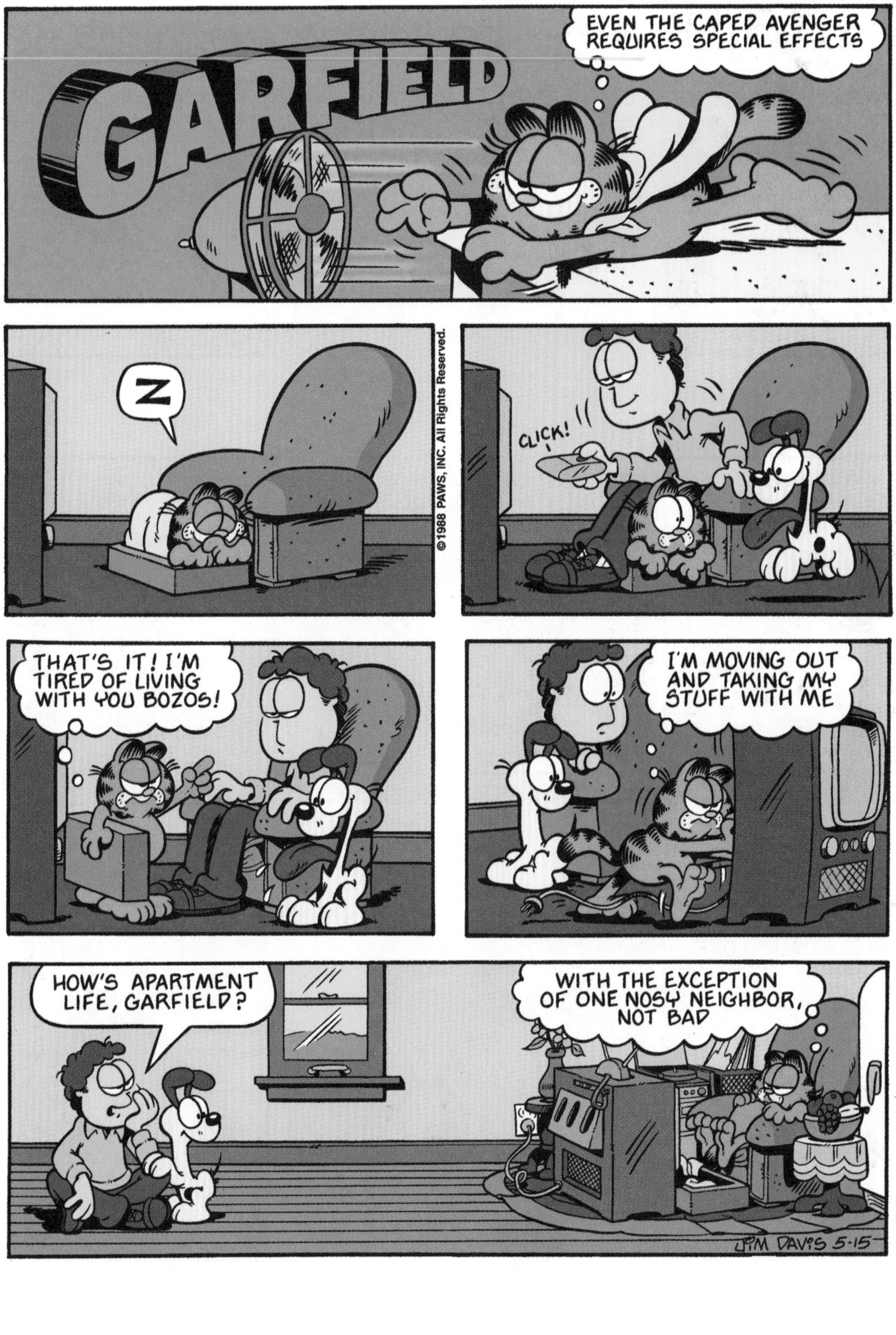
GARFIELD
EVEN THE CAPED AVENGER REQUIRES SPECIAL EFFECTS
Z
©1988 PAWS, INC. All Rights Reserved.
CLICK!
THAT'S IT! I'M TIRED OF LIVING WITH YOU BOZOS!
I'M MOVING OUT AND TAKING MY STUFF WITH ME
HOW'S APARTMENT LIFE, GARFIELD?
WITH THE EXCEPTION OF ONE NOSY NEIGHBOR, NOT BAD
JIM DAVIS 5-15

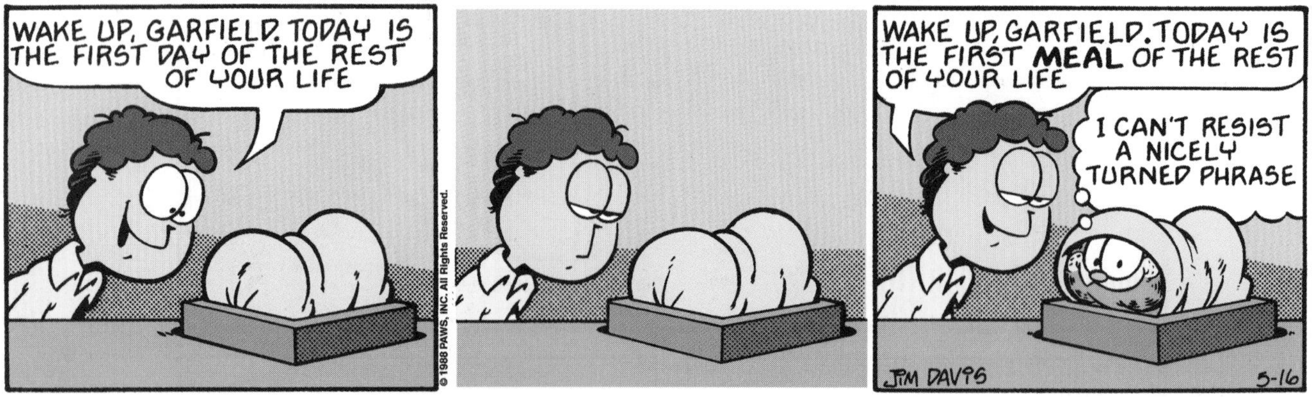
WAKE UP, GARFIELD. TODAY IS THE FIRST DAY OF THE REST OF YOUR LIFE
WAKE UP, GARFIELD. TODAY IS THE FIRST **MEAL** OF THE REST OF YOUR LIFE
I CAN'T RESIST A NICELY TURNED PHRASE
JIM DAVIS
5-16
© 1988 PAWS, INC. All Rights Reserved.

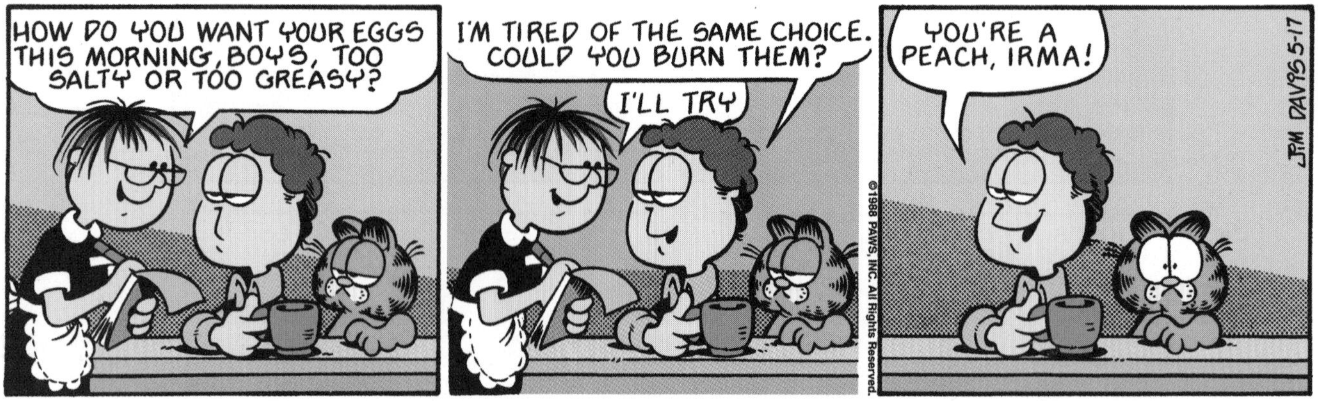
HOW DO YOU WANT YOUR EGGS THIS MORNING, BOYS, TOO SALTY OR TOO GREASY?
I'M TIRED OF THE SAME CHOICE. COULD YOU BURN THEM?
I'LL TRY
YOU'RE A PEACH, IRMA!
JIM DAVIS 5-17
© 1988 PAWS, INC. All Rights Reserved.

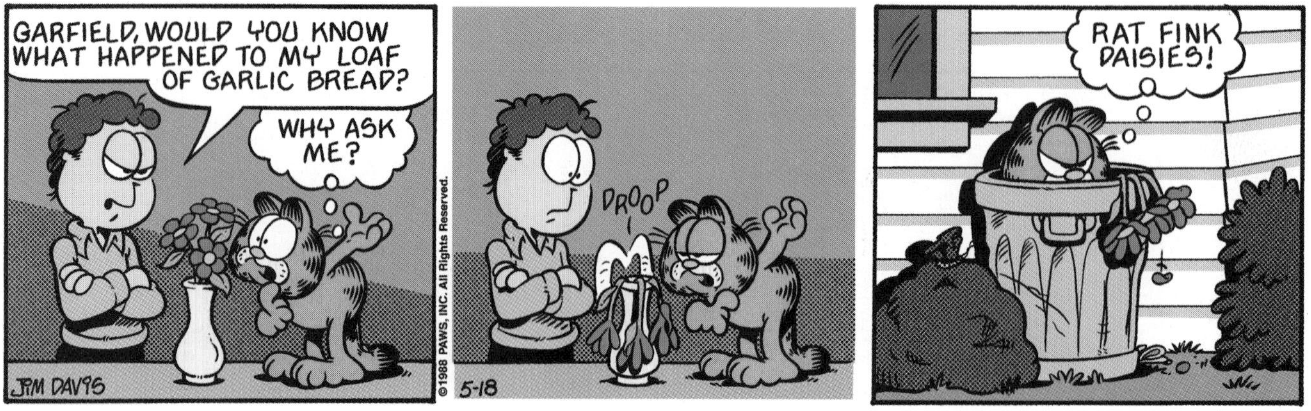
GARFIELD, WOULD YOU KNOW WHAT HAPPENED TO MY LOAF OF GARLIC BREAD?
WHY ASK ME?
JIM DAVIS
DROOP
5-18
RAT FINK DAISIES!
© 1988 PAWS, INC. All Rights Reserved.

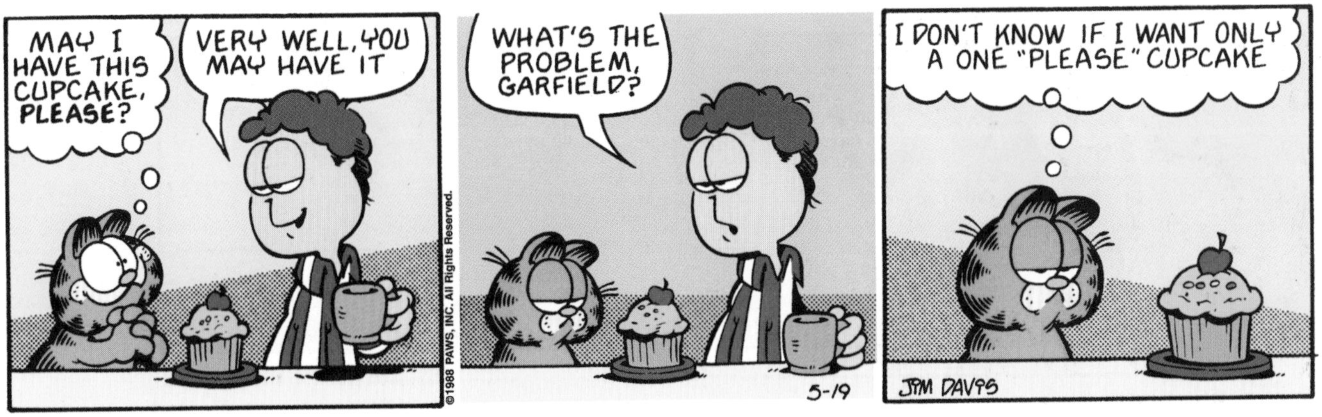
MAY I HAVE THIS CUPCAKE, PLEASE?
VERY WELL, YOU MAY HAVE IT
© 1988 PAWS, INC. All Rights Reserved.
WHAT'S THE PROBLEM, GARFIELD?
5-19
I DON'T KNOW IF I WANT ONLY A ONE "PLEASE" CUPCAKE
JIM DAVIS

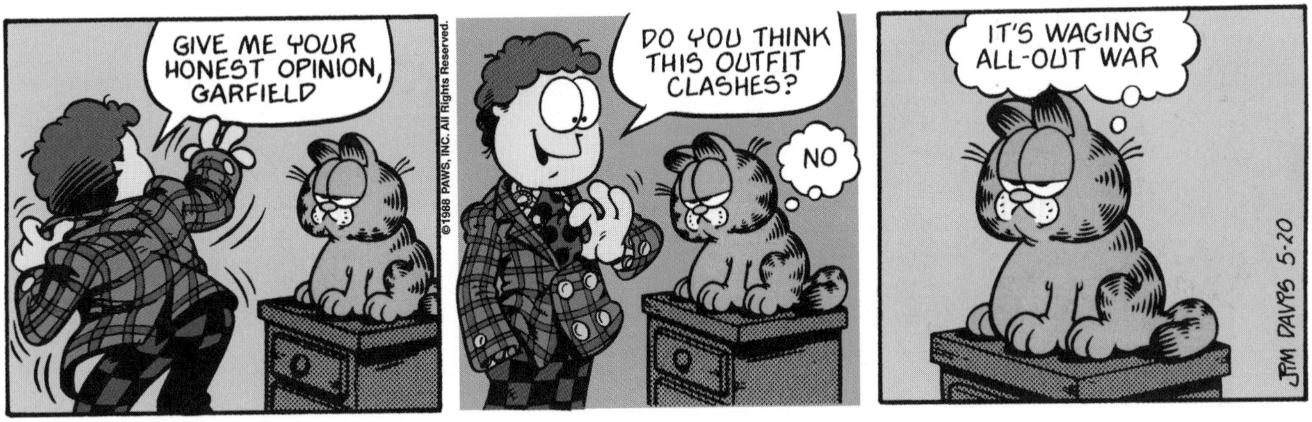
GIVE ME YOUR HONEST OPINION, GARFIELD
© 1988 PAWS, INC. All Rights Reserved.
DO YOU THINK THIS OUTFIT CLASHES?
NO
IT'S WAGING ALL-OUT WAR
JIM DAVIS 5-20

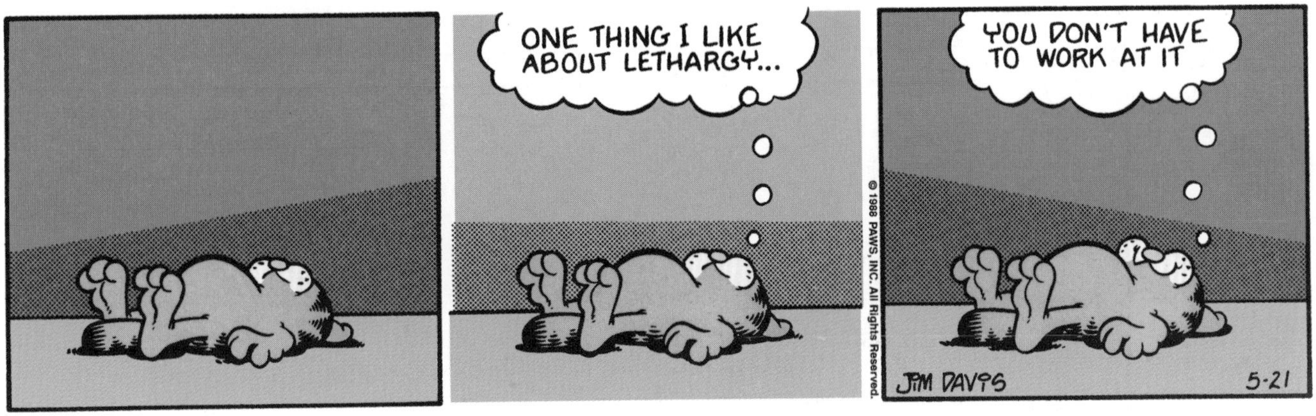
ONE THING I LIKE ABOUT LETHARGY...
© 1988 PAWS, INC. All Rights Reserved.
YOU DON'T HAVE TO WORK AT IT
JIM DAVIS
5-21

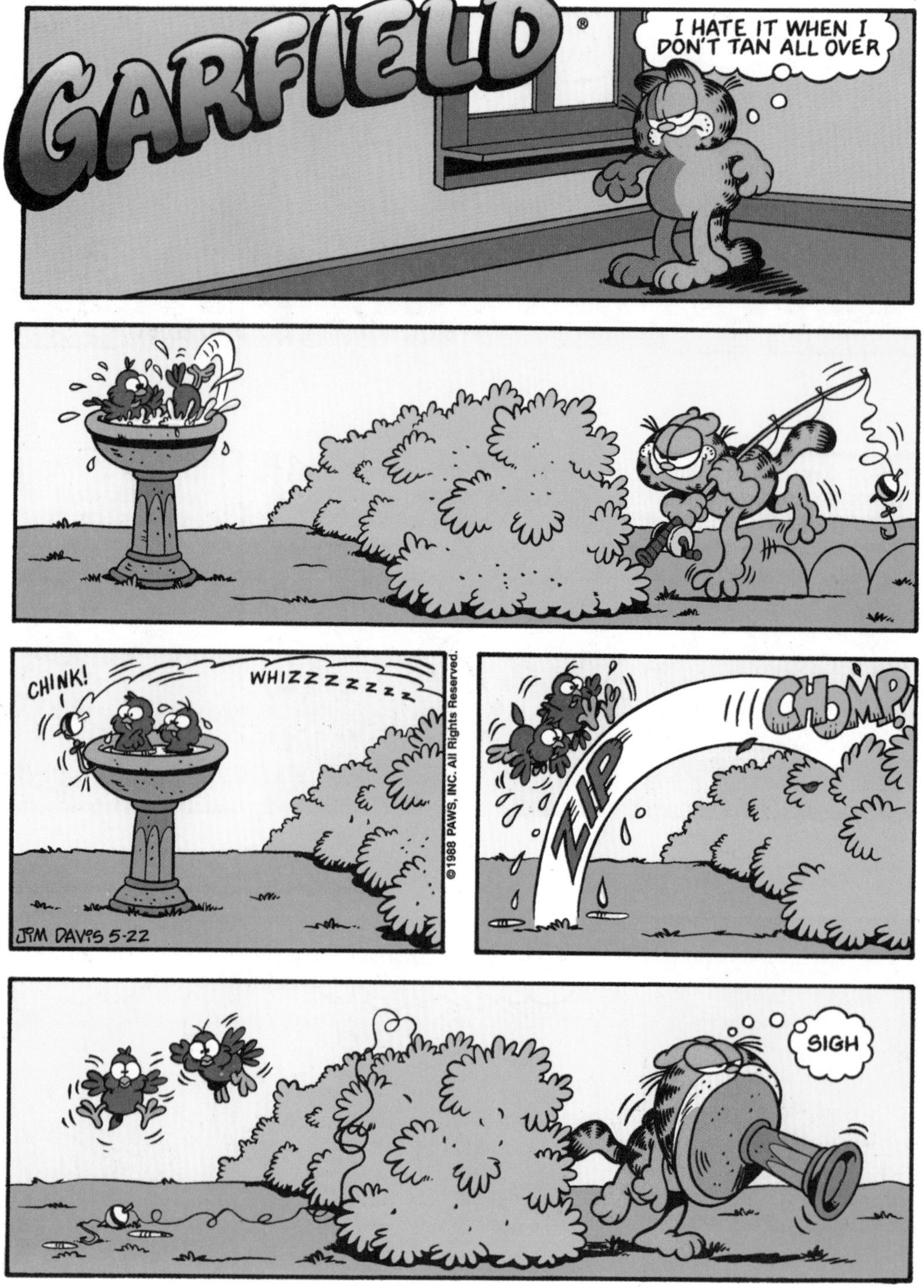
GARFIELD®
I HATE IT WHEN I DON'T TAN ALL OVER
CHINK!
WHIZZZZZZZ
JIM DAVIS 5-22
©1988 PAWS, INC. All Rights Reserved.
ZIP
CHOMP!
SIGH

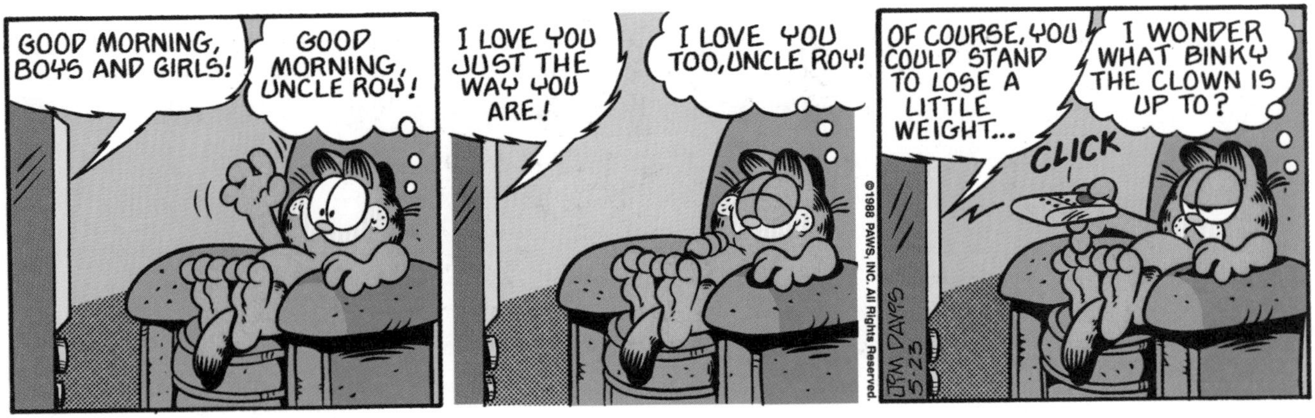
GOOD MORNING, BOYS AND GIRLS!
GOOD MORNING, UNCLE ROY!
I LOVE YOU JUST THE WAY YOU ARE!
I LOVE YOU TOO, UNCLE ROY!
OF COURSE, YOU COULD STAND TO LOSE A LITTLE WEIGHT...
CLICK
I WONDER WHAT BINKY THE CLOWN IS UP TO?
©1988 PAWS, INC. All Rights Reserved.
JIM DAVIS 5-23

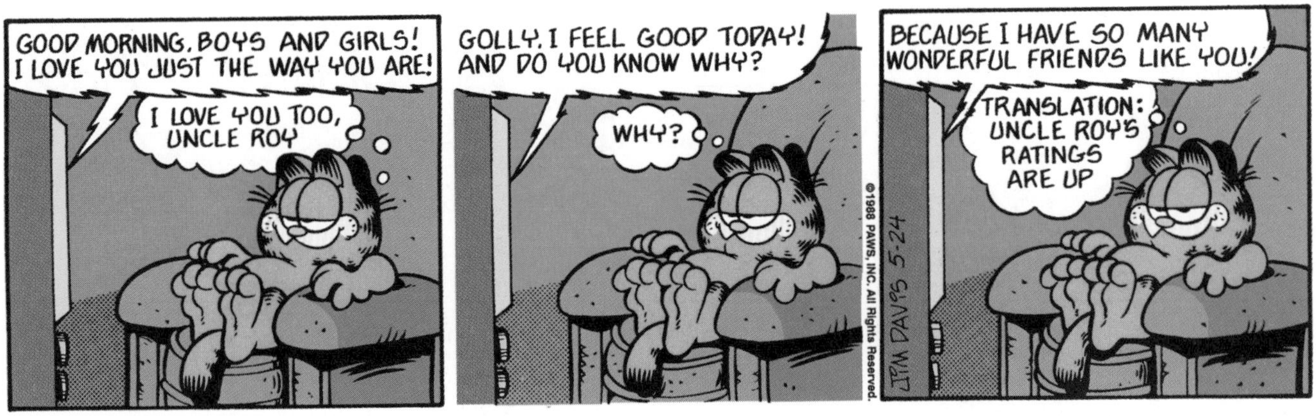
GOOD MORNING, BOYS AND GIRLS! I LOVE YOU JUST THE WAY YOU ARE!
I LOVE YOU TOO, UNCLE ROY
GOLLY, I FEEL GOOD TODAY! AND DO YOU KNOW WHY?
WHY?
BECAUSE I HAVE SO MANY WONDERFUL FRIENDS LIKE YOU!
TRANSLATION: UNCLE ROY'S RATINGS ARE UP
©1988 PAWS, INC. All Rights Reserved.
JIM DAVIS 5-24

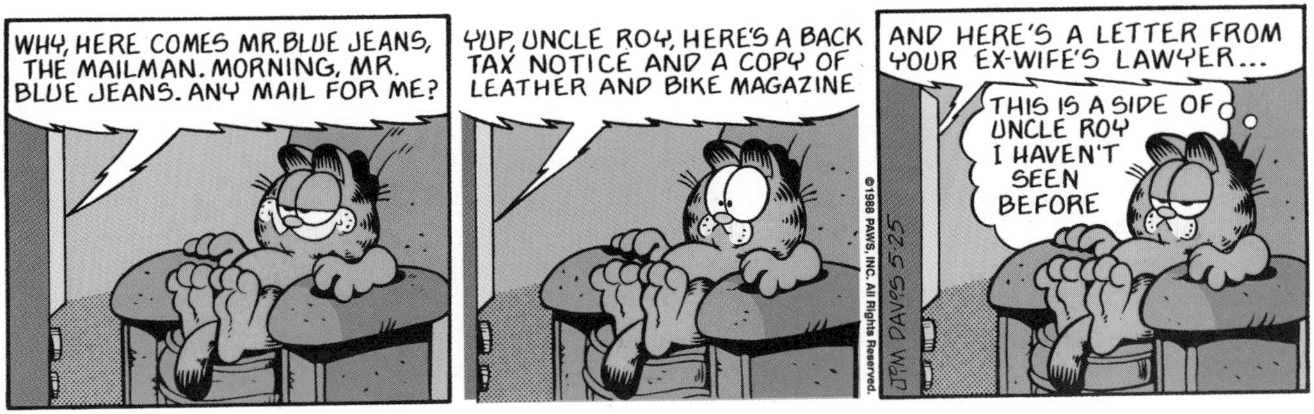
WHY, HERE COMES MR. BLUE JEANS, THE MAILMAN. MORNING, MR. BLUE JEANS. ANY MAIL FOR ME?
YUP, UNCLE ROY, HERE'S A BACK TAX NOTICE AND A COPY OF LEATHER AND BIKE MAGAZINE
AND HERE'S A LETTER FROM YOUR EX-WIFE'S LAWYER...
THIS IS A SIDE OF UNCLE ROY I HAVEN'T SEEN BEFORE
©1988 PAWS, INC. All Rights Reserved.
JIM DAVIS 5-25

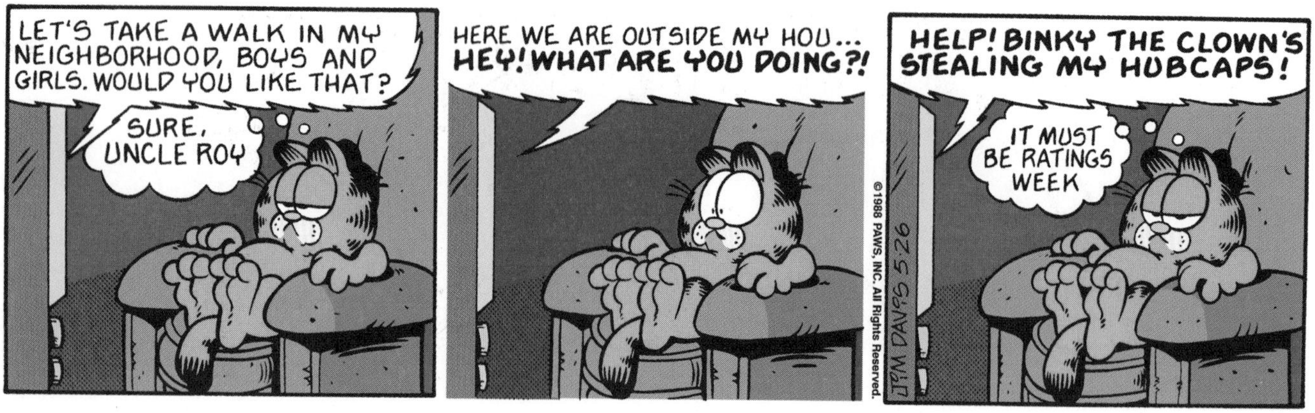
LET'S TAKE A WALK IN MY NEIGHBORHOOD, BOYS AND GIRLS. WOULD YOU LIKE THAT?
SURE, UNCLE ROY
HERE WE ARE OUTSIDE MY HOU... HEY! WHAT ARE YOU DOING?!
HELP! BINKY THE CLOWN'S STEALING MY HUBCAPS!
IT MUST BE RATINGS WEEK
©1988 PAWS, INC. All Rights Reserved.
JPM DAVPS 5-26

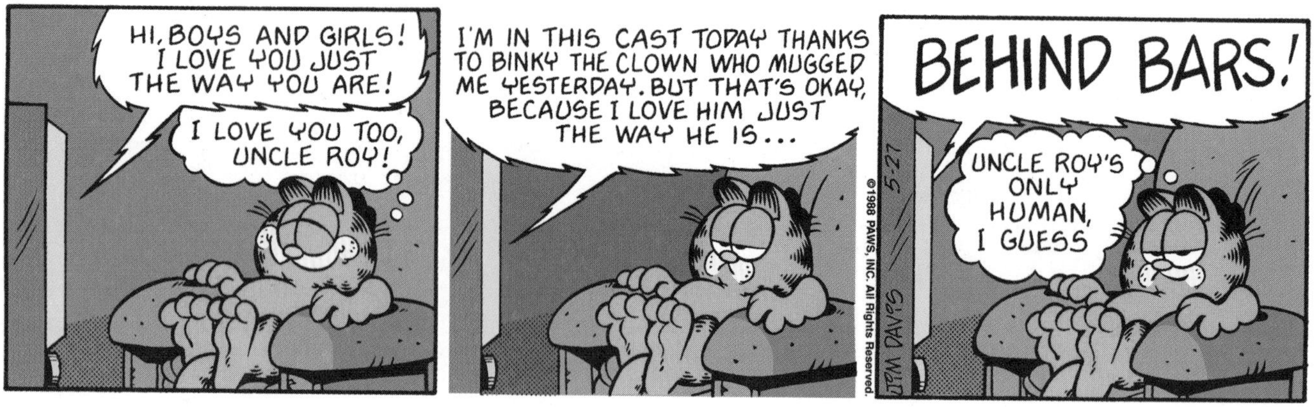
HI, BOYS AND GIRLS! I LOVE YOU JUST THE WAY YOU ARE!
I LOVE YOU TOO, UNCLE ROY!
I'M IN THIS CAST TODAY THANKS TO BINKY THE CLOWN WHO MUGGED ME YESTERDAY. BUT THAT'S OKAY, BECAUSE I LOVE HIM JUST THE WAY HE IS...
BEHIND BARS!
UNCLE ROY'S ONLY HUMAN, I GUESS
©1988 PAWS, INC. All Rights Reserved.
JPM DAVPS 5-27

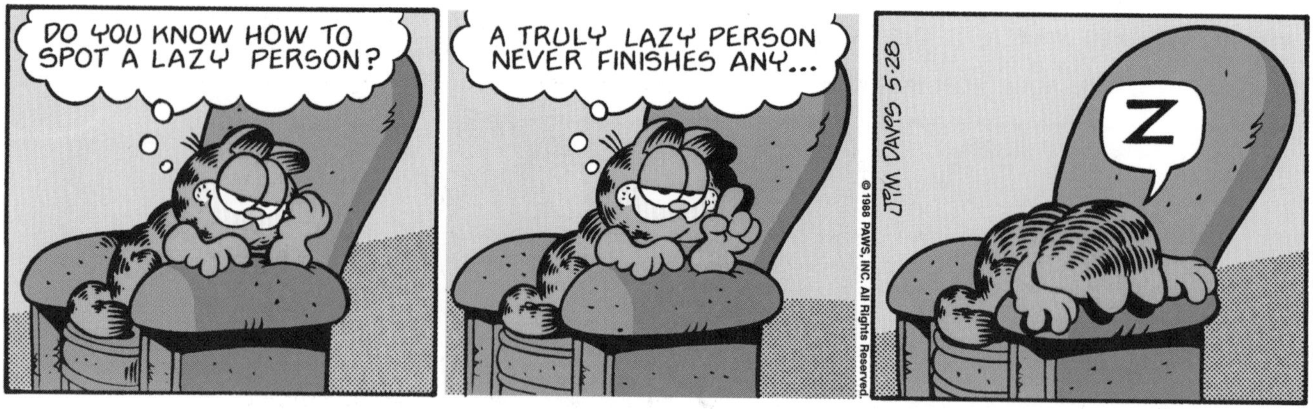
DO YOU KNOW HOW TO SPOT A LAZY PERSON?
A TRULY LAZY PERSON NEVER FINISHES ANY...
Z
©1988 PAWS, INC. All Rights Reserved.
JPM DAVPS 5-28

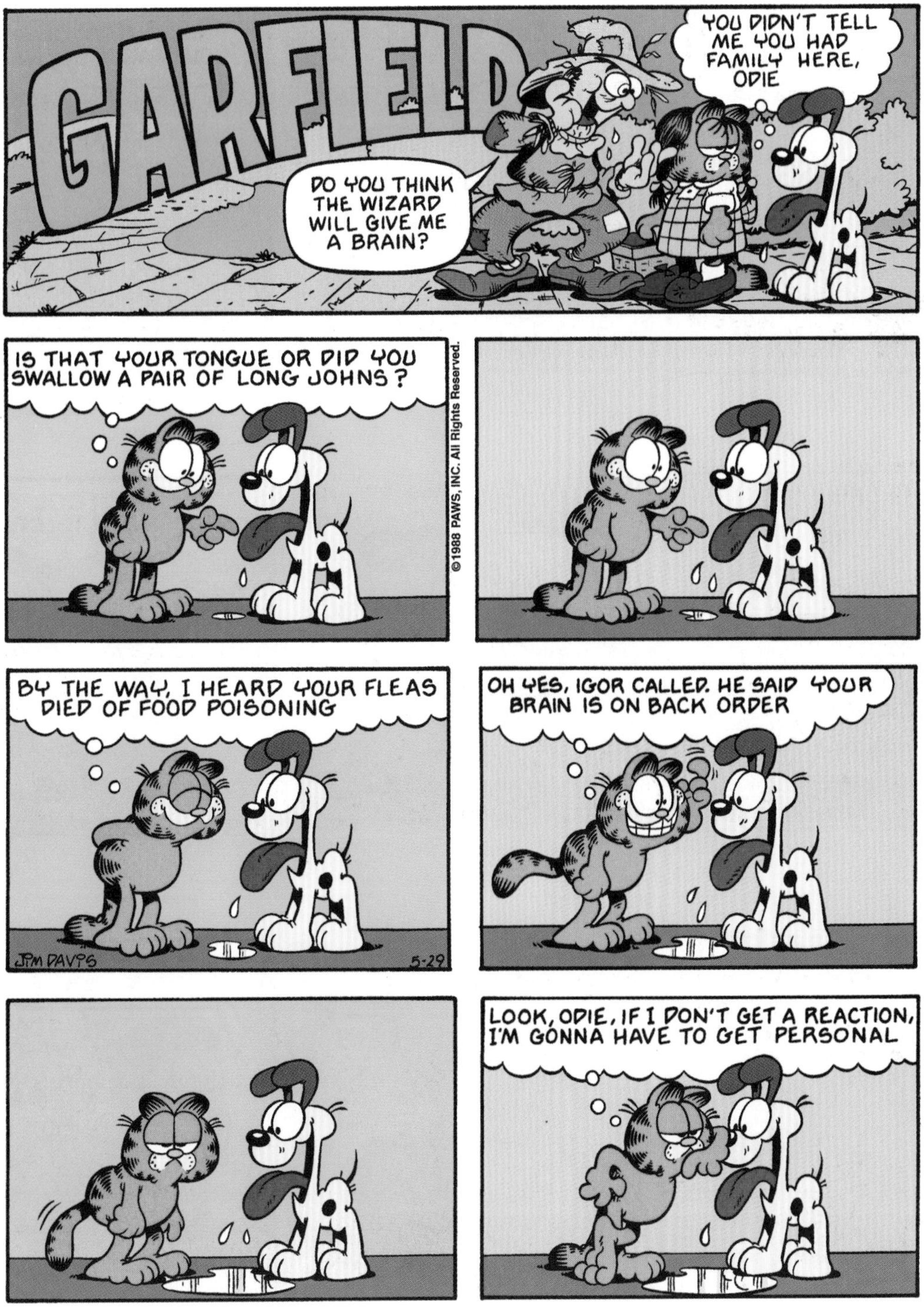
GARFIELD
DO YOU THINK THE WIZARD WILL GIVE ME A BRAIN?
YOU DIDN'T TELL ME YOU HAD FAMILY HERE, ODIE
IS THAT YOUR TONGUE OR DID YOU SWALLOW A PAIR OF LONG JOHNS?
BY THE WAY, I HEARD YOUR FLEAS DIED OF FOOD POISONING
OH YES, IGOR CALLED. HE SAID YOUR BRAIN IS ON BACK ORDER
JIM DAVIS
5-29
LOOK, ODIE, IF I DON'T GET A REACTION, I'M GONNA HAVE TO GET PERSONAL

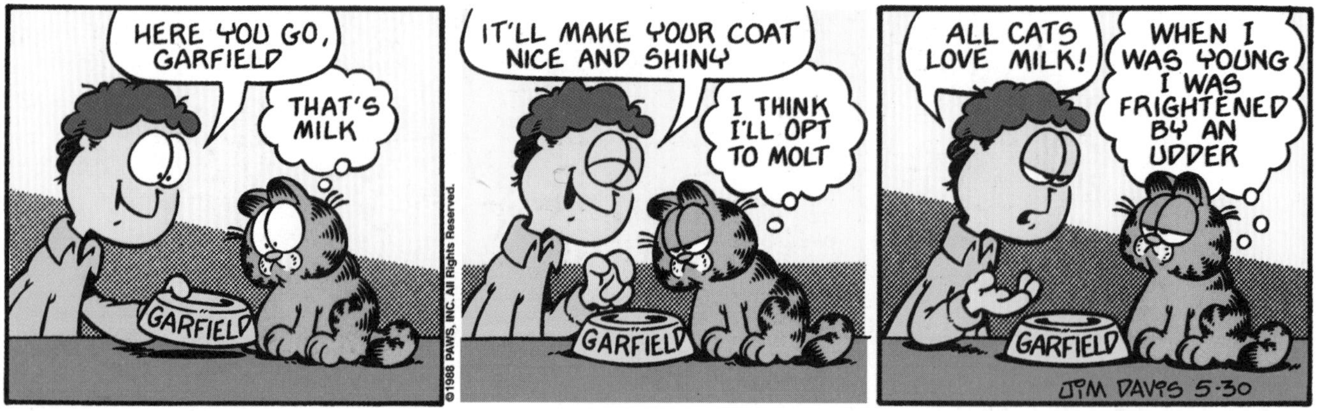
HERE YOU GO, GARFIELD
THAT'S MILK
IT'LL MAKE YOUR COAT NICE AND SHINY
I THINK I'LL OPT TO MOLT
©1988 PAWS, INC. All Rights Reserved.
ALL CATS LOVE MILK!
WHEN I WAS YOUNG I WAS FRIGHTENED BY AN UDDER
JIM DAVIS 5-30

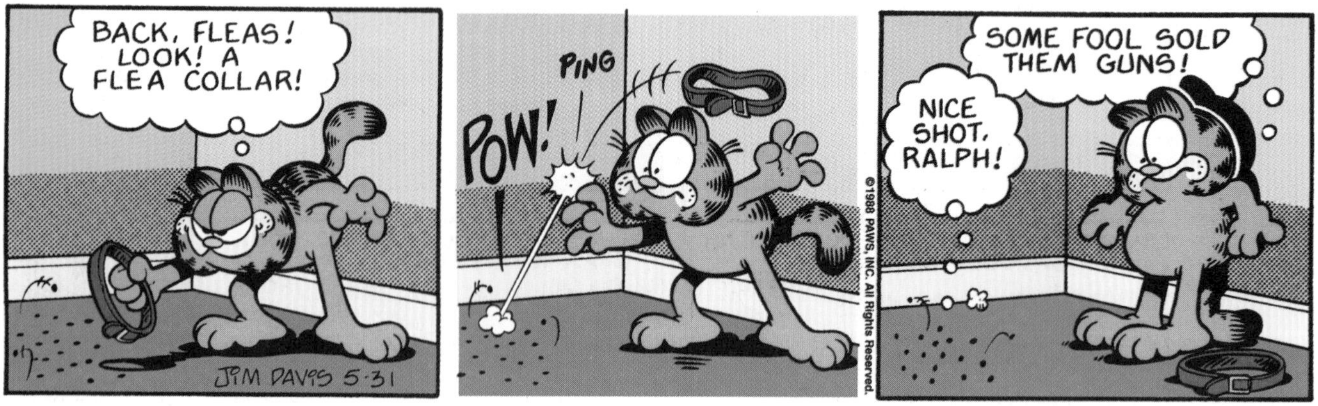
BACK, FLEAS! LOOK! A FLEA COLLAR!
JIM DAVIS 5-31
PING
POW!
©1988 PAWS, INC. All Rights Reserved.
SOME FOOL SOLD THEM GUNS!
NICE SHOT, RALPH!

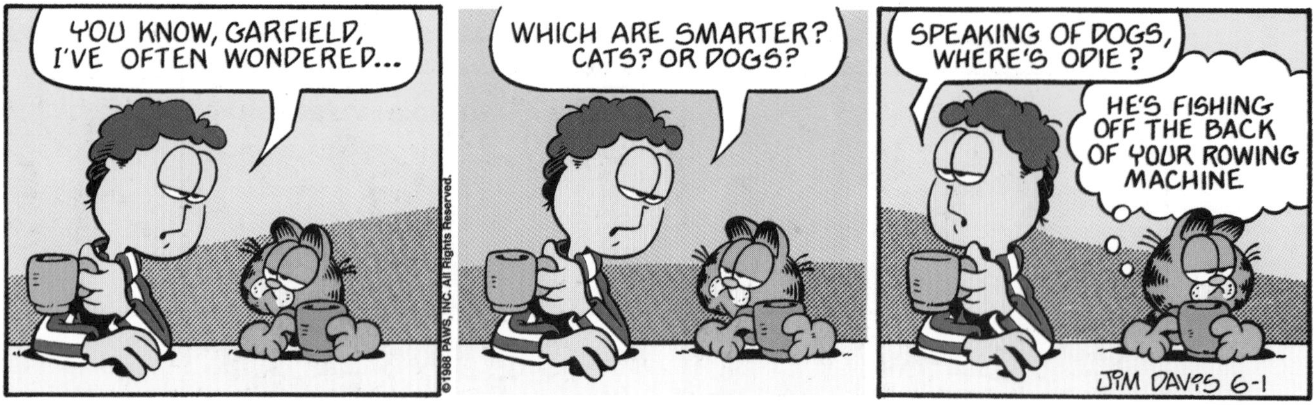
YOU KNOW, GARFIELD, I'VE OFTEN WONDERED...
©1988 PAWS, INC. All Rights Reserved.
WHICH ARE SMARTER? CATS? OR DOGS?
SPEAKING OF DOGS, WHERE'S ODIE?
HE'S FISHING OFF THE BACK OF YOUR ROWING MACHINE
JIM DAVIS 6-1

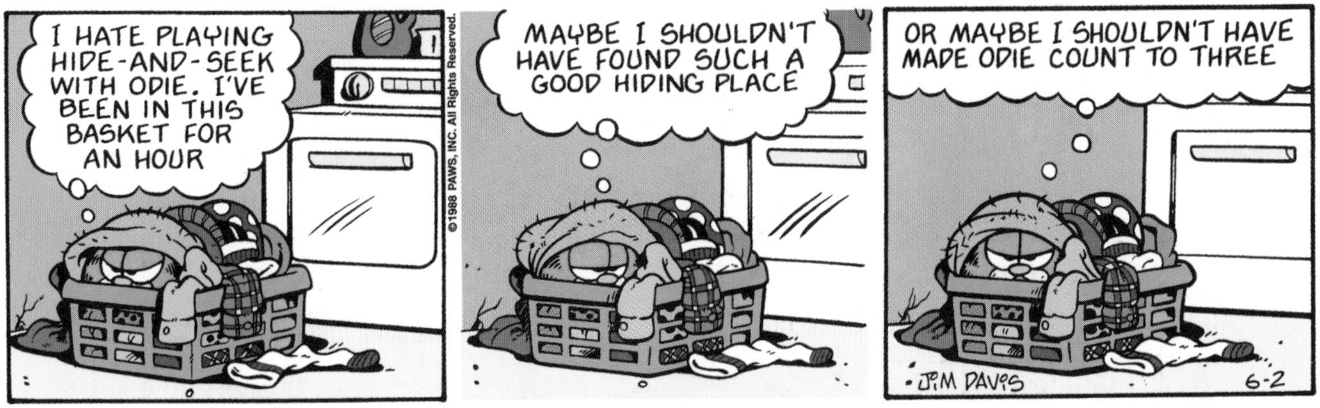
I HATE PLAYING HIDE-AND-SEEK WITH ODIE. I'VE BEEN IN THIS BASKET FOR AN HOUR
©1988 PAWS, INC. All Rights Reserved.
MAYBE I SHOULDN'T HAVE FOUND SUCH A GOOD HIDING PLACE
OR MAYBE I SHOULDN'T HAVE MADE ODIE COUNT TO THREE
JIM DAVIS 6-2

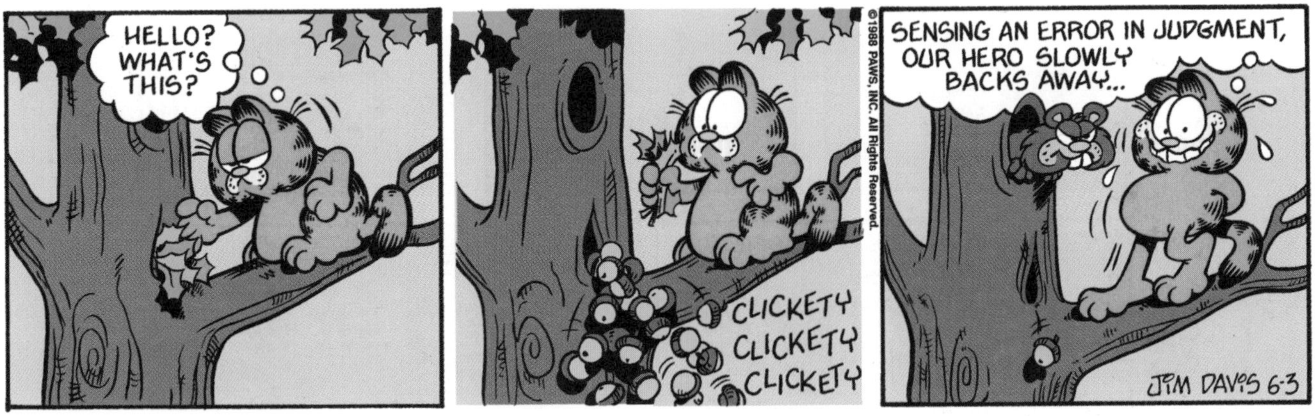
HELLO? WHAT'S THIS?
©1988 PAWS, INC. All Rights Reserved.
CLICKETY CLICKETY CLICKETY
SENSING AN ERROR IN JUDGMENT, OUR HERO SLOWLY BACKS AWAY...
JIM DAVIS 6-3

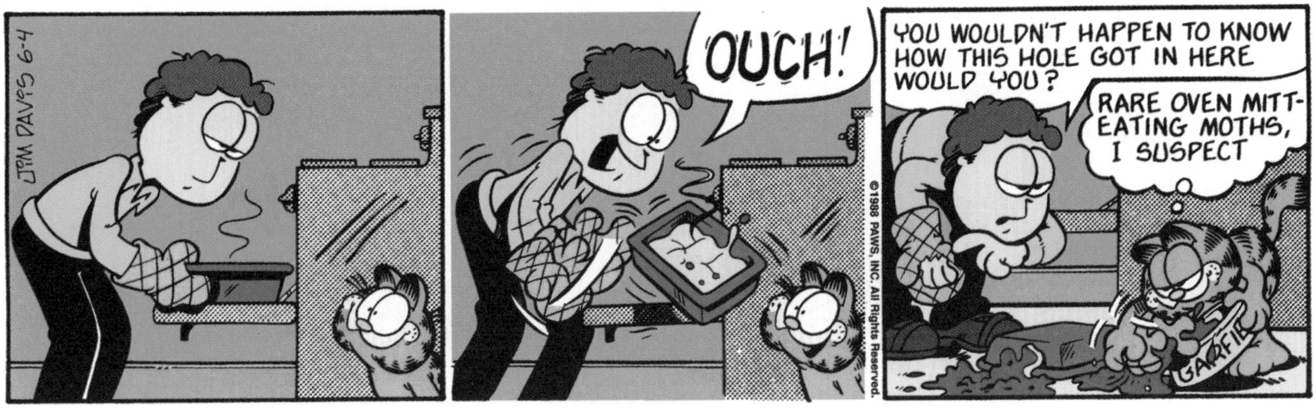
JIM DAVIS 6-4
OUCH!
©1988 PAWS, INC. All Rights Reserved.
YOU WOULDN'T HAPPEN TO KNOW HOW THIS HOLE GOT IN HERE WOULD YOU?
RARE OVEN MITT-EATING MOTHS, I SUSPECT

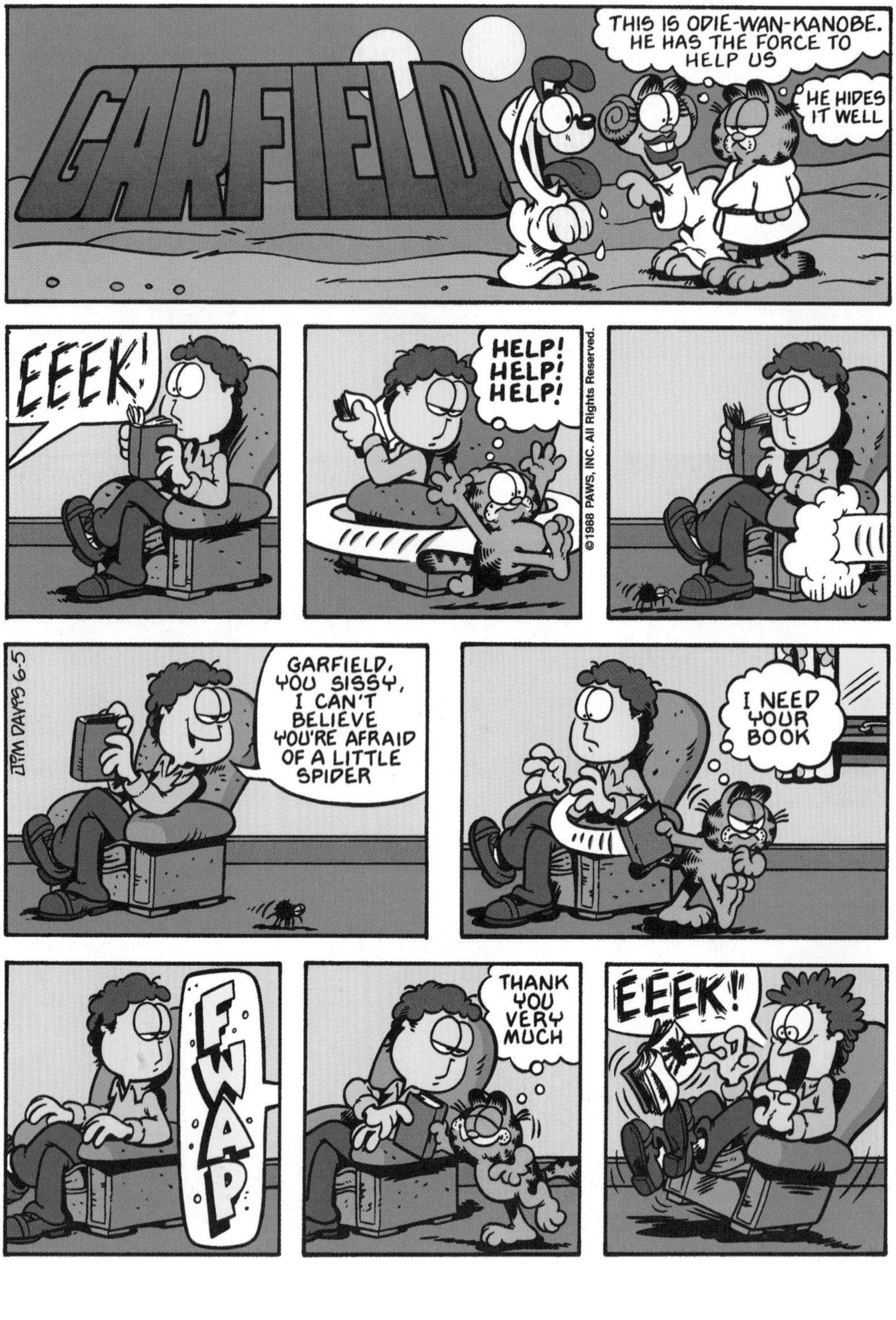
GARFIELD
THIS IS ODIE-WAN-KANOBE. HE HAS THE FORCE TO HELP US
HE HIDES IT WELL
EEEK!
HELP! HELP! HELP!
©1988 PAWS, INC. All Rights Reserved.
JPM DAVIS 6-5
GARFIELD, YOU SISSY, I CAN'T BELIEVE YOU'RE AFRAID OF A LITTLE SPIDER
I NEED YOUR BOOK
FWAP
THANK YOU VERY MUCH
EEEK!

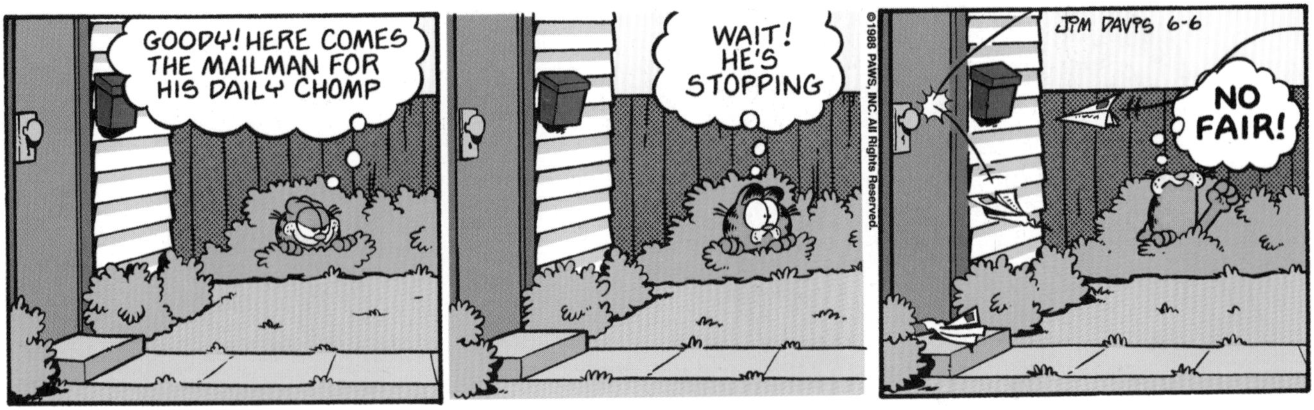
GOODY! HERE COMES THE MAILMAN FOR HIS DAILY CHOMP
WAIT! HE'S STOPPING
© 1988 PAWS, INC. All Rights Reserved.
JIM DAVIS 6-6
NO FAIR!

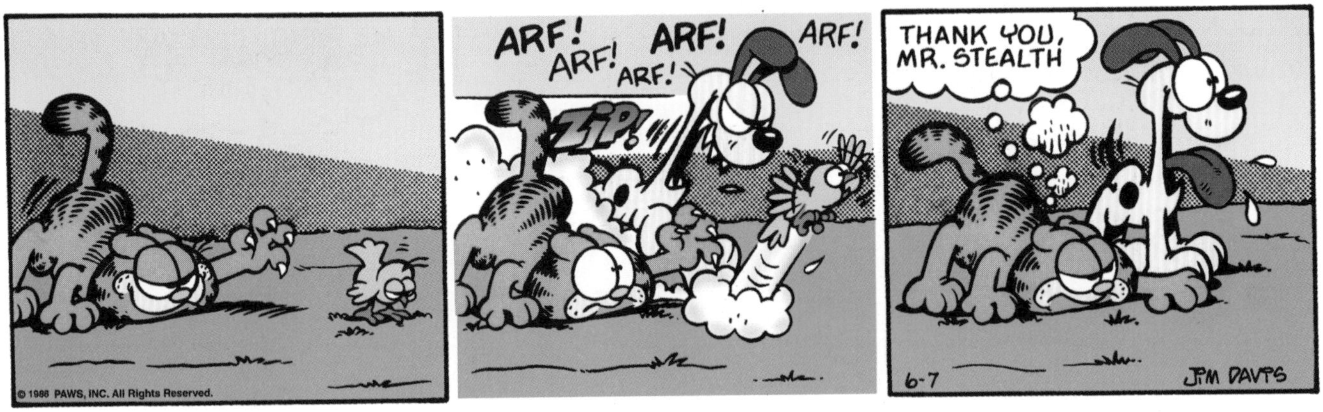
© 1988 PAWS, INC. All Rights Reserved.
ARF! ARF! ARF! ARF! ARF!
ZIP!
THANK YOU, MR. STEALTH
6-7
JIM DAVIS

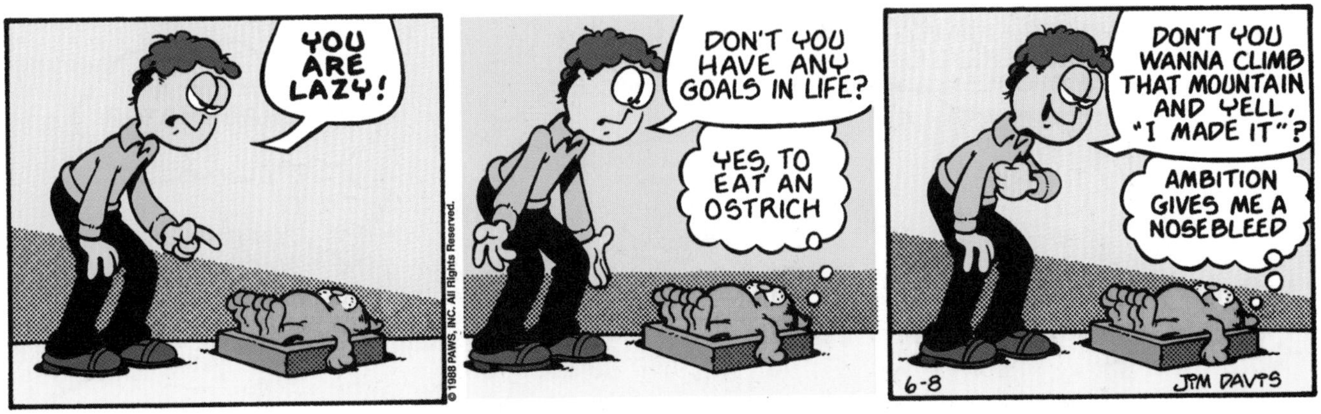
YOU ARE LAZY!
© 1988 PAWS, INC. All Rights Reserved.
DON'T YOU HAVE ANY GOALS IN LIFE?
YES, TO EAT AN OSTRICH
DON'T YOU WANNA CLIMB THAT MOUNTAIN AND YELL, "I MADE IT"?
AMBITION GIVES ME A NOSEBLEED
6-8
JIM DAVIS

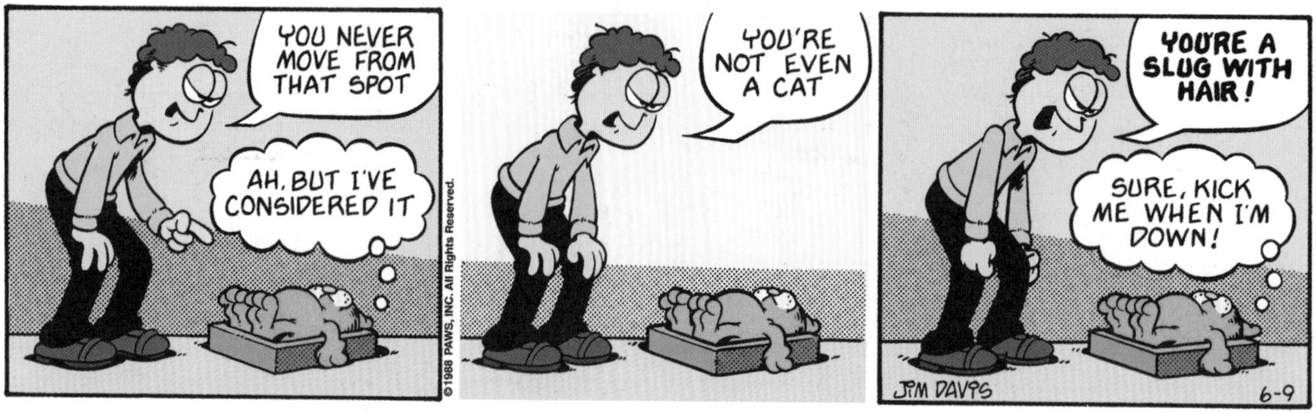
YOU NEVER MOVE FROM THAT SPOT
AH, BUT I'VE CONSIDERED IT
YOU'RE NOT EVEN A CAT
YOU'RE A SLUG WITH HAIR!
SURE, KICK ME WHEN I'M DOWN!
JIM DAVIS
6-9

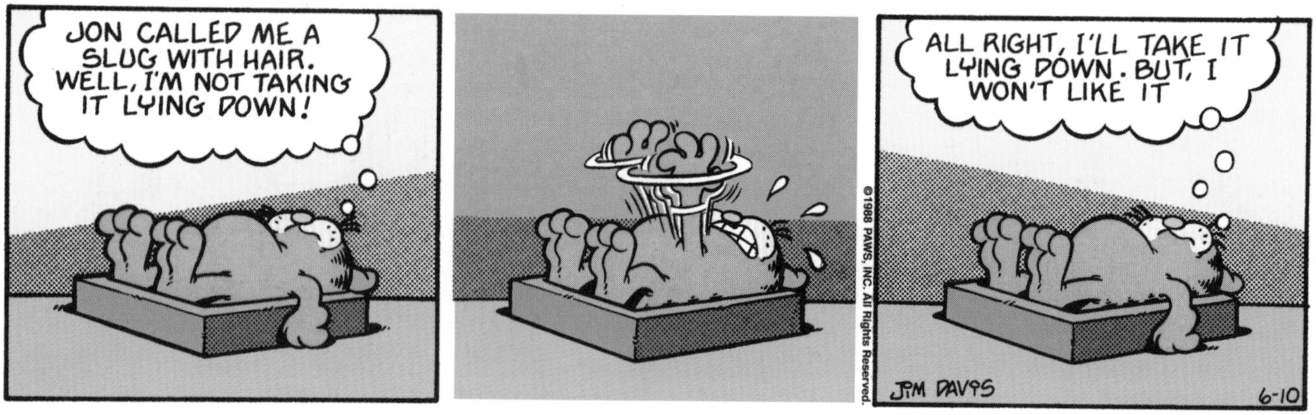
JON CALLED ME A SLUG WITH HAIR. WELL, I'M NOT TAKING IT LYING DOWN!
ALL RIGHT, I'LL TAKE IT LYING DOWN. BUT, I WON'T LIKE IT
JIM DAVIS
6-10

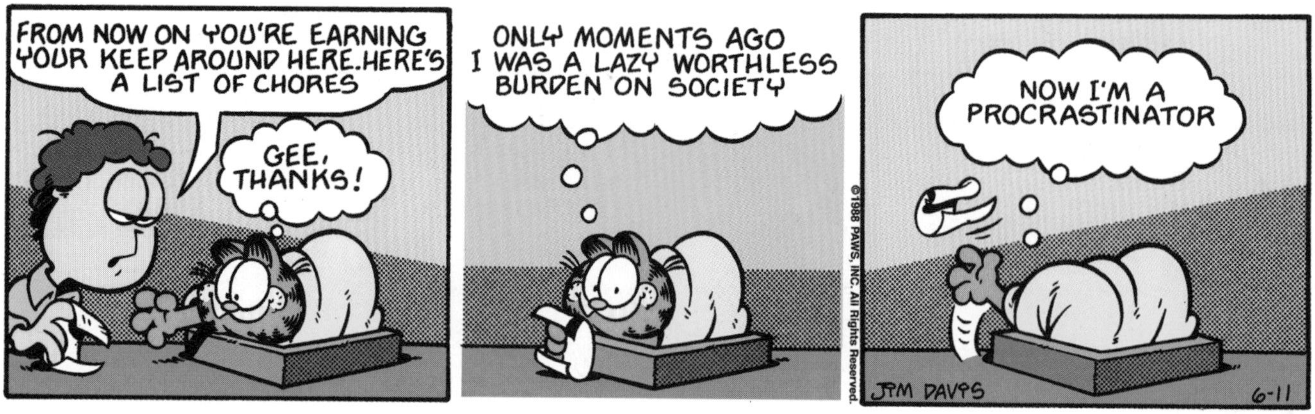
FROM NOW ON YOU'RE EARNING YOUR KEEP AROUND HERE. HERE'S A LIST OF CHORES
GEE, THANKS!
ONLY MOMENTS AGO I WAS A LAZY WORTHLESS BURDEN ON SOCIETY
NOW I'M A PROCRASTINATOR
JIM DAVIS
6-11

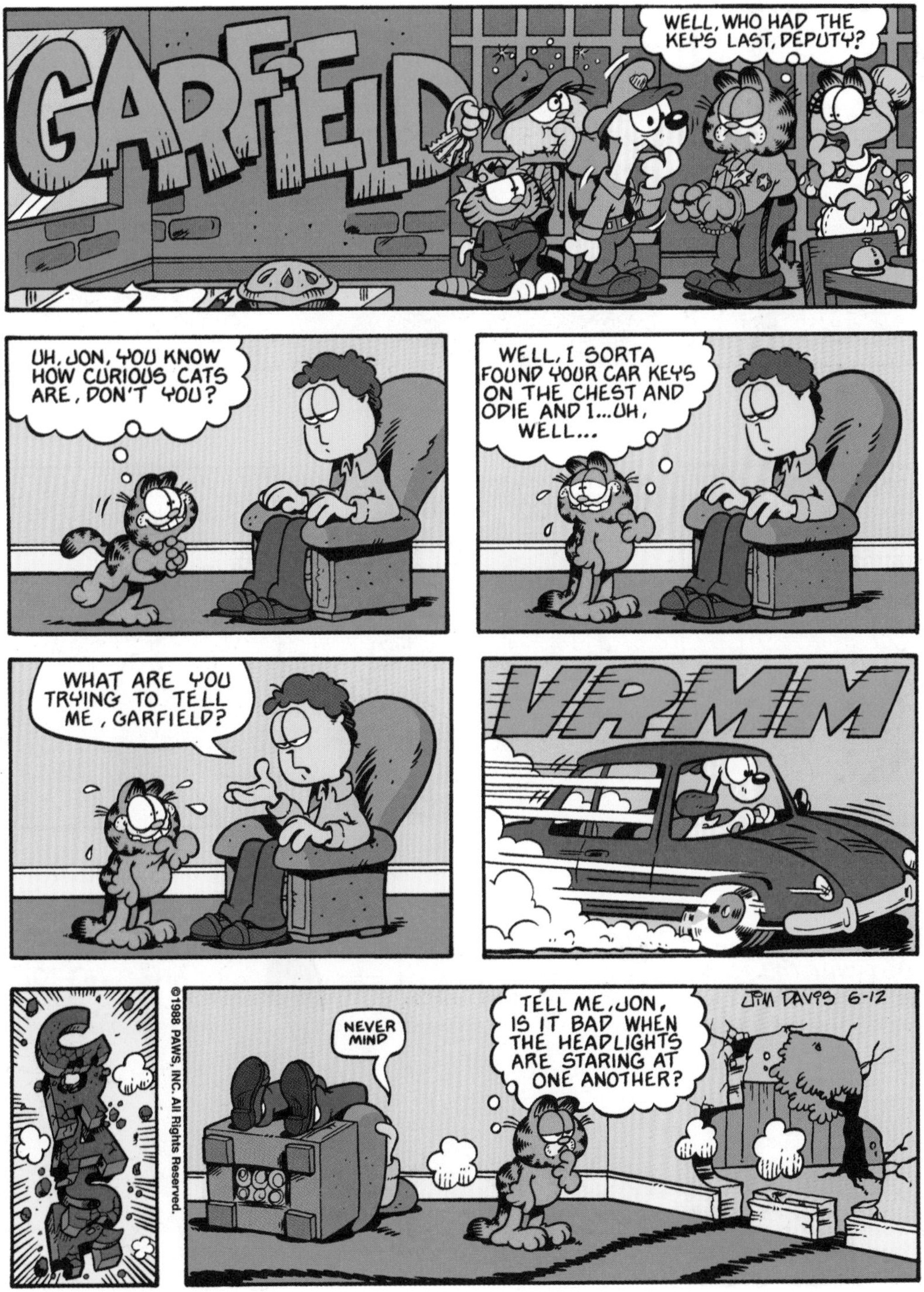
GARFIELD
WELL, WHO HAD THE KEYS LAST, DEPUTY?
UH, JON, YOU KNOW HOW CURIOUS CATS ARE, DON'T YOU?
WELL, I SORTA FOUND YOUR CAR KEYS ON THE CHEST AND ODIE AND I...UH, WELL...
WHAT ARE YOU TRYING TO TELL ME, GARFIELD?
VRMM
CRASH
NEVER MIND
TELL ME, JON, IS IT BAD WHEN THE HEADLIGHTS ARE STARING AT ONE ANOTHER?
JIM DAVIS 6-12
© 1988 PAWS, INC. All Rights Reserved.

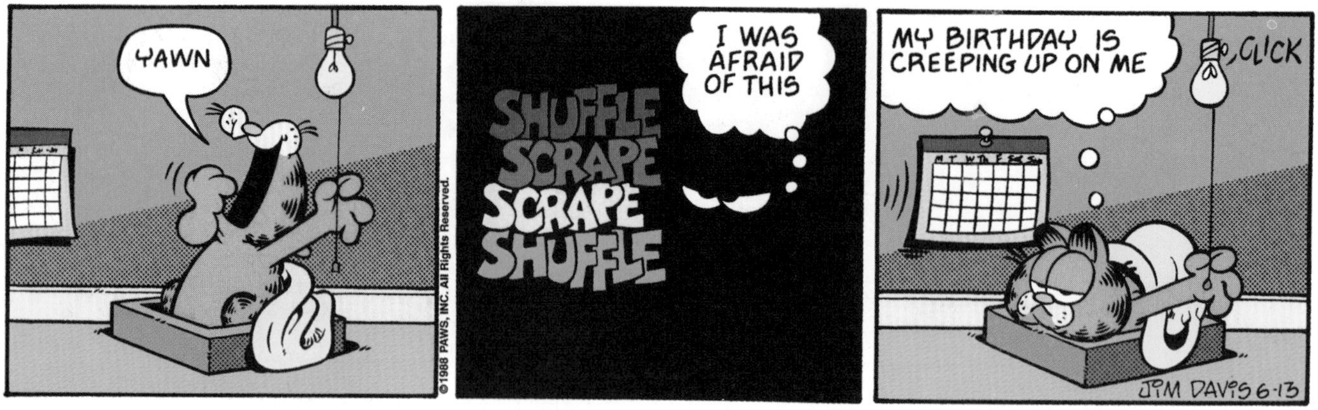
YAWN
©1988 PAWS, INC. All Rights Reserved.
SHUFFLE
SCRAPE
SCRAPE
SHUFFLE
I WAS AFRAID OF THIS
MY BIRTHDAY IS CREEPING UP ON ME
CLICK
JIM DAVIS 6-13

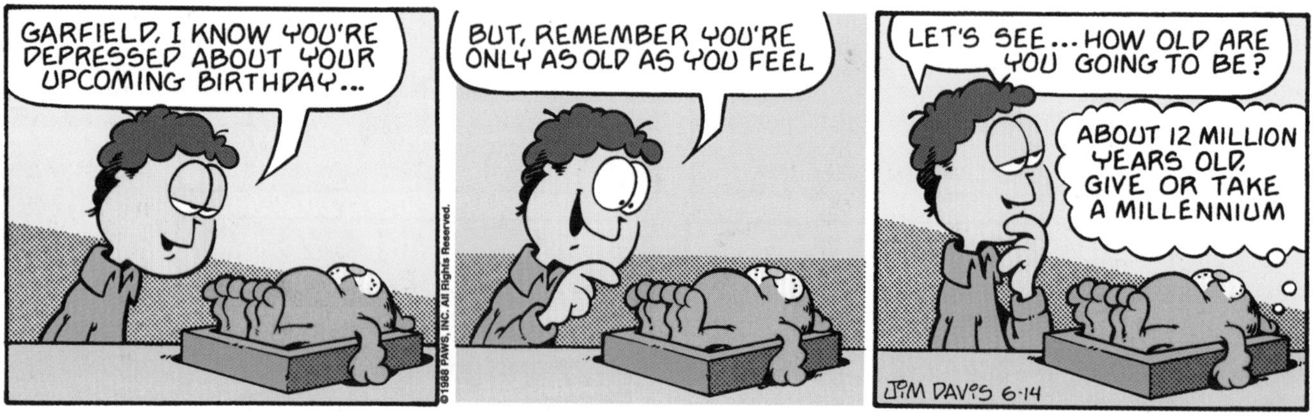
GARFIELD, I KNOW YOU'RE DEPRESSED ABOUT YOUR UPCOMING BIRTHDAY...
©1988 PAWS, INC. All Rights Reserved.
BUT, REMEMBER YOU'RE ONLY AS OLD AS YOU FEEL
LET'S SEE... HOW OLD ARE YOU GOING TO BE?
ABOUT 12 MILLION YEARS OLD, GIVE OR TAKE A MILLENNIUM
JIM DAVIS 6-14

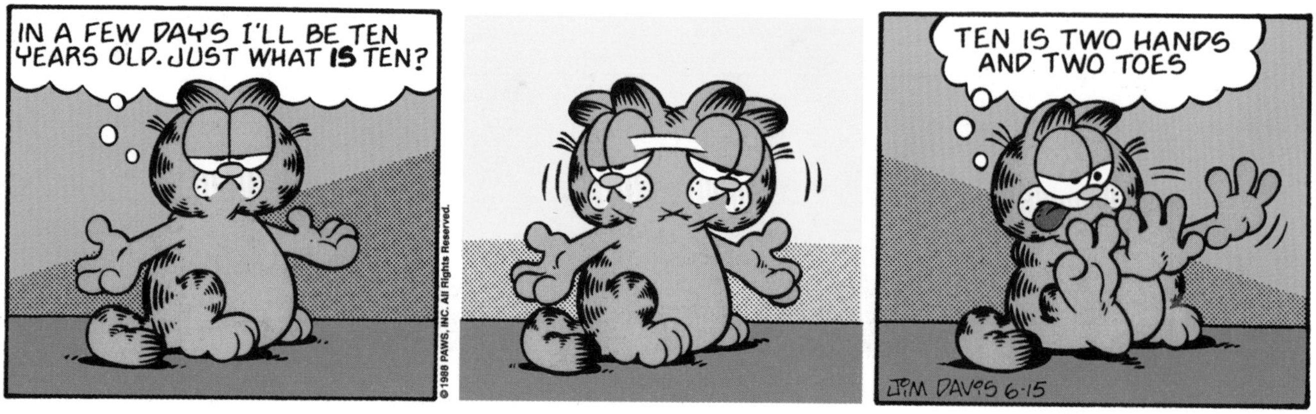
IN A FEW DAYS I'LL BE TEN YEARS OLD. JUST WHAT **IS** TEN?
©1988 PAWS, INC. All Rights Reserved.
TEN IS TWO HANDS AND TWO TOES
JIM DAVIS 6-15

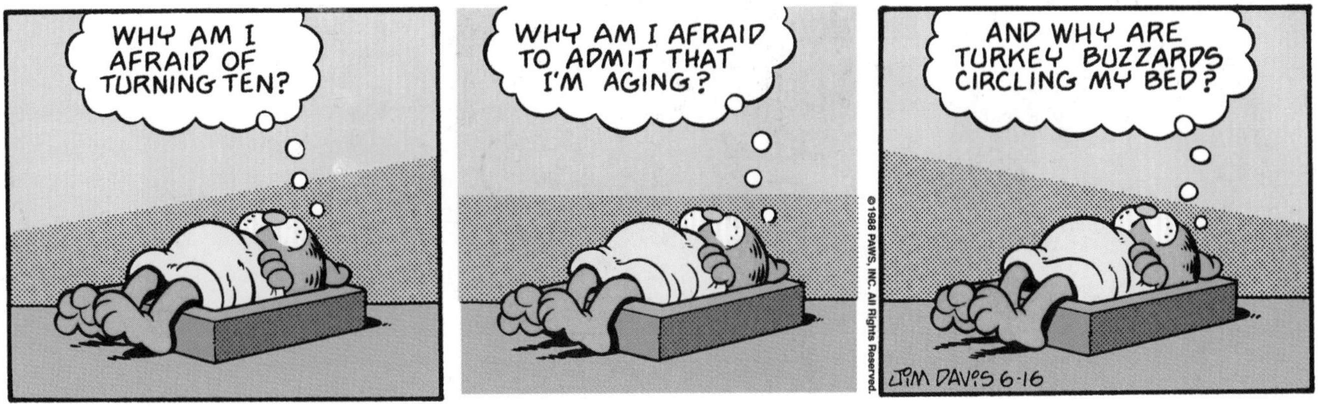
WHY AM I AFRAID OF TURNING TEN?
WHY AM I AFRAID TO ADMIT THAT I'M AGING?
AND WHY ARE TURKEY BUZZARDS CIRCLING MY BED?
©1988 PAWS, INC. All Rights Reserved.
JIM DAVIS 6-16

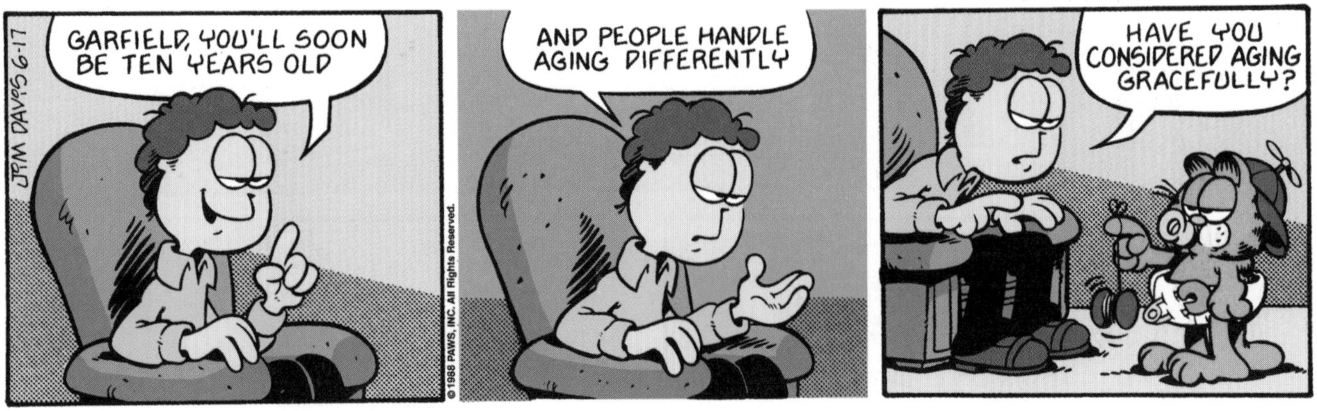
JIM DAVIS 6-17
GARFIELD, YOU'LL SOON BE TEN YEARS OLD
©1988 PAWS, INC. All Rights Reserved.
AND PEOPLE HANDLE AGING DIFFERENTLY
HAVE YOU CONSIDERED AGING GRACEFULLY?

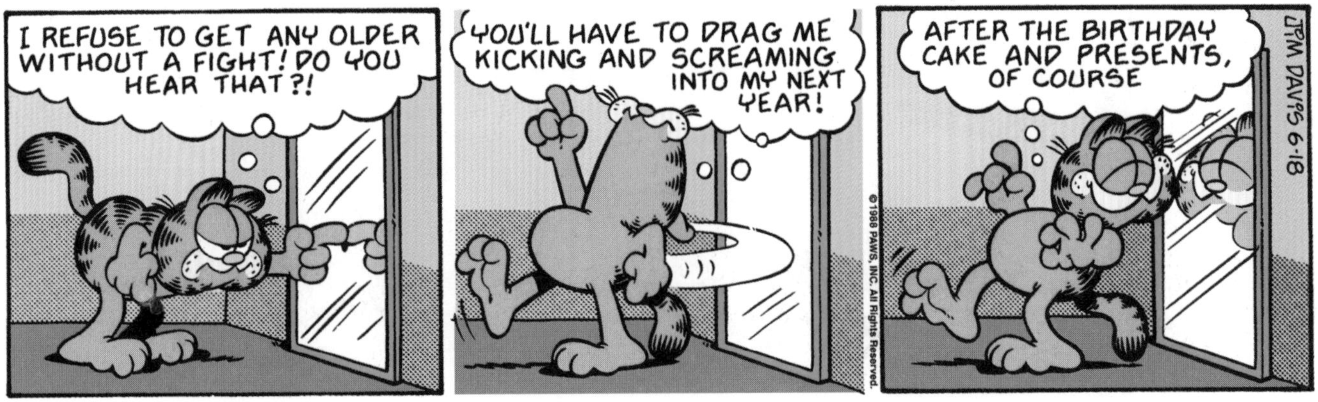
I REFUSE TO GET ANY OLDER WITHOUT A FIGHT! DO YOU HEAR THAT?!
YOU'LL HAVE TO DRAG ME KICKING AND SCREAMING INTO MY NEXT YEAR!
©1988 PAWS, INC. All Rights Reserved.
AFTER THE BIRTHDAY CAKE AND PRESENTS, OF COURSE
JIM DAVIS 6-18

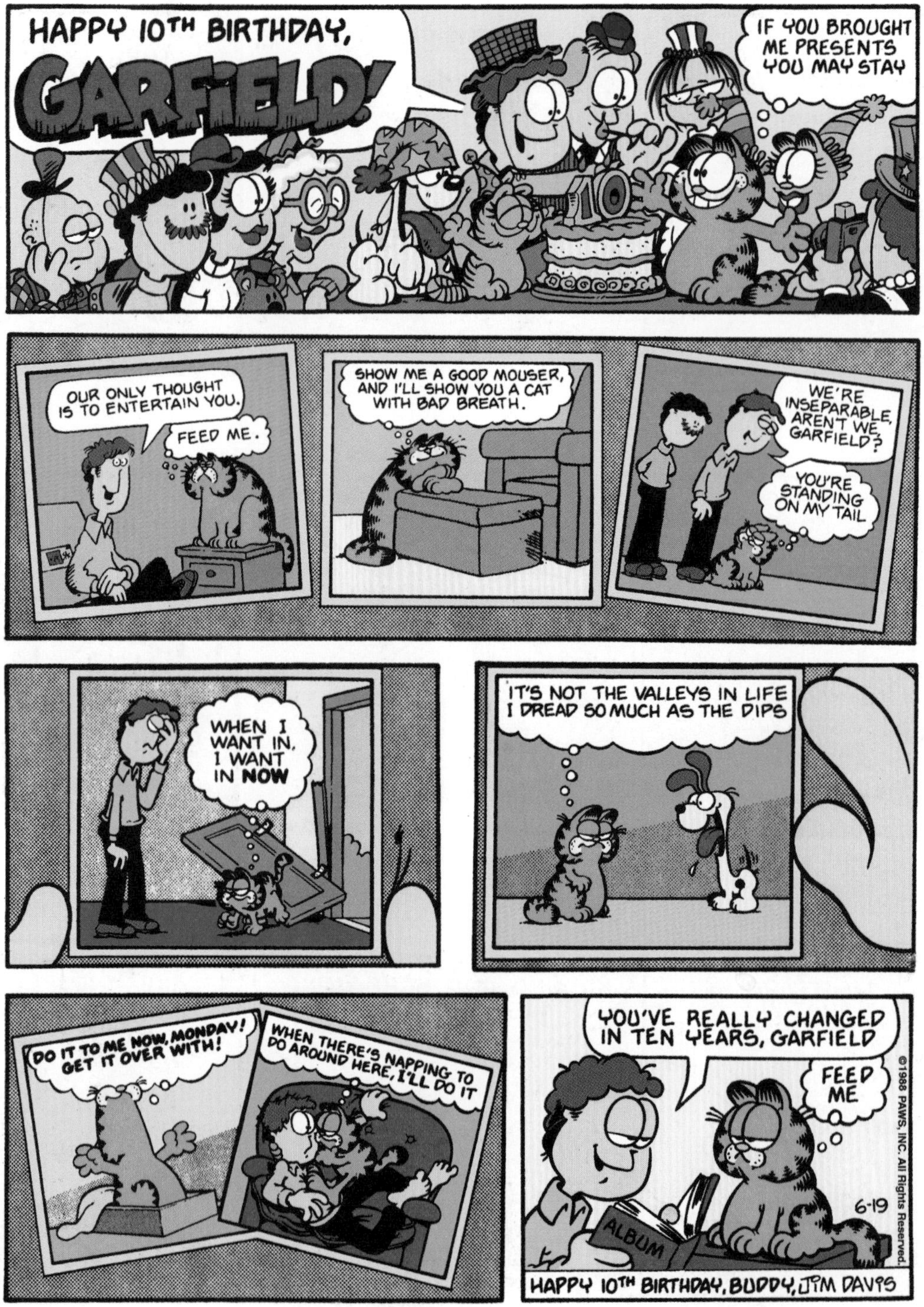
HAPPY 10TH BIRTHDAY, GARFIELD!
IF YOU BROUGHT ME PRESENTS YOU MAY STAY
OUR ONLY THOUGHT IS TO ENTERTAIN YOU.
FEED ME.
SHOW ME A GOOD MOUSER, AND I'LL SHOW YOU A CAT WITH BAD BREATH.
WE'RE INSEPARABLE, AREN'T WE, GARFIELD?
YOU'RE STANDING ON MY TAIL
WHEN I WANT IN, I WANT IN NOW
IT'S NOT THE VALLEYS IN LIFE I DREAD SO MUCH AS THE DIPS
DO IT TO ME NOW, MONDAY! GET IT OVER WITH!
WHEN THERE'S NAPPING TO DO AROUND HERE, I'LL DO IT
YOU'VE REALLY CHANGED IN TEN YEARS, GARFIELD
FEED ME
ALBUM
6-19
©1988 PAWS, INC. All Rights Reserved.
HAPPY 10TH BIRTHDAY, BUDDY, JIM DAVIS

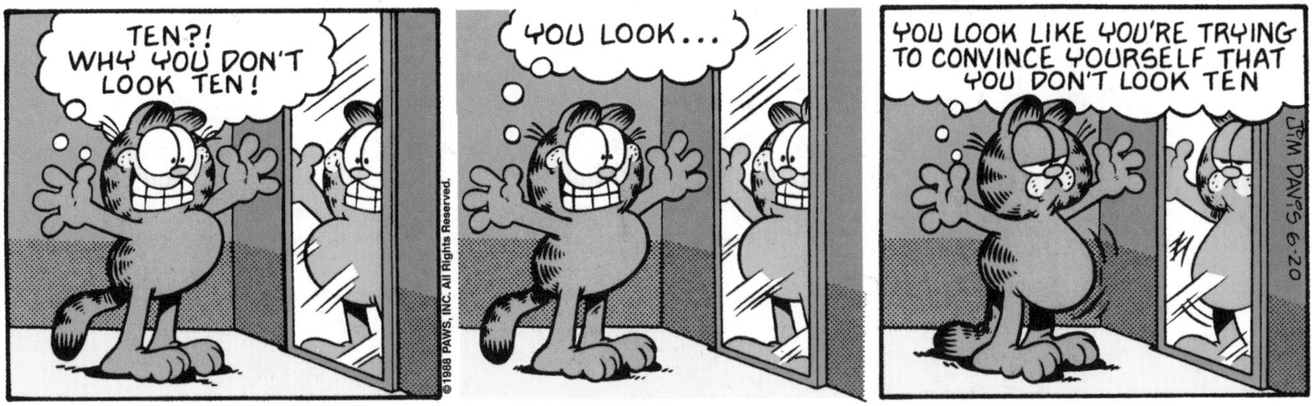
TEN?! WHY YOU DON'T LOOK TEN!
©1988 PAWS, INC. All Rights Reserved.
YOU LOOK...
YOU LOOK LIKE YOU'RE TRYING TO CONVINCE YOURSELF THAT YOU DON'T LOOK TEN
JIM DAVIS 6-20

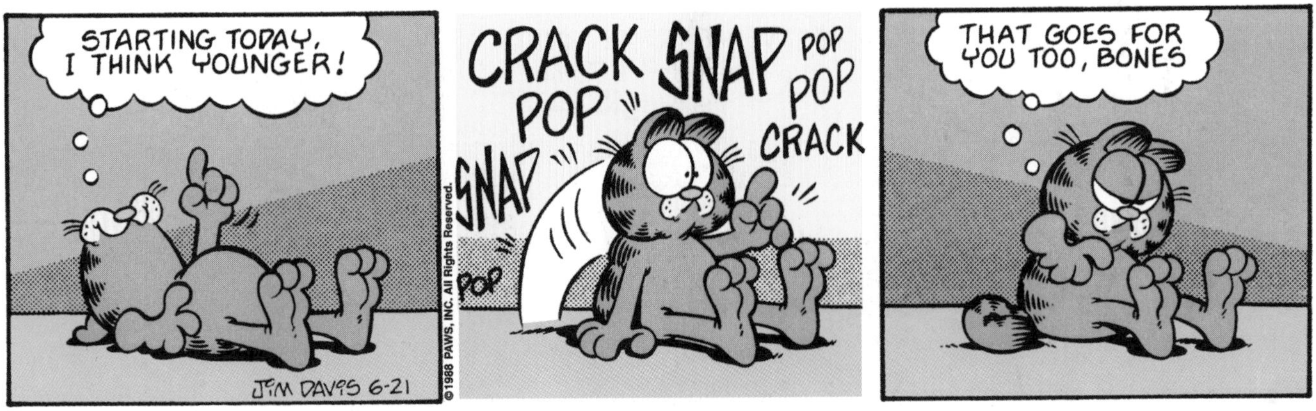
STARTING TODAY, I THINK YOUNGER!
JIM DAVIS 6-21
©1988 PAWS, INC. All Rights Reserved.
CRACK SNAP POP POP POP CRACK SNAP POP
THAT GOES FOR YOU TOO, BONES

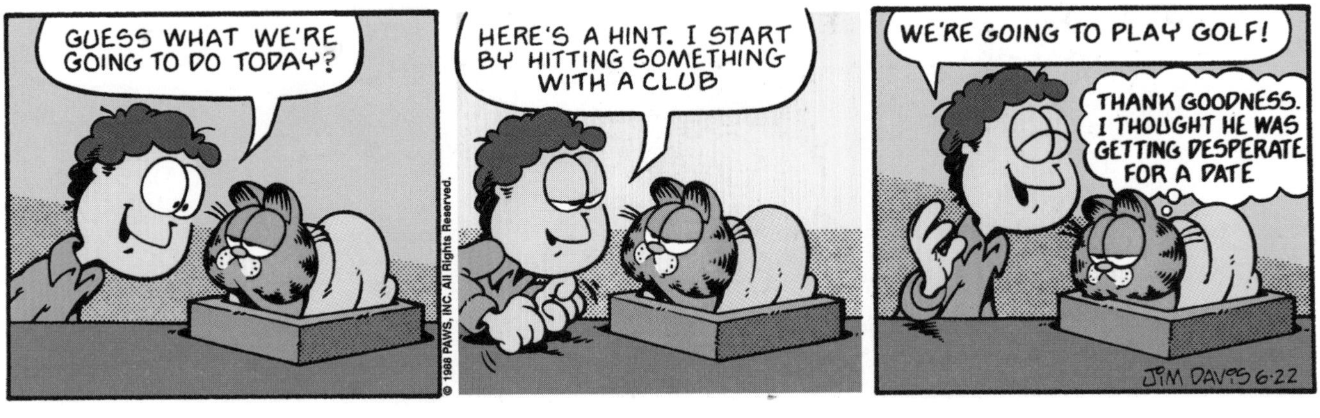
GUESS WHAT WE'RE GOING TO DO TODAY?
©1988 PAWS, INC. All Rights Reserved.
HERE'S A HINT. I START BY HITTING SOMETHING WITH A CLUB
WE'RE GOING TO PLAY GOLF!
THANK GOODNESS. I THOUGHT HE WAS GETTING DESPERATE FOR A DATE
JIM DAVIS 6-22

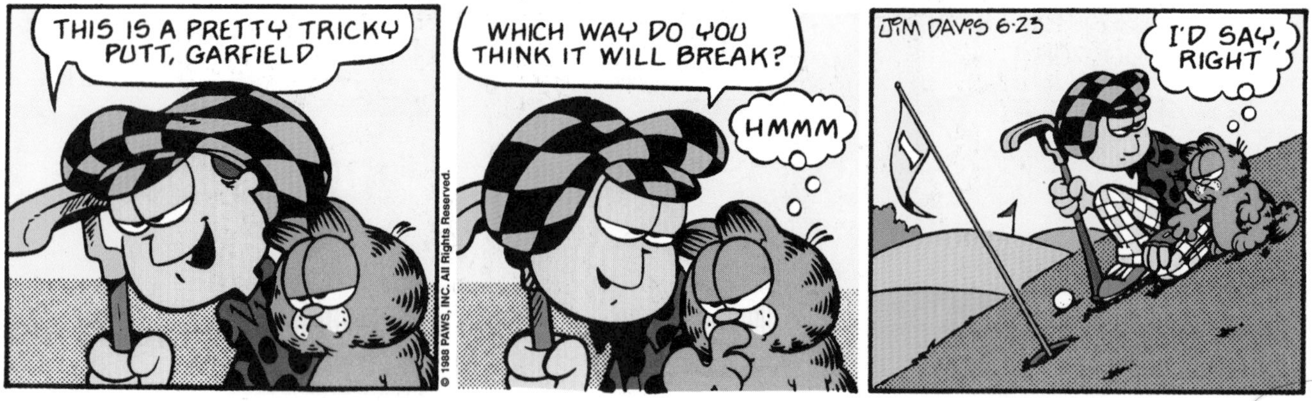
THIS IS A PRETTY TRICKY PUTT, GARFIELD
© 1988 PAWS, INC. All Rights Reserved.
WHICH WAY DO YOU THINK IT WILL BREAK?
HMMM
JIM DAVIS 6-23
I'D SAY, RIGHT

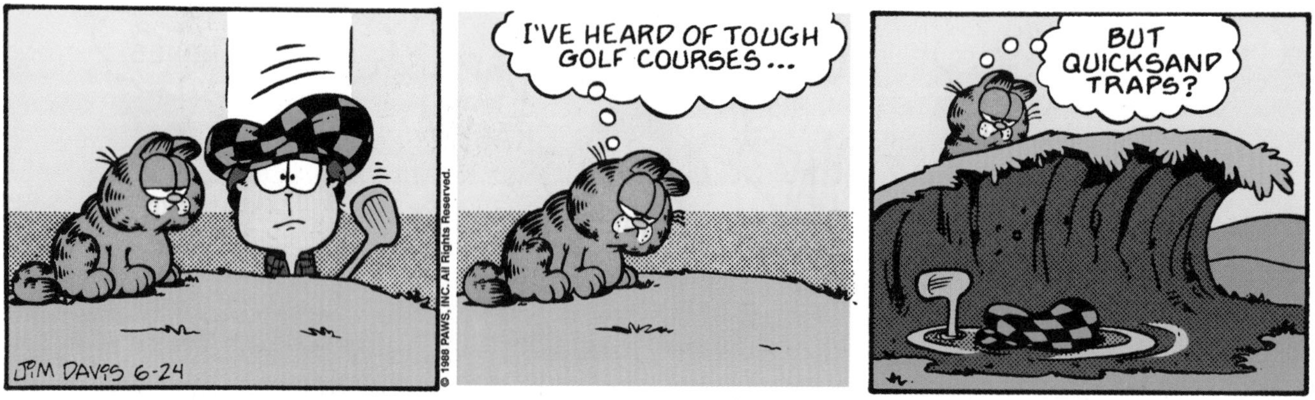
JIM DAVIS 6-24
© 1988 PAWS, INC. All Rights Reserved.
I'VE HEARD OF TOUGH GOLF COURSES...
BUT QUICKSAND TRAPS?

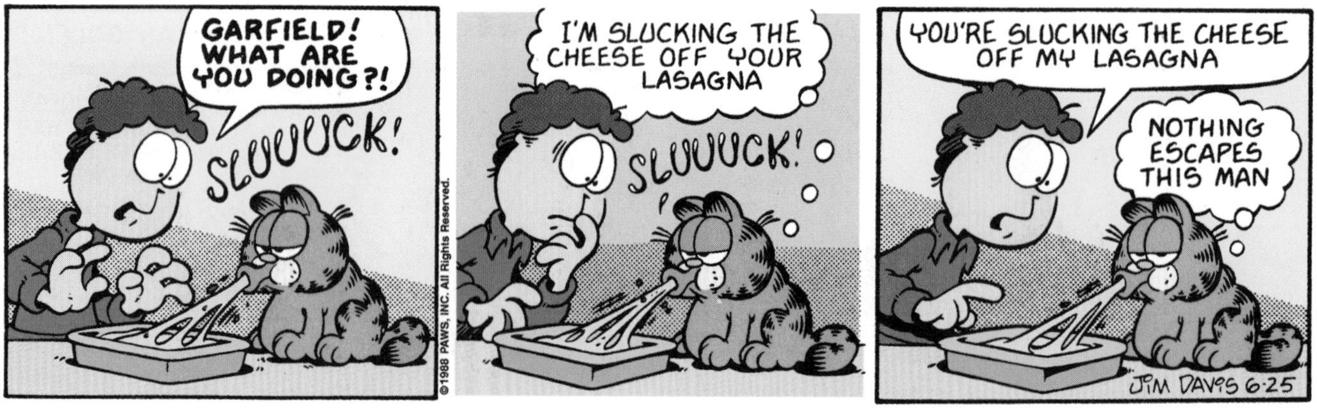
GARFIELD! WHAT ARE YOU DOING?!
SLUUUCK!
©1988 PAWS, INC. All Rights Reserved.
I'M SLUCKING THE CHEESE OFF YOUR LASAGNA
SLUUUCK!
YOU'RE SLUCKING THE CHEESE OFF MY LASAGNA
NOTHING ESCAPES THIS MAN
JIM DAVIS 6-25

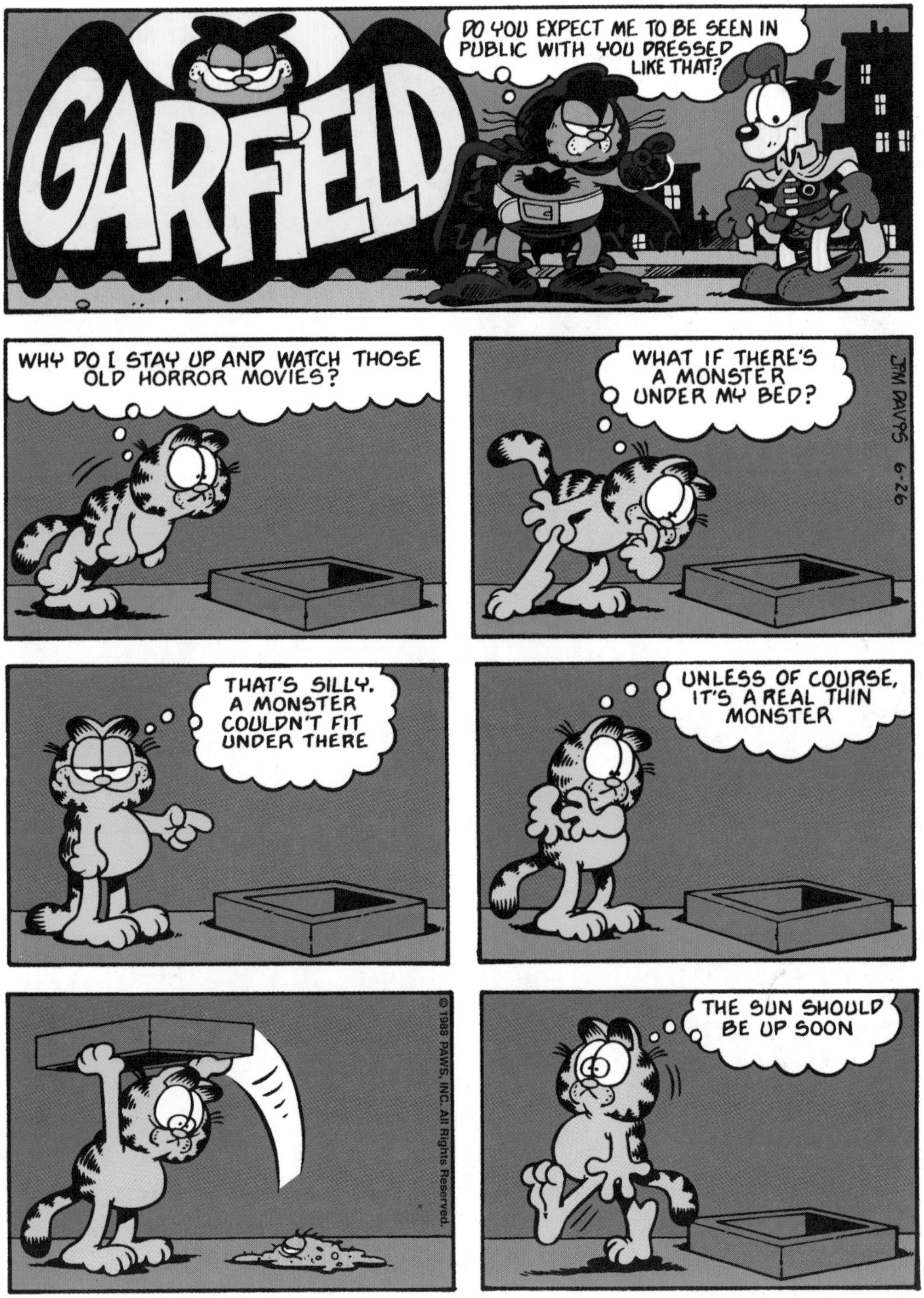
GARFIELD
DO YOU EXPECT ME TO BE SEEN IN PUBLIC WITH YOU DRESSED LIKE THAT?
WHY DO I STAY UP AND WATCH THOSE OLD HORROR MOVIES?
WHAT IF THERE'S A MONSTER UNDER MY BED?
JIM DAVIS 6-26
THAT'S SILLY. A MONSTER COULDN'T FIT UNDER THERE
UNLESS OF COURSE, IT'S A REAL THIN MONSTER
THE SUN SHOULD BE UP SOON

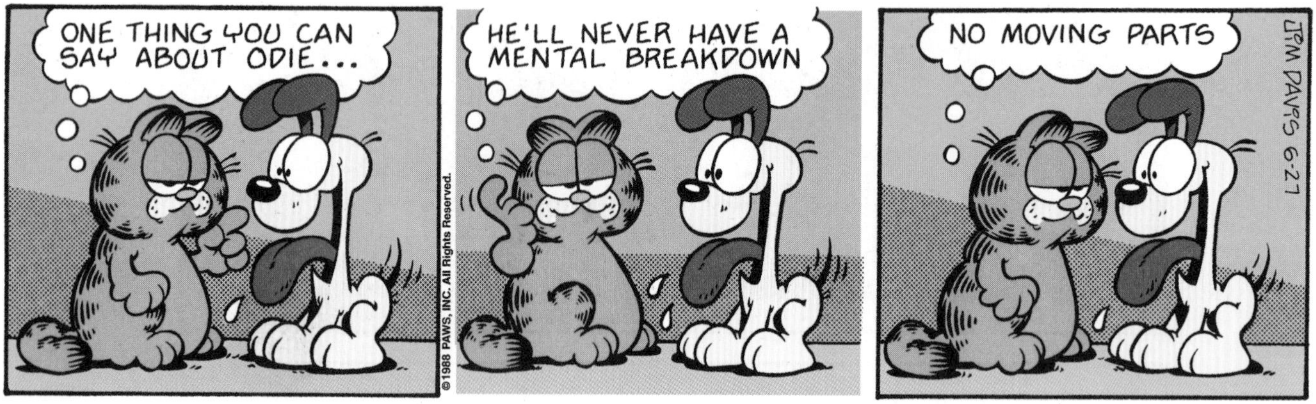
ONE THING YOU CAN SAY ABOUT ODIE...
©1988 PAWS, INC. All Rights Reserved.
HE'LL NEVER HAVE A MENTAL BREAKDOWN
NO MOVING PARTS
JIM DAVIS 6-27

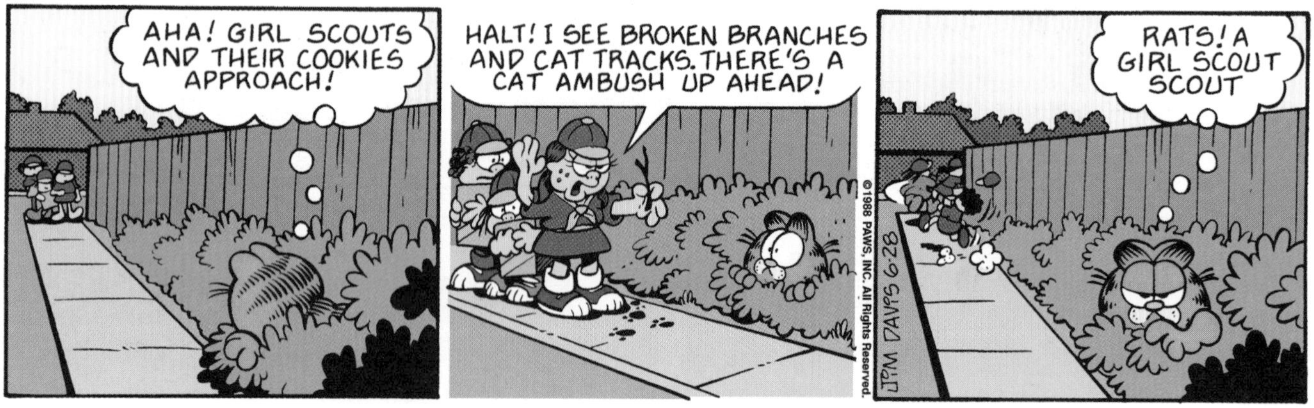
AHA! GIRL SCOUTS AND THEIR COOKIES APPROACH!
HALT! I SEE BROKEN BRANCHES AND CAT TRACKS. THERE'S A CAT AMBUSH UP AHEAD!
©1988 PAWS, INC. All Rights Reserved.
JIM DAVIS 6-28
RATS! A GIRL SCOUT SCOUT

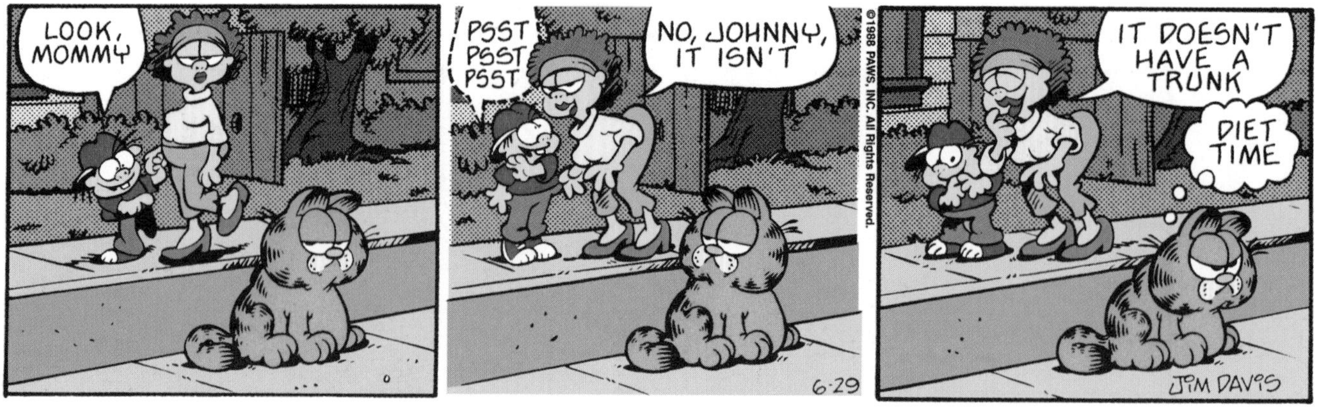
LOOK, MOMMY
PSST PSST PSST
NO, JOHNNY, IT ISN'T
6-29
©1988 PAWS, INC. All Rights Reserved.
IT DOESN'T HAVE A TRUNK
DIET TIME
JIM DAVIS

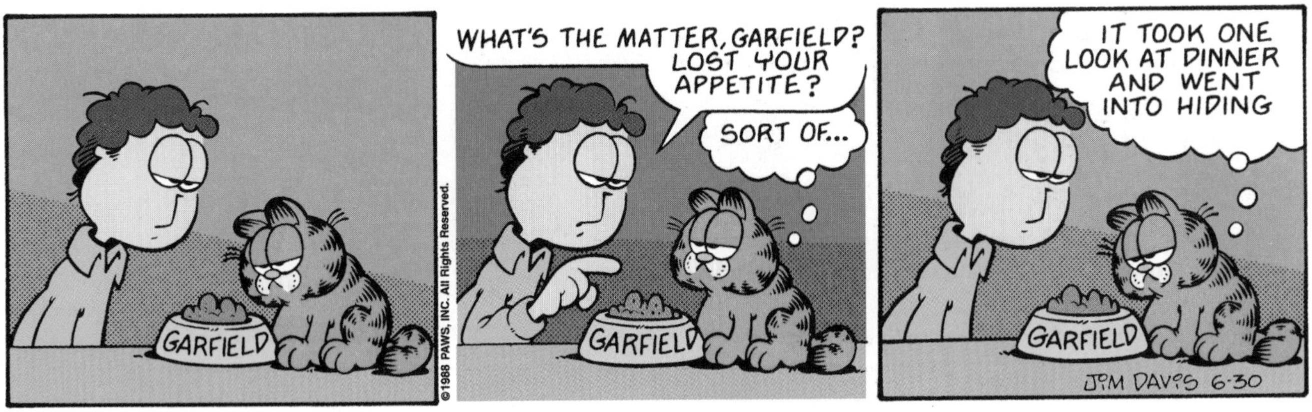
©1988 PAWS, INC. All Rights Reserved.
WHAT'S THE MATTER, GARFIELD? LOST YOUR APPETITE?
SORT OF...
IT TOOK ONE LOOK AT DINNER AND WENT INTO HIDING
JIM DAVIS 6-30

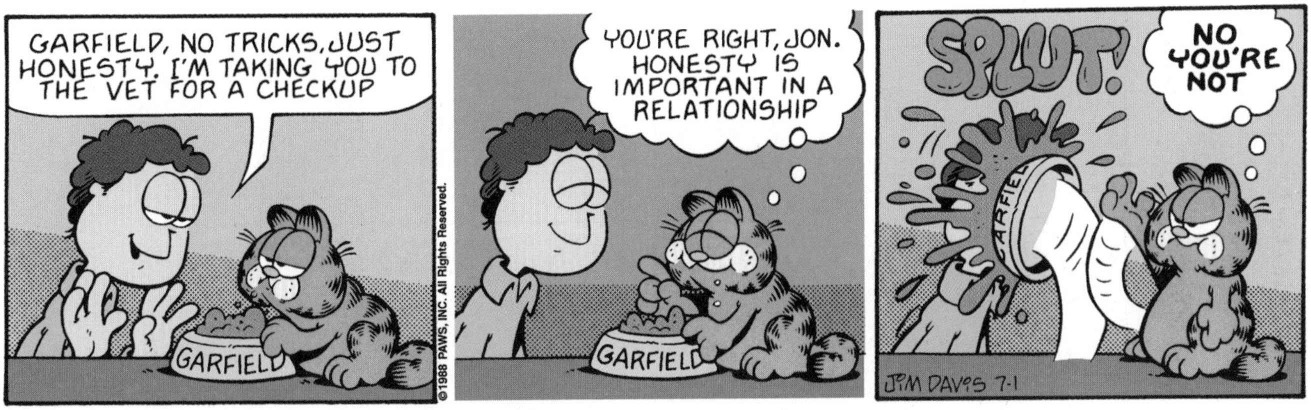
GARFIELD, NO TRICKS, JUST HONESTY. I'M TAKING YOU TO THE VET FOR A CHECKUP
©1988 PAWS, INC. All Rights Reserved.
YOU'RE RIGHT, JON. HONESTY IS IMPORTANT IN A RELATIONSHIP
SPLUT!
NO YOU'RE NOT
JIM DAVIS 7-1

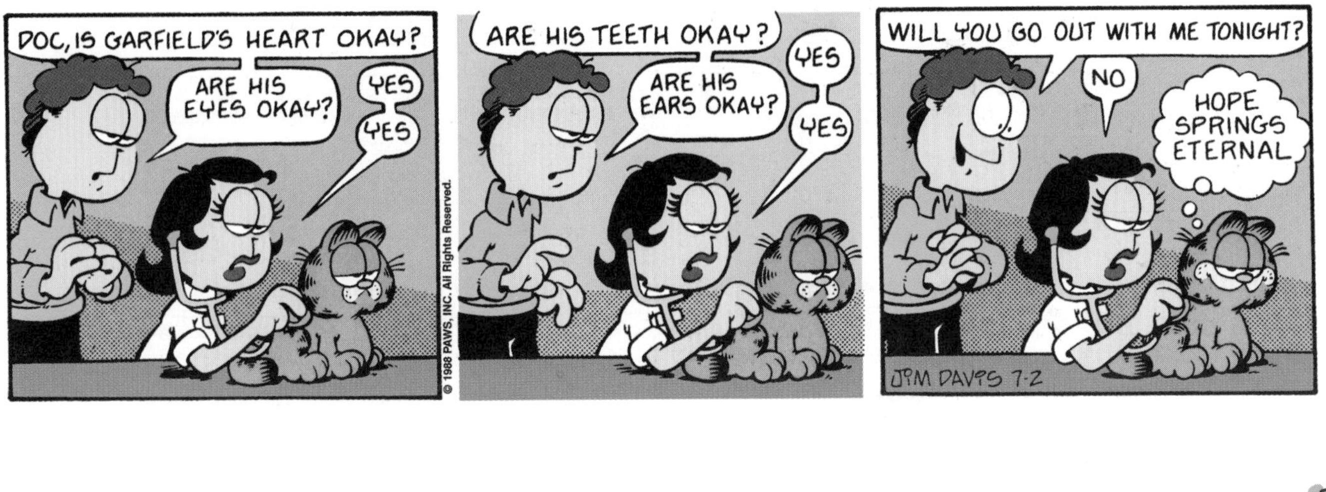
DOC, IS GARFIELD'S HEART OKAY?
ARE HIS EYES OKAY?
YES
YES
© 1988 PAWS, INC. All Rights Reserved.
ARE HIS TEETH OKAY?
ARE HIS EARS OKAY?
YES
YES
WILL YOU GO OUT WITH ME TONIGHT?
NO
HOPE SPRINGS ETERNAL
JIM DAVIS 7-2

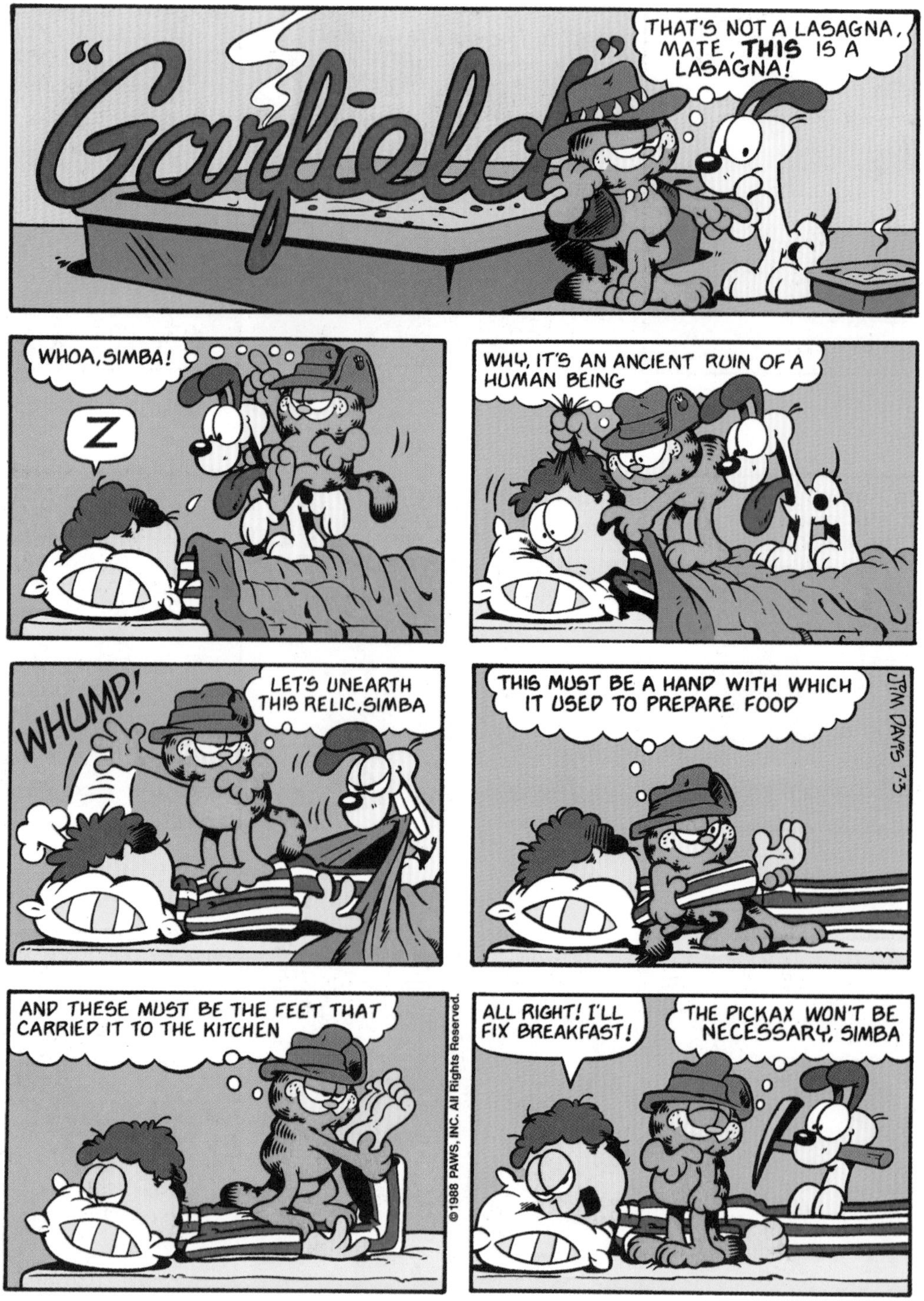
Garfield
THAT'S NOT A LASAGNA, MATE, THIS IS A LASAGNA!
WHOA, SIMBA!
Z
WHY, IT'S AN ANCIENT RUIN OF A HUMAN BEING
WHUMP!
LET'S UNEARTH THIS RELIC, SIMBA
THIS MUST BE A HAND WITH WHICH IT USED TO PREPARE FOOD
JIM DAVIS 7-3
AND THESE MUST BE THE FEET THAT CARRIED IT TO THE KITCHEN
ALL RIGHT! I'LL FIX BREAKFAST!
THE PICKAX WON'T BE NECESSARY, SIMBA

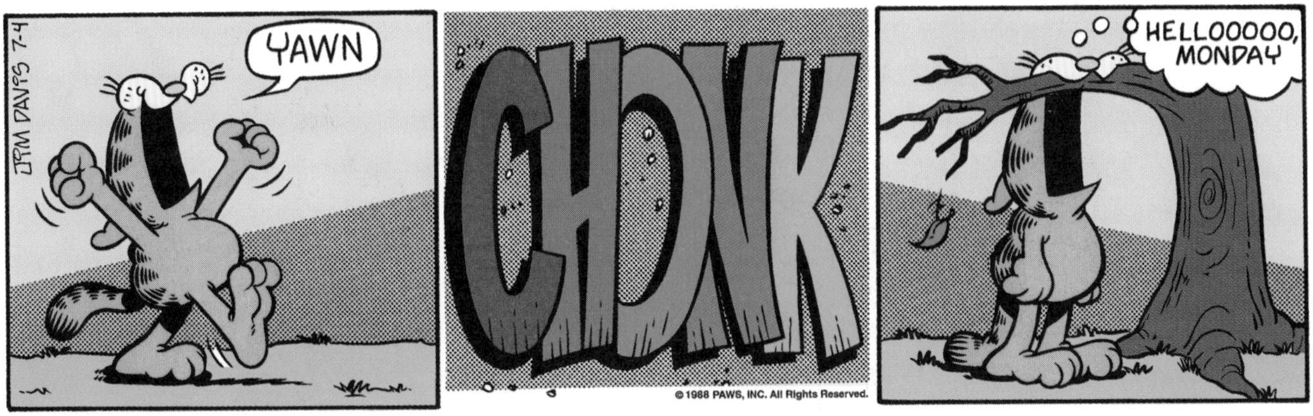
JIM DAVIS 7-4
YAWN
CHONK
HELLOOOOO, MONDAY

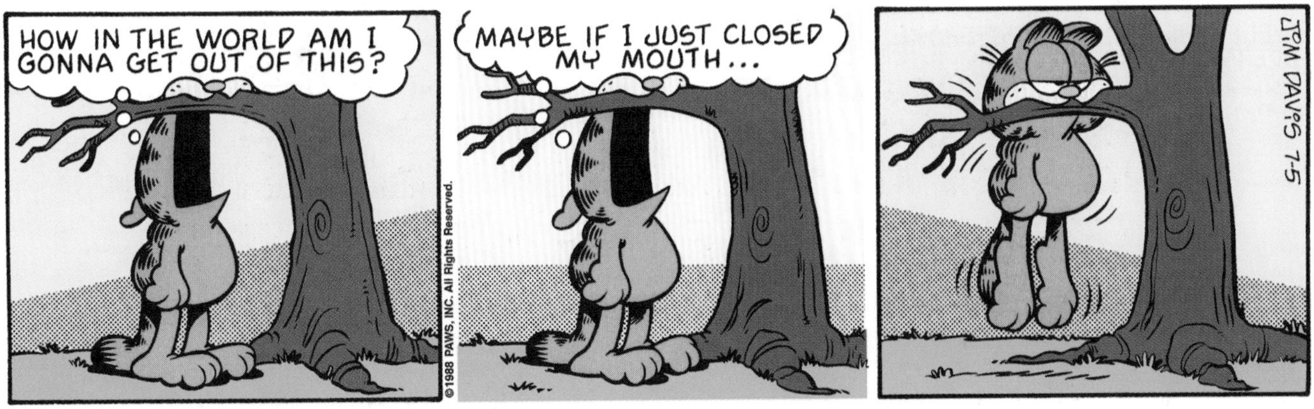
HOW IN THE WORLD AM I GONNA GET OUT OF THIS?
MAYBE IF I JUST CLOSED MY MOUTH...
JIM DAVIS 7-5

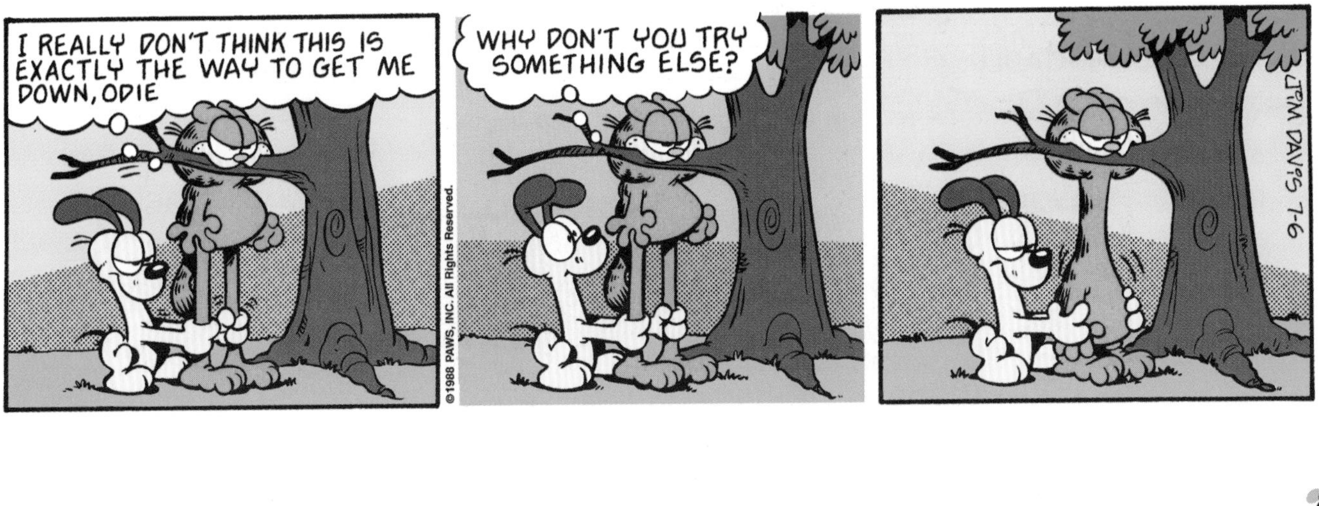
I REALLY DON'T THINK THIS IS EXACTLY THE WAY TO GET ME DOWN, ODIE
WHY DON'T YOU TRY SOMETHING ELSE?
JIM DAVIS 7-6

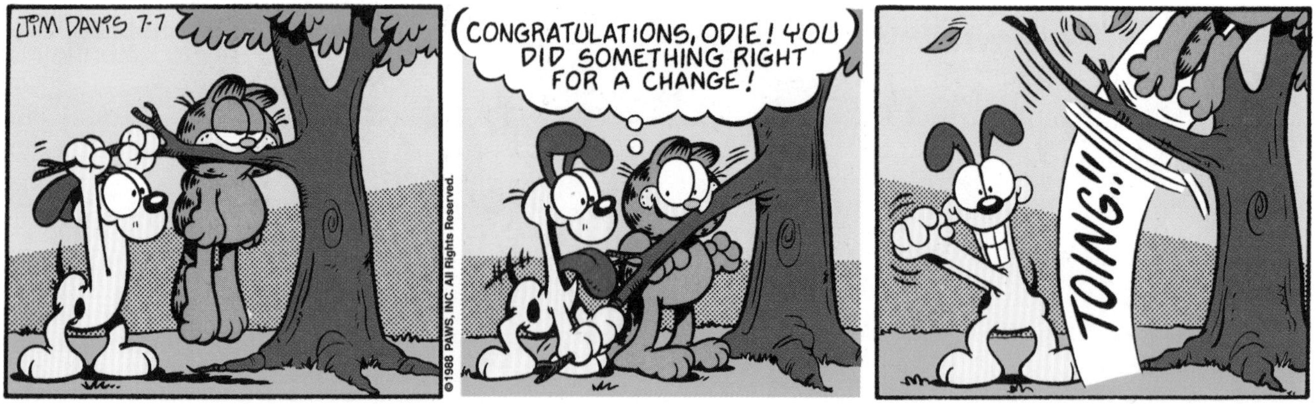
JIM DAVIS 7-7
© 1988 PAWS, INC. All Rights Reserved.
CONGRATULATIONS, ODIE! YOU DID SOMETHING RIGHT FOR A CHANGE!
TOING!!

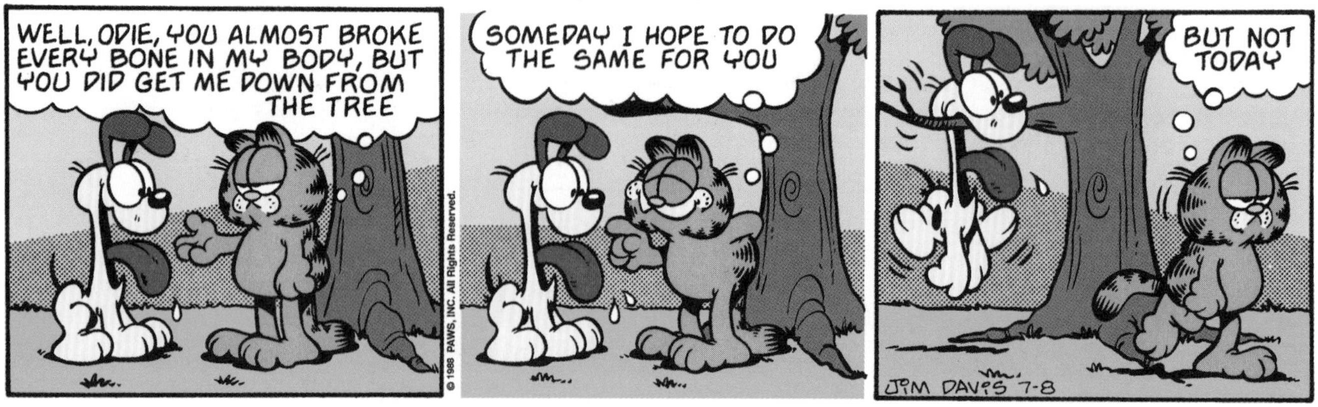
WELL, ODIE, YOU ALMOST BROKE EVERY BONE IN MY BODY, BUT YOU DID GET ME DOWN FROM THE TREE
© 1988 PAWS, INC. All Rights Reserved.
SOMEDAY I HOPE TO DO THE SAME FOR YOU
BUT NOT TODAY
JIM DAVIS 7-8

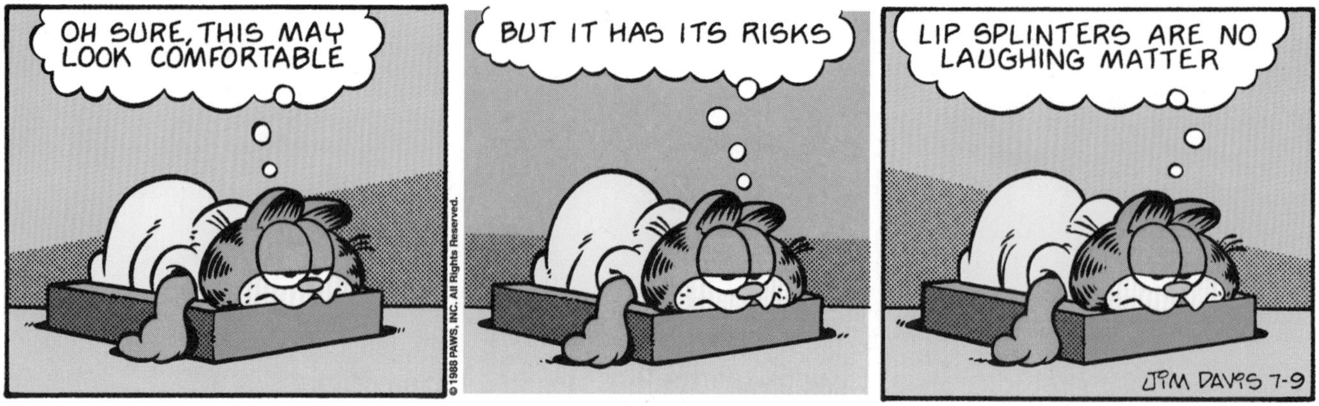
OH SURE, THIS MAY LOOK COMFORTABLE
© 1988 PAWS, INC. All Rights Reserved.
BUT IT HAS ITS RISKS
LIP SPLINTERS ARE NO LAUGHING MATTER
JIM DAVIS 7-9

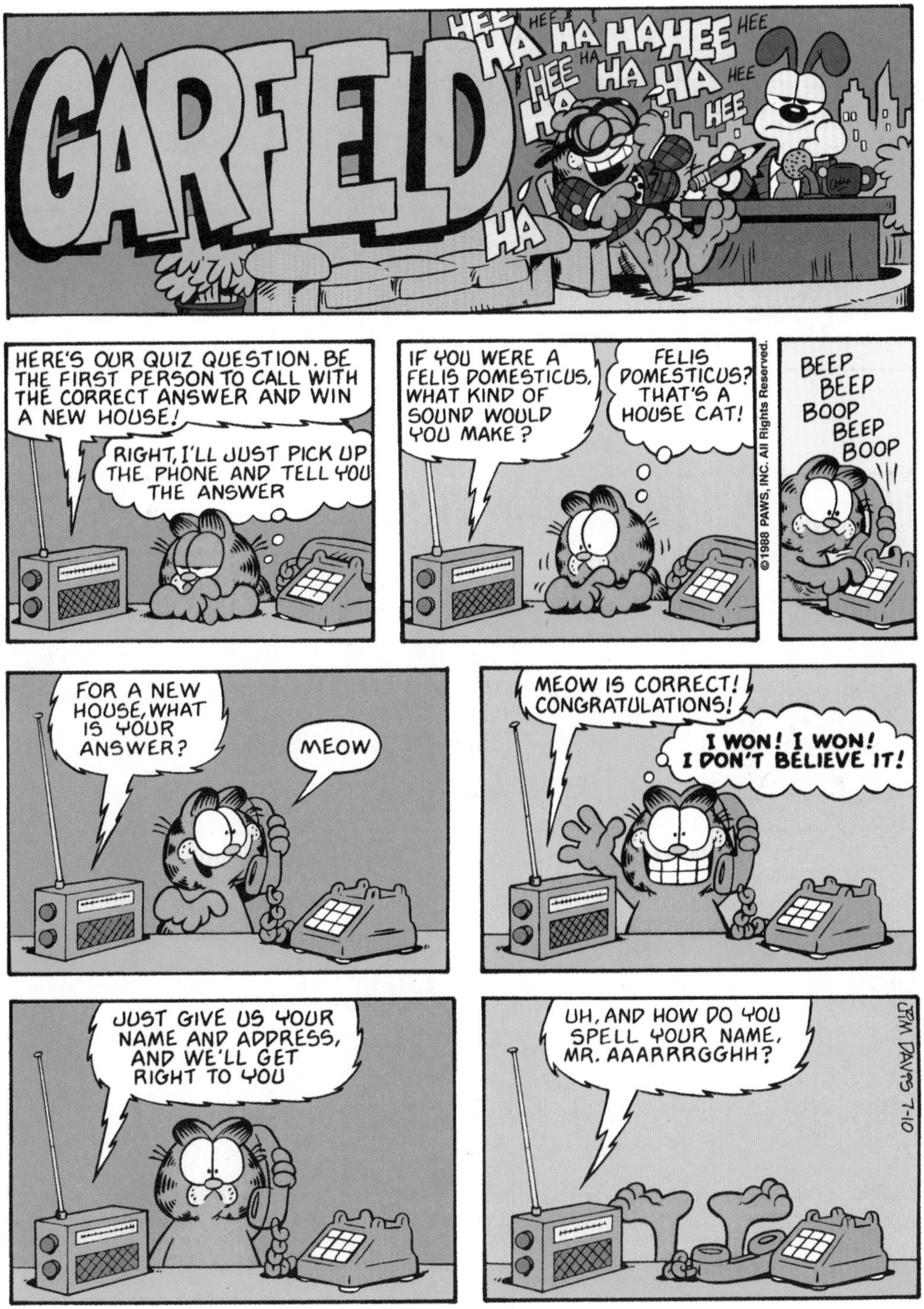
GARFIELD
HEE HA HA HA HEE HEE HA HEE HA HA HEE HA HEE HA
HERE'S OUR QUIZ QUESTION. BE THE FIRST PERSON TO CALL WITH THE CORRECT ANSWER AND WIN A NEW HOUSE!
RIGHT, I'LL JUST PICK UP THE PHONE AND TELL YOU THE ANSWER
IF YOU WERE A FELIS DOMESTICUS, WHAT KIND OF SOUND WOULD YOU MAKE?
FELIS DOMESTICUS? THAT'S A HOUSE CAT!
© 1988 PAWS, INC. All Rights Reserved.
BEEP BEEP BOOP BEEP BOOP
FOR A NEW HOUSE, WHAT IS YOUR ANSWER?
MEOW
MEOW IS CORRECT! CONGRATULATIONS!
I WON! I WON! I DON'T BELIEVE IT!
JUST GIVE US YOUR NAME AND ADDRESS, AND WE'LL GET RIGHT TO YOU
UH, AND HOW DO YOU SPELL YOUR NAME, MR. AAARRRGGHH?
JIM DAVIS 7-10

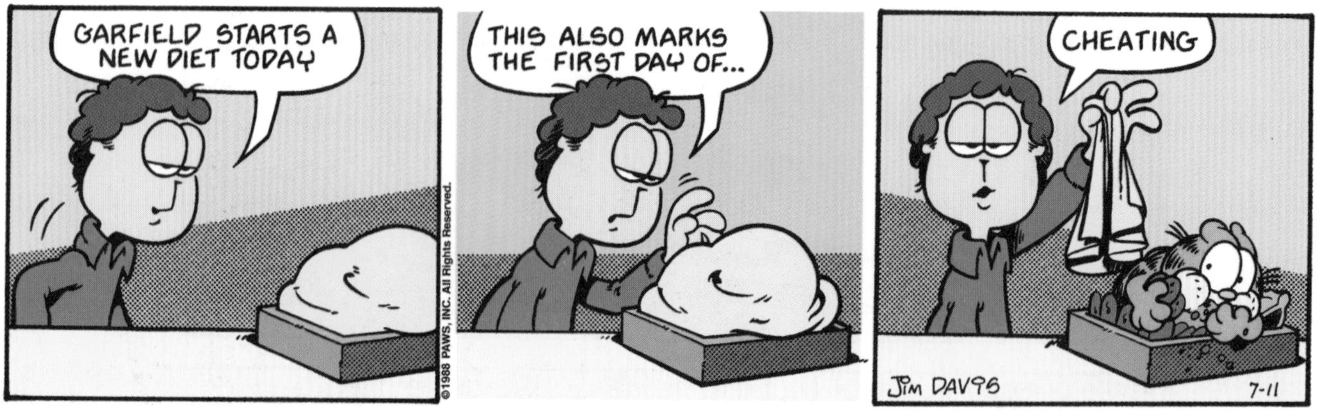
GARFIELD STARTS A NEW DIET TODAY
THIS ALSO MARKS THE FIRST DAY OF...
CHEATING
©1988 PAWS, INC. All Rights Reserved.
JIM DAVIS
7-11

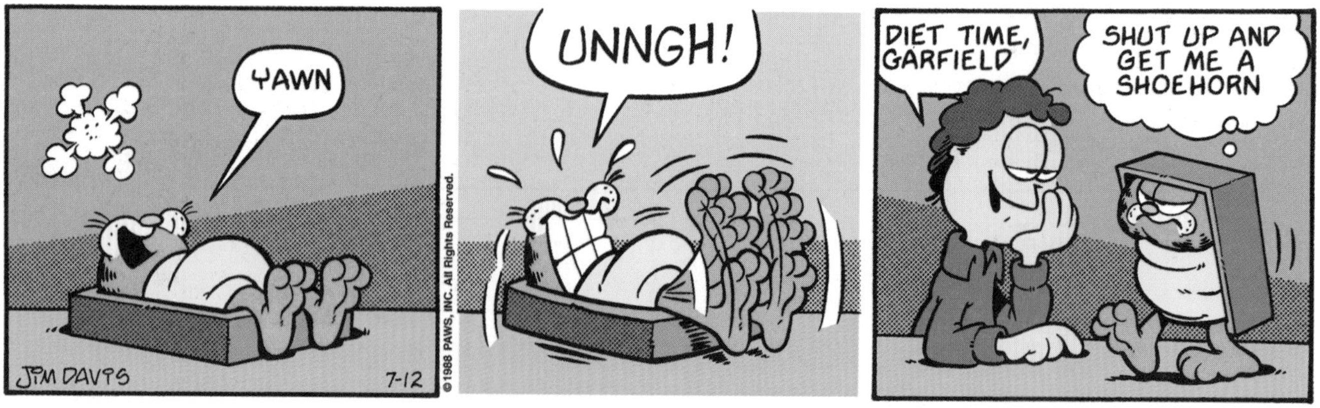
YAWN
JIM DAVIS
7-12
©1988 PAWS, INC. All Rights Reserved.
UNNGH!
DIET TIME, GARFIELD
SHUT UP AND GET ME A SHOEHORN

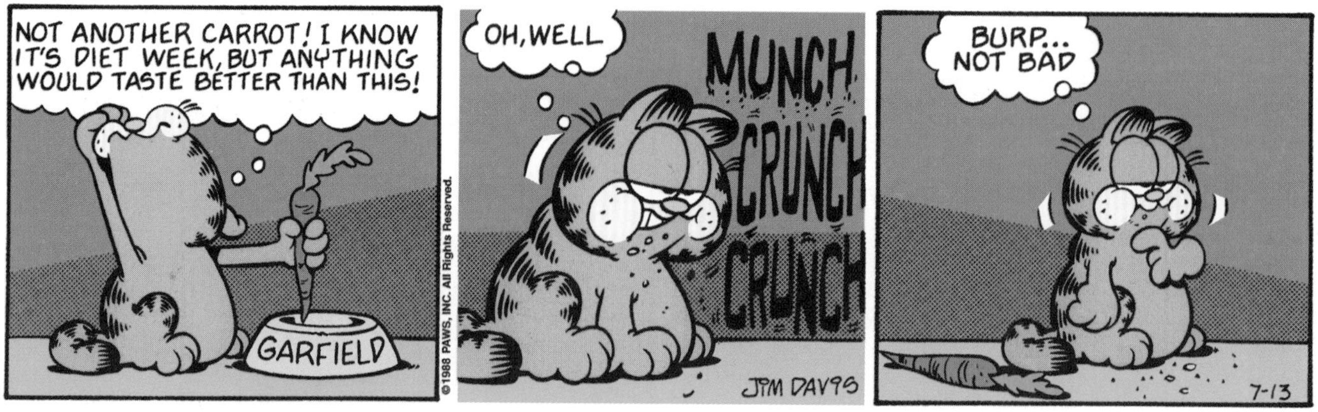
NOT ANOTHER CARROT! I KNOW IT'S DIET WEEK, BUT ANYTHING WOULD TASTE BETTER THAN THIS!
GARFIELD
©1988 PAWS, INC. All Rights Reserved.
OH, WELL
MUNCH
CRUNCH
CRUNCH
JIM DAVIS
BURP... NOT BAD
7-13

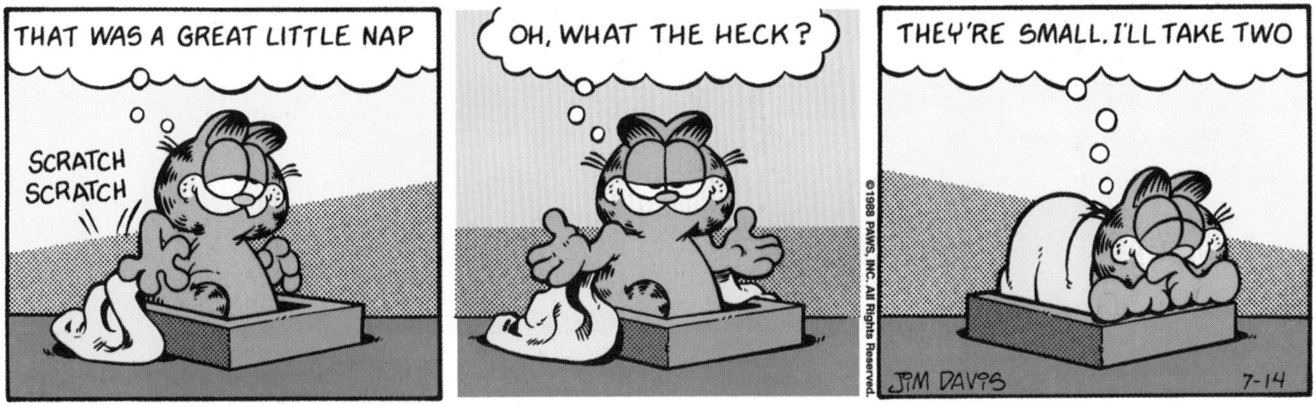
THAT WAS A GREAT LITTLE NAP
SCRATCH SCRATCH
OH, WHAT THE HECK?
©1988 PAWS, INC. All Rights Reserved.
THEY'RE SMALL. I'LL TAKE TWO
JIM DAVIS
7-14

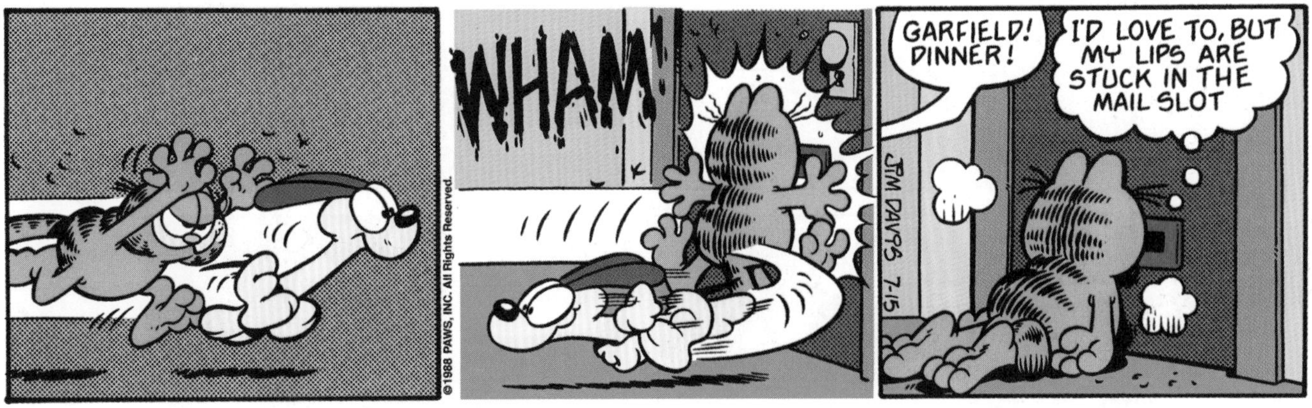
©1988 PAWS, INC. All Rights Reserved.
WHAM!
JIM DAVIS 7-15
GARFIELD! DINNER!
I'D LOVE TO, BUT MY LIPS ARE STUCK IN THE MAIL SLOT

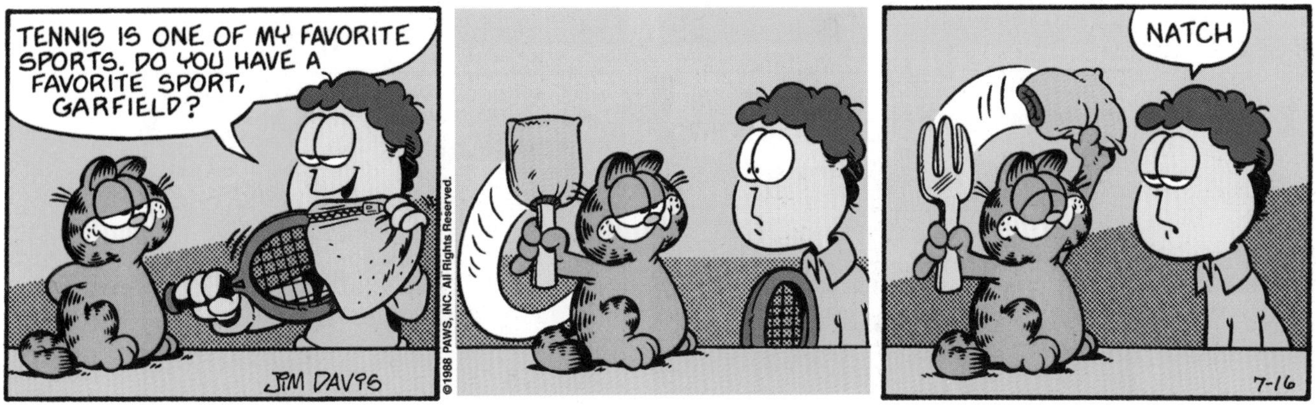
TENNIS IS ONE OF MY FAVORITE SPORTS. DO YOU HAVE A FAVORITE SPORT, GARFIELD?
JIM DAVIS
©1988 PAWS, INC. All Rights Reserved.
NATCH
7-16

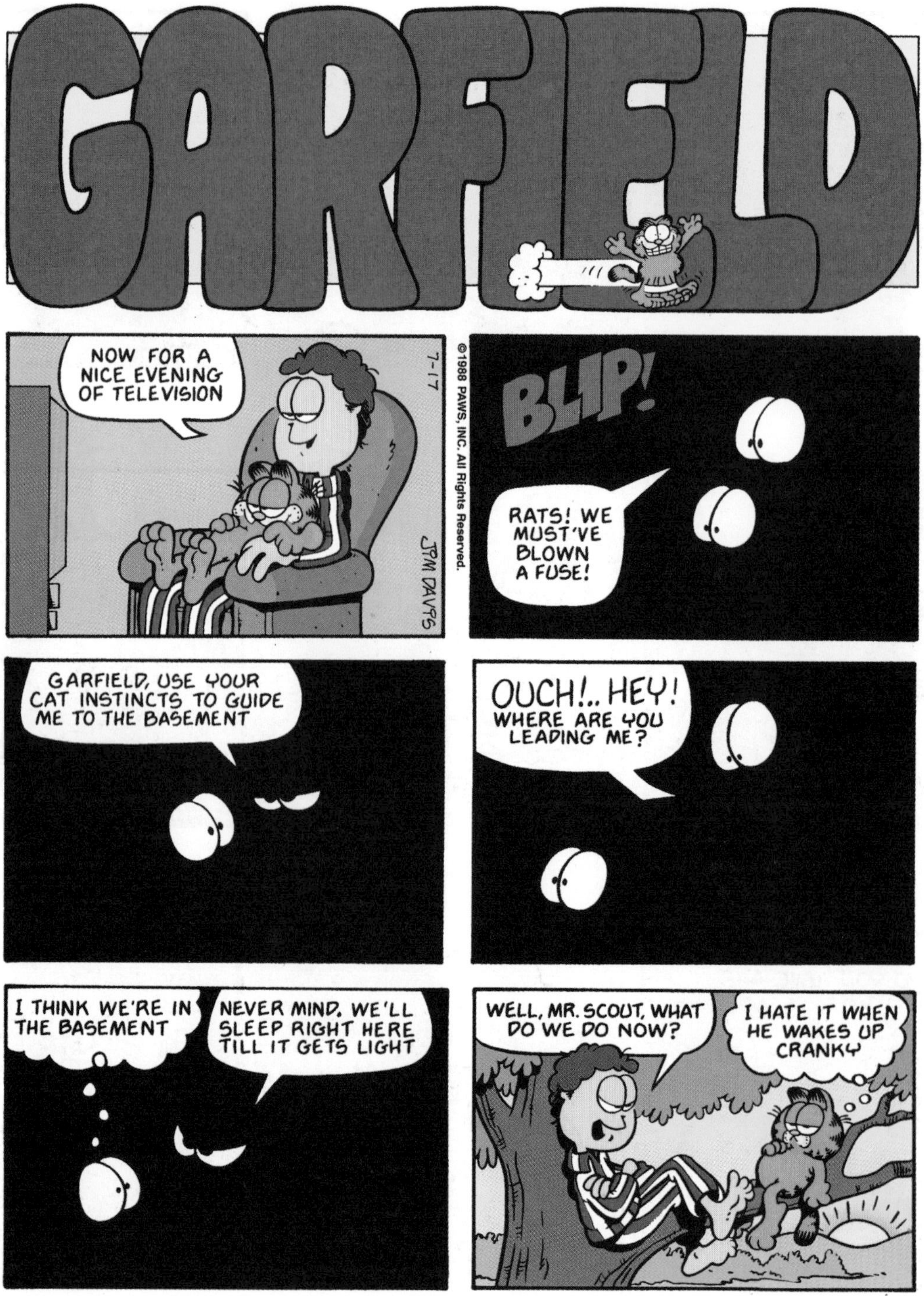

GARFIELD
NOW FOR A NICE EVENING OF TELEVISION
7-17
JPM DAVPS
©1988 PAWS, INC. All Rights Reserved.
BLIP!
RATS! WE MUST'VE BLOWN A FUSE!
GARFIELD, USE YOUR CAT INSTINCTS TO GUIDE ME TO THE BASEMENT
OUCH!.. HEY! WHERE ARE YOU LEADING ME?
I THINK WE'RE IN THE BASEMENT
NEVER MIND, WE'LL SLEEP RIGHT HERE TILL IT GETS LIGHT
WELL, MR. SCOUT, WHAT DO WE DO NOW?
I HATE IT WHEN HE WAKES UP CRANKY

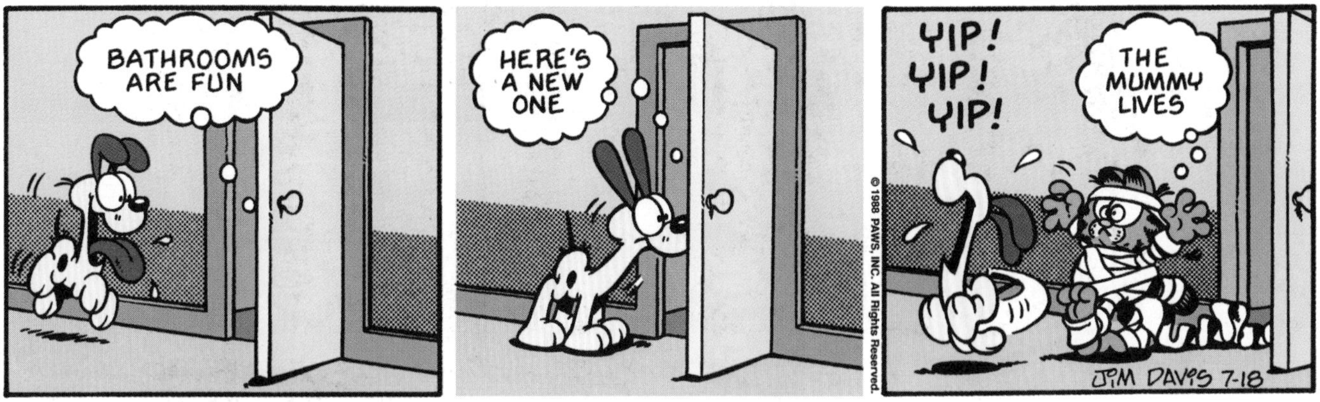
BATHROOMS ARE FUN
HERE'S A NEW ONE
© 1988 PAWS, INC. All Rights Reserved.
YIP! YIP! YIP!
THE MUMMY LIVES
JIM DAVIS 7-18

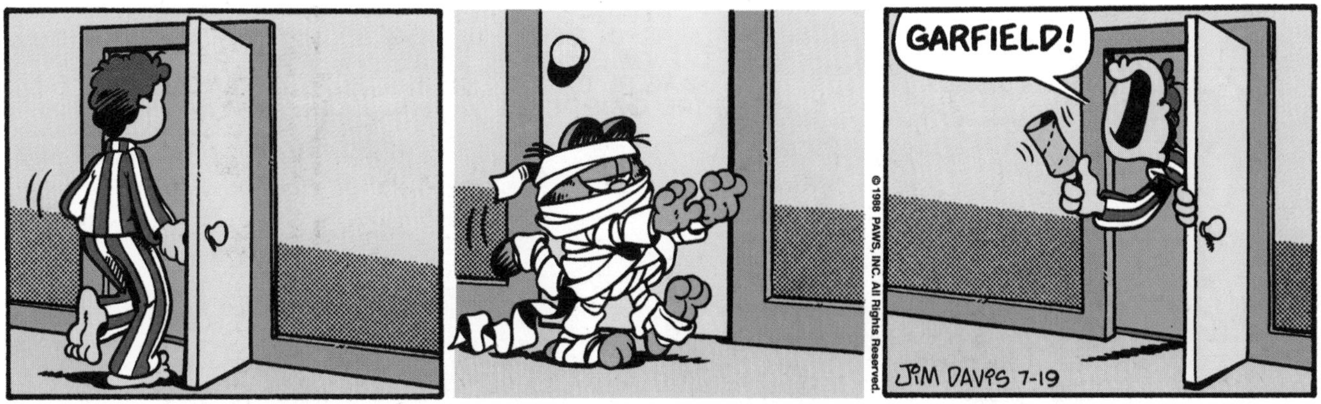
© 1988 PAWS, INC. All Rights Reserved.
GARFIELD!
JIM DAVIS 7-19

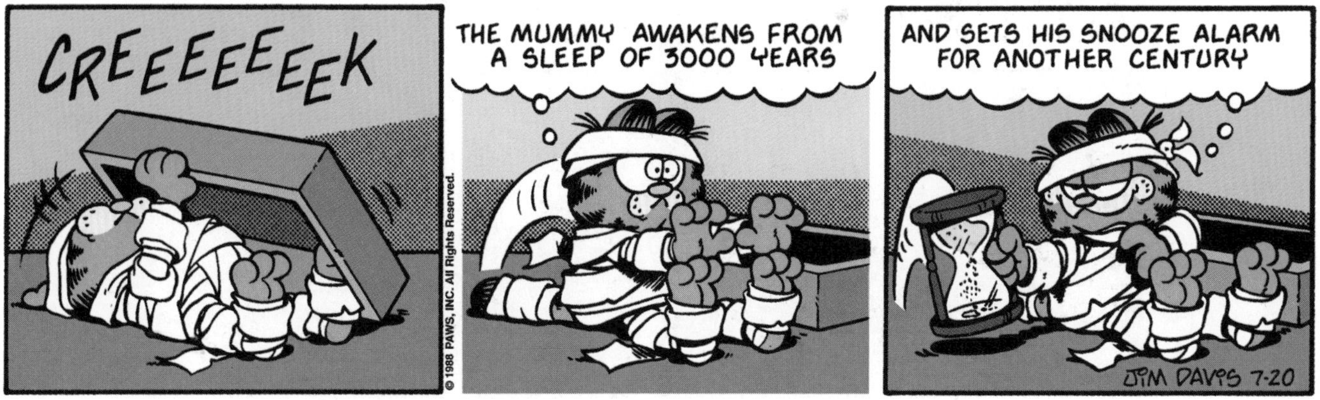
CREEEEEEEEK
© 1988 PAWS, INC. All Rights Reserved.
THE MUMMY AWAKENS FROM A SLEEP OF 3000 YEARS
AND SETS HIS SNOOZE ALARM FOR ANOTHER CENTURY
JIM DAVIS 7-20

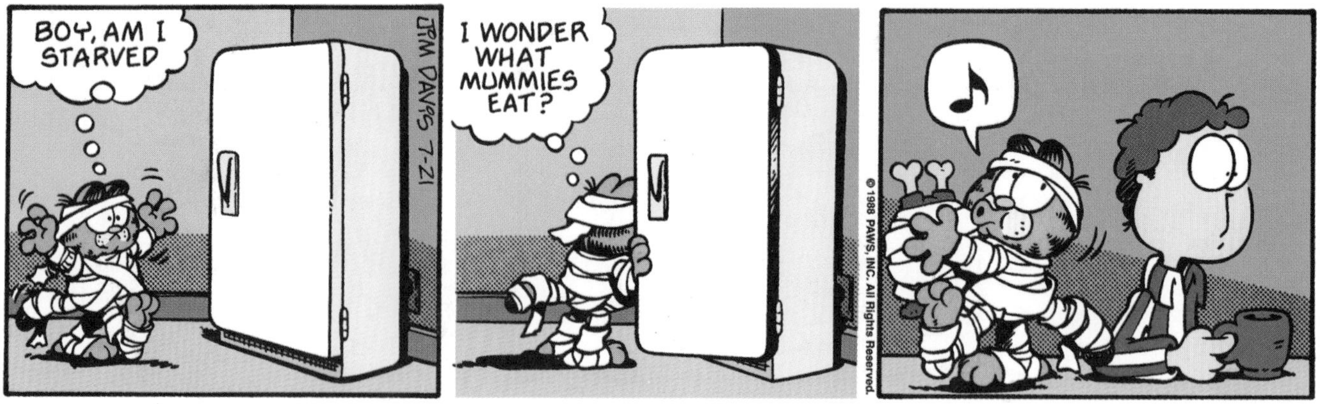
BOY, AM I STARVED
JIM DAVIS 7-21
I WONDER WHAT MUMMIES EAT?
© 1988 PAWS, INC. All Rights Reserved.
♪

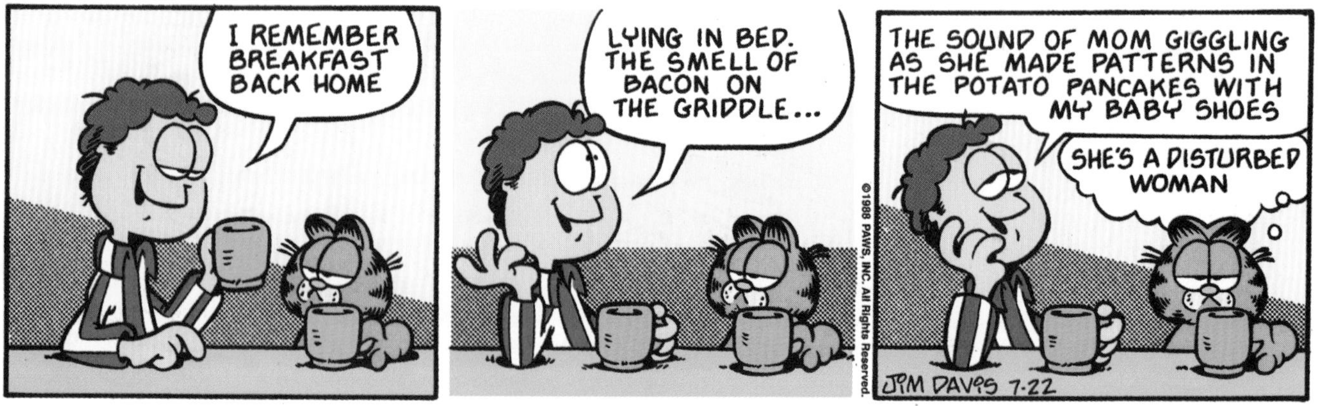
I REMEMBER BREAKFAST BACK HOME
LYING IN BED. THE SMELL OF BACON ON THE GRIDDLE...
© 1988 PAWS, INC. All Rights Reserved.
THE SOUND OF MOM GIGGLING AS SHE MADE PATTERNS IN THE POTATO PANCAKES WITH MY BABY SHOES
SHE'S A DISTURBED WOMAN
JIM DAVIS 7-22

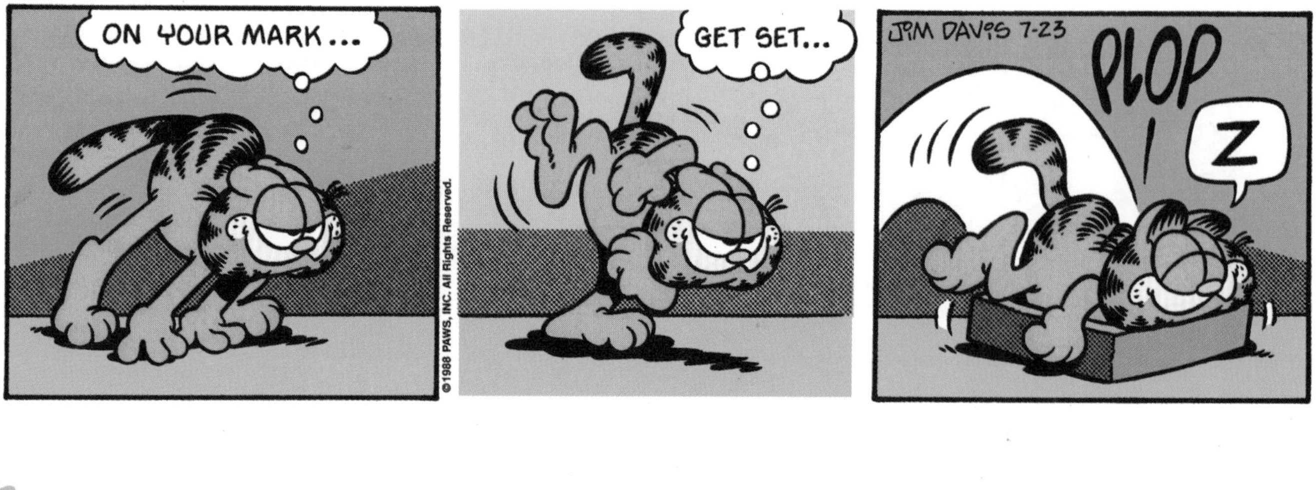
ON YOUR MARK...
© 1988 PAWS, INC. All Rights Reserved.
GET SET...
JIM DAVIS 7-23
PLOP
Z